# Healing
# Humanity

# Healing Humanity

## Confronting Our Moral Crisis

Edited by
Archpriest Alexander F. C. Webster, PhD,
Professor Alfred Kentigern Siewers, PhD,
and Professor David C. Ford, PhD

HOLY TRINITY PUBLICATIONS
Holy Trinity Seminary Press
Holy Trinity Monastery
Jordanville, New York
2020

Printed with the blessing of His Eminence,
Metropolitan Hilarion First Hierarch
of the Russian Orthodox Church Outside of Russia

The opinions expressed by individual contributors are not necessarily those
of the editors or publisher.

## HOLY TRINITY
## SEMINARY PRESS

An imprint of

HOLY TRINITY PUBLICATIONS
Holy Trinity Monastery
Jordanville, New York 13361-0036
www.holytrinitypublications.com

ISBN: 978-1-942699-29-3 (paperback)
ISBN: 978-1-942699-31-6 (ePub)
ISBN: 978-1-942699-32-3 (Mobipocket)

Library of Congress Control Number 2020940596

Dedicated to all those Orthodox Christians—saints, hierarchs, clergy, monastics, and laity—who stood for and stand for Orthodox Christian Tradition with God's grace and ascetic struggle, especially in America, but also worldwide: a true "cloud of witnesses."

# Contents

# Foreword

"You are the salt of the earth; but if the salt loses its flavor,
how shall it be seasoned? It is then good for nothing but to be thrown out
and trampled underfoot by men."
—Matthew 5:13

These words of our Lord and Saviour Jesus Christ are addressed to His faithful people. They were true at the time He uttered them two thousand years ago, and they still stand to challenge our faithfulness to the Gospel of salvation and the hope it brings if we would only follow it. We see abundant signs of the fruit of human sin and disobedience to God's commandments all around and sometimes feel like Lot in Sodom for whom the Lord promised his uncle Abraham that He (God) would spare the city if ten righteous men could be found in it (see Genesis 18:32). But such a number could not be found. So, to be the salt of the world we must rise to the challenge of amending our own way of life and by the Grace of God to live by His Laws. "Blessed art Thou, O Lord; Teach me Thy statutes" (Psalm 118:12).

The times in which we live are most accurately described as those of rampant agnosticism where fear and uncertainty are pervasive, and people struggle to find coherent belief or a faith to live by. Our own failure to live the Gospel contributes to this and demonstrates how essential is our own repentance. If we do not manifest the life of Christ to the world, then we are the salt that has lost its savor and so should not be shocked to find ourselves and our belief "trampled underfoot."

This volume presents a collection of essays from a diverse group of contemporary Orthodox voices—both ordained clergy and articulate lay believers, many of whom hold teaching positions in academic institutions across the United States. Their varied contributions address some of the causes of our current ethical and moral dilemmas and to offer ways of bringing our own lives more into conformity with "*the image that He* [Christ] *made in the beginning*" (From the troparion of the pre-feast of Christmas).

What is written here may fly in the face of contemporary political correctness, but it is offered not to hurt but to heal. Because a pill may at first be bitter to our taste it should not prevent us from swallowing it in order to receive healing from our sickness. Thus, however much it may receive spitting and insults for what it confesses the Church must live and proclaim the Truth of God the Holy Trinity and our humanity, knowing that "the creation itself also will be delivered from the bondage of corruption into the glorious liberty of the children of God" (Romans 8:21).

Holy Trinity Monastery
Great Lent 2020

# Preface

Orthodox Christian scholars and writers, both clergy and laity, from four Orthodox jurisdictions in North America, gathered at Holy Trinity Orthodox Seminary in Jordanville, New York, during Cheesefare Week of March 2019. They joined faculty and students of the seminary and the monastic community living there, together with other attendees, for a three-day conference focused on the application of Orthodox Christian doctrinal, moral, spiritual, and pastoral teachings to contemporary challenges posed by secular Western culture, especially in its American context, with particular reference to the impact these have upon the Church.

Together with the Rector and the Dean of Holy Trinity Orthodox Seminary, the President of St Vladimir's Orthodox Theological Seminary, and the Dean of St Tikhon's Orthodox Theological Seminary were present and delivered papers. The other major Orthodox seminary in North America—Holy Cross Greek Orthodox School of Theology in Brookline, Massachusetts—was also represented by a faculty member who gave a presentation.

The presentations were given before a daily attendance of approximately 100 in that secluded rural upstate New York location and were recorded for global access online via Ancient Faith Radio. The speakers offered both scholarly and pastoral perspectives, informed by current social trends pertaining to sexuality, anthropology, and human nature. Each reflected prayerful preparation and strove to convey a traditional Orthodox *phronema* (or "mind"), coupled with compassion for struggling Orthodox Christians and families, as well as all those facing spiritual shipwreck in our culture today. The speakers were able to share their research freely as a public offering of collective scholarly and experiential insights under the aegis of Holy Trinity Seminary.

Each presentation provided an opportunity for candid conversation among Orthodox Christians of common mind. At a time when secular methodologies and assumptions have impacted even some Orthodox scholars in academia, this collection serves as a reminder that Orthodox anthropology and morality are alive and well both in theory and practice, rooted in an experiential encounters with "the Way, the Truth, and the Life," Who is the Person of our Lord Jesus Christ made manifest in His Church.

The papers fell naturally into the two-part division of this volume, namely diagnoses and cure. The first part grapples with the ideas and behaviors that increasingly challenge Orthodox Christian clergy, academics, and students in the secular world, by dissecting increasingly aggressive secular ideologies with the scalpel of the two thousand years of accumulated wisdom found in the Church. The second part follows from the first: Orthodox *theoria* integrates with *praxis*, applying Orthodox teachings to the contemporary home and parish and to our interactions with the secular world in education, professions, and community. Both sections necessarily involve theory and application, given Orthodoxy's experiential epistemology and synergy of grace and ascetic struggles. But they offer different solutions that relate, we hope, to all of us in varied arenas of struggle in our lives, sometimes simultaneously.

The conference organizing committee included, in addition to the three coeditors of this volume, Professor David Bradshaw and Professor Mary Ford, whose contributions are included herein.

We are grateful especially to His Grace Bishop Luke of Syracuse for hosting the conference on the grounds of Holy Trinity Seminary and Monastery, and to the many clergy, monks, seminary faculty, administrators, and students, who, with their hospitality and generous volunteer labor, contributed to its success. In addition, we thank Isaac Beck for his assistance with digital aspects of the conference, and his Russian Orthodox mission parish of St John of Shanghai and San Francisco (in Lewisburg, Pennsylvania) and its Treasurer Cam Mazeski for handling donations to support the conference, as well as Holy Trinity Publications, particularly Rdr Nicholas and Nina Chapman, for making this volume possible.

All nineteen presenters were invited to contribute written versions of their talks for publication. All but a few of the presentations from the conference are collected in this volume, revised and adapted for scholarly and, we hope, accessible publication. May any errors contained herein be harmless and the reader be blessed.

Archpriest Alexander F. C. Webster, Ph.D.
Professor Alfred Kentigern Siewers, Ph.D.
Professor David C. Ford, Ph.D.

The Feast of Theophany, Jan. 6/19, 7528/2020

# PART ONE

## Diagnoses: Chastity, Purity, and Integrity

# The Beauty of Chastity

## Prof. David Bradshaw

The beauty of chastity is one of the great themes of Western literature. The Arthurian romances turn on the contrast between the adulterous love of Lancelot and Guinevere and the chastity of Sir Galahad. They present vividly the contrast between the ugliness of a passion that destroys a kingdom and the beauty of soul that enables Sir Galahad to attain the Holy Grail. In another great medieval work, *Sir Gawain and the Green Knight*, it is Sir Gawain's chaste refusal of temptation that saves him from the uncanny threat posed by the Green Knight. Perhaps the finest flower of chivalric literature is Edmund Spenser's *Faerie Queene*, a vast tapestry of symbolically charged chivalrous adventure that was partly inspired by Greek patristic writings.[1] For Spenser the virtue of chastity figures centrally, not only for its own sake, but as an emblem of fidelity to God. Further examples could be multiplied, from Shakespeare through novelists such as Austen, Dickens, and Trollope. All present us with characters whose chastity and integrity elicit our admiration, even as these virtues place them in danger—sometimes, as in *Othello*, with tragic results.

That chastity is a central virtue was an unquestioned assumption of Western civilization for almost two thousand years. Nonetheless, as society began to move away from its Christian moorings, a new sexual ethic inevitably followed. Already in the seventeenth century, freethinkers, deists, and the so-called "rakes" of the court of Charles II began to advance the idea that all morality is merely a human invention. Often this belief was accompanied by a rosy optimism about what life would be like if only Christian inhibitions could be cast aside. Faramerz Dabhoiwala has described the gradual triumph of such ideas in his *The Origins of Sex: A History of the First Sexual Revolution*.[2] He points out that already by the early nineteenth century they had spread broadly and were embraced by many of the avant-garde of the time. As Percy Bysshe Shelley wrote in a note to his popular poem "Queen Mab" (1813): "Love withers under constraint: its very essence is liberty . . . That which will result from the abolition of marriage, will be natural and right, because choice and change will be exempted from restraint."[3]

Today it is hard to be so optimistic. Two generations have gone by since the sexual revolution of the 1960s put into practice what the rakes, romantics, and freethinkers had long advocated. We have passed from the initial heady sense of liberation of the 1960s and 1970s, through the consequent explosion of abortion, divorce, cohabitation, and single motherhood, to the hook-up culture of the 1990s, and finally to the so-called rape culture of today. I say "so-called" because it is facile to think that the current sense of mistrust and alienation between the sexes is due simply to male sexual violence. Nonetheless, the phrase does rightly highlight that many young men today have grown up watching pornography that glamorizes rape and other forms of sexual perversion. This is a subterranean influence that has done much to poison relations between the sexes. Coming on top of the rest of the chain of events that followed the sexual revolution, the result has been what a recent writer for *The Atlantic* has called a "sex recession"—a state in which young adults are having less sex, not because of moral scruples, but because they find the very idea of it unappealing.[4]

Of course, it is hardly a new discovery to say that the sexual mores of our culture are in sad disarray. What can Orthodoxy contribute to overcoming the troubles that we now face? I will say, first of all, that I do not think that Orthodoxy has any distinctive *teaching* about chastity or purity. Our teaching on this subject is drawn from the same biblical and classical sources as that of Western Christianity, and it is at home in the same world as the great works of literature just mentioned.

Instead I would suggest that what Orthodoxy offers is a way of life in which the real beauty of chastity is both more readily apparent, and more accessible, than it would be otherwise. What is important here is not just Orthodox sexual ethics, but the way that this ethics is embedded in practices of worship, repentance, forgiveness, and self-denial. It is these that make the ideal of chastity at once attractive and realistic. Apart from them this same ideal must—at least typically, given the conditions of modern society—appear as no more than an arbitrary imposition.

My thinking on this subject was spurred by a comment I saw some time ago on a blog. I will repeat it here *not* because I know it to be true (I do not), but because I found it thought-provoking. The comment was offered by a man who identified himself as a gay Catholic. He said that he thought the sudden upsurge in militant homosexuality that began in the late 1960s would not have occurred had it not been for the collapse of Roman Catholic liturgy following Vatican II. He made the simple point that people need beauty, and when they cease to find it where it has traditionally been most evident, in the Church, they will look elsewhere. The result, in his view, was that people (and young men, in particular) began to seek beauty in the idealized male form, much as had the ancient Greeks.

As I said, I cannot vouch for the truth of this theory. However, I believe the author was right on at least this point, that people need beauty. One has only to look at the world around us today—our architecture, our traffic, our music, our pop culture, our very clothes—to recognize that beauty is in short supply. That is not to say that it cannot be found if one knows where to look. But how is one to know, given that our educational system has no concern for beauty and acts as if it does not exist? For us as Orthodox this should be of particular concern, because we believe that Beauty is one of the names of God. Indeed, according to St Dionysius the Areopagite, it is (along with the Good) the *first* name of God, prior even to Being.[5] We should, therefore, be particularly concerned that the world we live in is one that is starved of beauty. The absence of beauty deprives the soul of the opportunity to recognize and respond to the divine presence in creation—that presence by which, according to Dionysius, God is in all creatures, calling us to Himself.[6]

What about the beauty of chastity, in particular? Granted that this is not an explicit theme in most Orthodox theology and liturgy, it does figure prominently in at least one important text. This is the climactic hymn of the *Akathist to the Theotokos* sung on the first five Fridays of Lent in the Greek tradition, and the fifth Friday in the Russian tradition. The Akathist both begins and ends with the Archangel Gabriel at the Annunciation, marveling at what God has done. Let us consider the ending hymn first, for it is the one most relevant to our topic. Gabriel exclaims:

> Astounded by the comeliness of your virginity, and the exceeding splendor of your purity, Gabriel cried out to you, O Theotokos: What hymn of praise is fitting for me to present to you? What name shall I give you? I am lost and stand in wonder. Wherefore, as I was commanded, I cry to you: Hail, O Bride Unwedded![7]

The term translated "comeliness" here is *hōraiotēs*, the beauty of one who is *hōraios*, in the bloom of life. Unlike other terms that can be translated as beauty (such as *kallos* and *kallonē*), it refers not simply to that which is pleasing to the eye, but to internal soundness and vigor as they are externally manifest. It is the beauty that the old admire in the young, and the sick in the healthy. It is striking, then, to find that an angel, who is himself possessed of heavenly radiance, marvels at the *hōraiotēs* of the Theotokos.

The other key term is "purity," *hagneia*. Originally this meant ritual purity. In the Old Testament, *hagneia* is used of the purity of one who has taken the vows of a Nazarite and of one who is authorized to enter the sanctuary, as well as that of the sanctuary itself.[8] From ritual purity it is a short step to moral purity, including chastity, and by the time of the New Testament *hagneia* had acquired this further sense. Saint Paul speaks of his desire to present the Corinthian church to Christ as a chaste virgin (*parthenon hagnēn*, II Cor. 11:2). He likewise urges St Timothy to be a model of purity (*hagneiai*, I Tim. 4:12) and to address young women "as sisters, with all purity" (*en pasēi hagneiai*, 5:2).

The Latin equivalent of *hagneia* is *castitas*, the source of "chastity" in English. Thus the ideal of moral purity is one root of our concept of chastity. However, it is not the only one. Another term that is often translated as "chastity," particularly in patristic literature, is *sōphrosunē*. This is the virtue of temperance or self-control, one of the traditional four cardinal virtues. By the Imperial era, its most common meaning had narrowed to *sexual* temperance or self-control, or, in other words, chastity.[9] Although *hagneia* and *sōphrosunē* often overlapped in Christian usage, they retained distinctive connotations.[10] *Hagneia* indicates the purity of a way of life that is set apart from that of the world, particularly that of consecrated virgins, widows, and monastics, as well as that of the Church itself. *Sōphrosunē* indicates the habit of sexual self-control that is expected of everyone, although the form it takes naturally varies depending on one's station and walk of life.

I find this distinction helpful in thinking about the beauty of chastity. *Sōphrosunē* is beautiful in the way that any virtue is beautiful. It is one of the qualities that St John Chrysostom advises a wise husband to praise in his bride, along with her propriety, gentleness, discretion, openness, and piety.[11] Good though it is, it has no distinctive beauty that is not also possessed by these other traits. *Hagneia* is different. It possesses a very distinctive kind of beauty, one that had to be discovered, so to speak, in the course of Christian experience. Part of what is so noble and edifying about the Akathist service is that it leads us through this very process of discovery.

I return now to the Akathist, because I think we find here the key to what is missing from the way chastity is viewed in society today. As I mentioned earlier, the service begins (following the Small Compline) with the Annunciation as seen through the eyes of Gabriel. Here we see Gabriel primarily in the role of a dutiful servant obeying the commands of his master. He marvels at the Virgin, to be sure, but less because of any trait intrinsic to her than because of what his Master has done: "With mystic apprehension of the divine commandment, the bodiless angel quickly appeared in the house of Joseph, and said to the unwedded Virgin: Lo, He who in His descent bowed the heavens is housed unchanged and whole in thee. As I behold Him in thy womb taking on the form of a servant, I marvel and cry unto thee: Hail, O Bride Unwedded!"[12]

Beauty is not mentioned here. Nonetheless, what Gabriel describes is profoundly beautiful. Indeed, it is perhaps the highest form of beauty that can be apprehended by the human mind—the unlooked for, undeserved, and deeply mysterious act of God becoming man, solely out of the abundance of love. Gabriel can only obey in awestruck wonder the command he has been given, marveling all the while at the Virgin in whose womb the eternal God now makes His abode.

Much like Gabriel, we learn much here. We learn, in the first place, the incredible, unfathomable depth of divine love. We learn the exalted place that this love has given to an otherwise unknown Jewish maiden. And we learn something about the nature of beauty itself: that it consists, not only in the manifestation of the divine nature (as philosophers had long believed), but, more specifically, in the manifestation of divine love. It is for this reason that God's act itself is a supreme form of beauty. Thus, among the many things that the Incarnation revolutionizes, there is our understanding of beauty itself.

The Canon that follows this opening hymn amplifies profusely the marvel of the Virgin containing God. She is the "mountain of spiritual riches seasoned by the Spirit," "the ladder elevating all from earth by grace," the "fiery chariot of the Logos," the "living paradise, having the Lord, the Tree of Life, in [her] midst."[13] But soon there is another element as well. At the start of the Seventh Ode, the focus shifts to the three holy youths in the fire:

> The godly-minded youths did not worship the creature instead of the Creator; but valiantly rejecting the threat of the fire, they joyfully sang: "Blessed art Thou, most praised Lord, and God of our fathers."[14]

This sudden shift is not explained until the subsequent Ode, where it is linked to the theophany at the burning bush:

> Verily Moses comprehended in the bush the great mystery of thy birth-giving. The youths prefigured this most clearly, standing in the midst of the fire without being burned, O pure and holy Virgin; wherefore we praise you unto all the ages.[15]

Much is said here, and even more is implied. The point is not only that the youths in the fire, like the burning bush, prefigured the Theotokos, who contained God in her womb but was not consumed. We must bear in mind as well that the youths were kept safe in the fire only because of their single-minded refusal to surrender to temptation. The youths thus prefigure the Theotokos, not only by the miracle of their remaining unburnt in the fire, but by their purity and their fitness to receive God.

Of course, we too face temptation, and we too may someday find ourselves in the situation of the three youths. The hymn thus invites us to see ourselves as called, in our own way, to prefigure the Theotokos—or, perhaps better (since we are subsequent to her in time), to partake of her purity. There is thus now a personal link between us and her. We have moved from marveling at the divine act and the exalted place it has given her, to turning to her as our model and guide.

The subsequent hymns make this clear. Above all, there is the magnificent Kontakion addressed to the Theotokos by the imperial city of Constantinople, "To Thee, Our Champion":

> To thee our champion, Queen of war,
> The battle trophies won
> Thy people rescued by thine aid from peril
> Dedicate as our offering of thanksgiving, O Theotokos.
> As thou hast might
> Which none by war can overcome,
> From all forms of danger do thou deliver me,
> That I may cry unto thee: Hail, O Bride Unwedded![16]

According to tradition, this hymn was first sung in the Church of the Theotokos in Constantinople in 626 AD, following the miraculous deliverance of the city from the siege of the Avars. The emperor and the army were still away from the city fighting the Persians, so further danger could descend at any time. The hymn in effect places us there, as we both give thanks to the Theotokos and beseech her further aid.

Of course, not all enemies are barbarians outside the city gates. The most dangerous are those that lie within: our own gluttony, fear, pride, anger, self-love, and other passions. Against these we fight our most consequential battle, for they can destroy not only our lives but our very souls. And it is above all against these that we seek the aid of our champion, the Queen of war.

Seeing the hymn in this light, we may wonder why it cloaks, as it were, spiritual struggle under the image of the deliverance of the city. But surely the answer is not far to seek. One of the most insidious lies of the devil is that we fight alone. My gluttony, my fear, my pride, my anger—are they not mine alone? What good would it do to speak of them to anyone else? Would it not just bring me shame? The Apostle already answered this lie when he wrote, "no temptation has overtaken you except such as is common to man" (I Cor. 10:13). We are all of the same flesh and suffer the same passions. So the hymn places us first of all in the position of the city, seeking a common deliverance from our common enemy.

These thoughts prepare us for the *Akathist's* next and most sobering turn. Near the end of the service, following the "Akathist" proper and the second singing of the Kontakion, but before the final hymn of Gabriel, there are five prayers that are addressed alternately to the Theotokos and to Christ. In the Greek practice these are typically read, respectively, by a laywoman before the icon of the Theotokos and a layman before the icon of Christ; but in any case, even when they are read by the priest, they present a striking contrast to the sense of wonder and exuberance in the earlier hymns. Here is the beginning of the first prayer:

> O spotless, undefiled, incorruptible, pure, and chaste (*hagnē*) Vir-
> gin-Bride of God, who by your wondrous conception united God the
> Logos with man, and joined our fallen nature with the Heavens; the only
> hope of the hopeless, and the help of the persecuted; the ever-ready to
> rescue all that flee to you, and the refuge of all Christians, spurn me not,
> the branded sinner, who by shameful thoughts, words, and deeds, have
> made my whole being useless, and through indolence have enslaved my
> judgement to the pleasures of this life. But as the mother of the merciful
> God, mercifully show compassion to me, the sinner and prodigal, and
> accept my supplication which is offered unto you from impure lips.[17]

In this prayer we no longer imagine ourselves in the place of Gabriel, nor even in that of the imperial city. Instead each of us stands before the Theotokos alone as a suppliant, seeking the aid that we desperately need. And we do so now, not with the joy and wonder of the previous hymns, but out of deep contrition, recognizing the contrast between her purity and our own shameful and defiled life.

This is the final step in which we learn to recognize the real beauty of the Theotokos—and through her, that of chastity itself. We no longer appreciate this beauty as something from which we stand apart in disinterested admiration. It is worthy of admiration, to be sure, but we now recognize in it that which we desperately need, as we recognize also, in the Theotokos, our only help. Not, of course, that there is not help in Christ, to Whom we also pray, and in God the Father, Whose boundless love worked the Incarnation. But she is the loving mother who especially hears us in our need. The final hymn of the service, which we quoted at the outset, brings all of these strands together. There we see Gabriel at last marveling at both the wonder of the Incarnation and the beauty of the Theotokos, still finding no words that are sufficient to praise her.

I said earlier that the Orthodox way of life is one that makes the ideal of chastity not only attractive but realistic. It should be apparent now how this is the case. The prayer of penitence leads us to reflect critically on our own lives. If it is uttered sincerely, it leads us to repent in humility, not just of particular wrongs we have done, but of our whole shameful and degraded state of being. The paradox is that, far from leading to lethargy or despair, such penitence brings a new kind of strength. Sexual sin is never merely sexual, but always has motives that are rooted in the passions—whether the need to be loved, or the lust for domination, or the desire to prove oneself attractive, or any of a dozen other motives that come readily to mind. Nothing more fully deflates such passions than the humility of the penitent. The penitent recognizes that he is not worthy to be loved, has no right to domination, and, if truth be known, is deeply and shamefully ugly. He seeks not self-gratification but forgiveness and healing.

It is rare to achieve such penitence through one's whole being, and rarer still to be fully transformed by it. Most of us oscillate between partial repentance and a return to the passions that at other times we loathe. Orthodoxy is a way of life that constantly summons us, through example, precept, and the rhythm of worship, to a deeper and truer repentance. Granted that not all Orthodox are saints, even so, to the extent that one enters into the Orthodox way of life, chastity becomes realistic, because it is the natural concomitant of everything else that one does.

I emphasize this point because one of the reasons that people have turned against chastity is that they believe it to be impossible. Countless stories in our literature and pop culture, from *The Scarlet Letter* to *Animal House*, have taught us to think that anyone who aspires to sexual purity must be a fool or a hypocrite, or both. Perhaps such a perception was inevitable once chastity was removed from the way of life in which it is naturally at home. But the right response is not to despise it, but to seek to recover that fuller way of life.

I trust it will now be plain why I say that Orthodoxy does not have so much a distinctive teaching about chastity as a distinctive way of life in which chastity is appreciated and pursued. That way of life is one of prayer, worship, and reverence for the saints, especially the Theotokos. It is also one of repentance and confession, along with fasting and other ascetic disciplines. Within this way of life, the beauty of chastity shines forth at almost every turn. Apart from it, chastity becomes merely *sōphrosunē*, self-control, as it was for the ancient pagans. The element of other-worldly beauty is lost, and with it the power of chastity to withstand the pressure to conform to the world.

We Orthodox today have our work cut out for us: to speak from within this ancient and holy way of life to a modern world that is in desperate need. To many the beauty of chastity, which is so apparent to us, seems like sheer fantasy. Yet it is hard to look honestly at the state of the world and think that the alternative it offers truly has much appeal. As always, it is only by entering more fully into the Orthodox way of life that we become able to share its riches with others. That is the task, and the privilege, that lies before us.

# The Splendor of Purity

## Kh. Frederica Mathewes-Green

Back in my college days, when dinosaurs roamed the earth, I was a hippie and a spiritual seeker. The range of spiritual options on campus was broad, and I sampled a bit of everything: Hinduism, Ananda Marga Buddhism, Zen Buddhism, Hare Krishna, Transcendental Meditation. I say I was a "seeker," but that's not exactly right; I didn't expect to reach a destination. I was, more accurately, a spiritual *explorer*, always journeying toward a new horizon.

There's something about that era that I don't understand, though. My friends and I savored all the more-esoteric religions, but for some reason we hated Christianity. We ridiculed it automatically, reflexively. The Jesus Freak movement had arrived on campus and, when I ran into newly born-again students, I enjoyed trying to shake their faith. I'd tell them that the myth of a dying-and-rising god isn't unique to Christianity, but appears in religions around the world. I savored any opportunity for unsettling them and sowing doubts.

I don't know why, but Christianity roused in us a kind of malicious delight. Somebody donated stacks of the paperback New Testament, *Good News for Modern Man*, and they were placed in all the dorm lobbies. My friend George, at his dorm, tore them up. When bystanders objected, he said, "It's a bad translation." We thought this was hilarious—a witty bit of revolutionary theater.

What's more, we felt that Christians *deserved* this treatment. We felt that it was right to hurt them, but also felt that it would somehow "do them good." I can't remember now how hearing their faith insulted was supposed to help them. It was some inner spark of mischief that made us want to embarrass and sadden them. Other religions didn't stir up this zestful cruelty; only Christians roused our desire to wound and gloat. The hostility was so inexplicable, and so intense, that you'd almost think it was an outbreak of some unseen spiritual battle.

We told each other that Christians were stuffy and judgmental, but the Jesus Freaks on campus weren't like that, actually. They looked like us, like hippies, and were generally humble, cheerful, and amiable. And we found that annoying. I would say, "There's something wrong with those Christians. They're *too clean.*"

◆ ◆ ◆

Looking back, I think the "cleanness" that irritated me was their *purity.* There's something about purity that awakens in those who don't share it a kind of malicious delight. And this desire to hurt them feels justified, even righteous; even when purity is just minding its own business, it feels like they're preaching at you. So you want to see them shocked and hurt. It would be sweet to see their tears.

Our culture's appreciation of purity hasn't increased over the intervening decades; on the contrary, it seems like *everything* has been sexualized. And if it's not specifically sexualized, it's crude. I stopped shopping for greeting cards some years ago (I just make my own), because almost every one I picked up was organized around a fart joke. I stopped going out to see new movies, because gross-out scenes so often jump out with no warning. When this coarsening began, a couple of decades ago, it seemed flatly juvenile, as if everything was being marketed at thirteen-year-old boys. But, in time, that passed. I don't mean the crudity; what passed was the sense that it was juvenile. Now it's marketed at *everybody.*[18]

Perhaps the biggest factor in this general coarsening is the overwhelming amount of porn now available. Pastors like my husband know all too well how pornography destroys marriages, friendships, families—in short, destroys people. It is addictive, of course; it's designed to be.[19] It is cumulative, of course, and when addicts become inured to shocking images, they are hit with something more shocking still. The trend is toward increasing degrees of violence.

When author Martin Amis was assigned to write an article about the porn industry, he had to watch some videos and filming. He wrote, "I kept worrying about something. I kept worrying that I'd like it."[20] Porn targets, he said, the "near-infinite chaos of human desire," and if you unknowingly harbor some sexual demon, "sooner or later porn will identify it" and bid it come forth.

Given all the varieties of sexual upheaval today, critics tend to focus on gay marriage, saying that it destroys traditional marriage. But in terms of sheer numbers, porn is *overwhelmingly* more destructive. And most viewers of porn are straight, for the simple reason that most people are straight. About two-thirds of American men tune in to porn at least monthly.[21]

Men are more likely than women to be enslaved by porn, but that doesn't mean they alone suffer its effects. When I'm out with my little granddaughters, I'm aware that nearly any man we pass could have terrible images burned into his brain. That's the world they will have to live in. When they're a little older, they may unknowingly date such men. They may unknowingly marry one. (Remember, the next step is violence.) All their lives, my granddaughters will be walking through a porn-saturated world.

But that considers only the impact on them. What about the effect on the men themselves? What is it like to feel that your mind is no longer under your control, that you can no longer stop the rushing thoughts that repulse and frighten you?

Yet it's so easy to begin. At the University of Maryland a few years ago, two student groups, Christian and atheist, held a debate. At one point the pastor made a reference to porn, and suddenly the room was filled with hooting and applause. I was shocked; I guess I'm just naïve. I didn't know this was something young men are *proud* of. But that brief reference to porn got the most enthusiastic audience response of the evening.

◆ ◆ ◆

That brings us back to the question of why purity would be hated. Those who continue to think, quaintly, that it is beautiful and worthy of honor, are no threat to anybody's freedom; their private opinion doesn't restrict anyone else. We are at a rare (perhaps unique) moment in history, in which everyone is free to seek any kind of sex they want. The old moral standards are long gone. How could it be possible for the pendulum swing back, and an understanding of the beauty of purity be recovered?

Our impulse, naturally, is to find a better way to argue for it, to develop better rhetorical terms. But let's start by making a distinction that became very clear to me in the pro-life cause, that there is a difference between being a *proclaimer* and being a *persuader*.

For a number of years in the 90's, I was vice president of Feminists for Life, a pro-life feminist organization. In summit meetings with leaders of other pro-life groups, I noted that many of my allies fell into the camp of "Proclaimer," for they were dedicated to the goal of speaking their beliefs. We certainly felt bombarded by pro-choice arguments and assumptions in the common culture; it had become the fashionable position to hold, and the pro-life cause was broadly derided. So they were determined to proclaim their stubbornly contrary convictions, on the principle that both sides have a right to be heard.

I felt then, and still feel, that that was a misguided approach. It's undeniably gratifying to proclaim your despised belief, but that doesn't necessarily advance the cause. If we're going to ever change things, we'll have to *persuade* people. In a democracy, you don't get ahead except by winning people to your side, and they only come voluntarily. So we need to listen to the reasons people give for being pro-choice, and come up with persuasive responses. Our insistence on saying "It's a baby" doesn't make people think "It's a baby," but rather, "Right, we already know you think it's a baby." We need to craft instead the kind of rhetoric that persuades, and draws converts in.

So that's what I did for a decade or so, mostly in the 1990s, when abortion was still a lively public issue. (It was replaced for a long time by the gay issue, though it has lately returned as states pass various abortion laws.) I helped found a "Common Ground" movement where pro-life and pro-choice people could meet and talk about the reasons for their beliefs. (It wasn't "common ground" in the sense of "compromise," but "safe ground" where differing beliefs could be expressed and received.) In these sessions I kept listening to pro-choice arguments, gathering insights for a persuasive response.

Over the years I spoke on every Ivy League campus and dozens of others, presenting a secular, feminist argument against abortion. The following Q & A sessions were invaluable for testing the rhetoric I was developing, and so I kept fine-tuning it, seeking to persuade hearers and not merely proclaim my beliefs. I believed that, if I found the right language, I could draw pro-choice and undecided people toward the pro-life goal.

Well, I failed. Over and over, I saw that people would pay no attention to what I actually said. They didn't want to. The lines were so bright in their minds—pro-choice good, pro-life bad—that the "pro-life" label was itself sufficient to show I wasn't worth listening to. If it was a debate, I would explain why abortion was a bad thing, but then my opponent wouldn't say why abortion was a good thing; she would say why I was a bad *person*. She didn't defend abortion; she attacked me.

And the really heartbreaking thing was, the audience loved her for it. They were looking for a reason, any reason, not to listen to me. Maybe what I was saying was starting to make too much sense. They wanted to run back under the safety of the pro-choice label, and my opponent showed them a way to do so. For that, they were thunderously grateful.

And my attempts to phrase things persuasively, to find new angles, to address concerns about women, say, were actually seen as duplicitous. I recall a TV host telling me, "Other anti-choicers at least are honest, because they admit they only care about the fetus; but you're worse, because you lie and pretend you care about women." In their mind all pro-lifers are bad guys, and anything I did to disrupt that prejudice just amounted to being *sneaky*.

I painfully realized that, with the abortion issue (and probably with the cause of purity), what we're up against is good old peer pressure. Humans are herd animals[22], and prefer to remain within the safety of the ruling herd. Pro-choice good, pro-life bad, as the *Animal Farm* piggies would say. This was a bitter realization to me, I have to say, because I spent years thinking that I just hadn't yet found the best way of expressing the argument. I polished and rephrased diligently, believing the rhetoric that said people think deeply about the abortion issue, and having faith that the right way of presenting it could draw them to our side. Realizing that instead this was a matter of peer pressure, a pre-intellectual need to cling to the ascendant social label, and that I could reformulate arguments endlessly without a shred of success, was, as I said, a bitter thing to grasp.

◆ ◆ ◆

Where, then, can we find hope? I'm a fan of old movies, especially the old black-and-whites from the past mid-century. And I came to notice that they sometimes take for granted, or even celebrate, behaviors that we would disapprove today. As hard as it is to believe, sometimes the older generation embraced values that we today frown on, and the pendulum swung back toward a more conservative morality.

One example would be drinking to excess, to the point of drunkenness. There was a period, during Prohibition and afterward, when it was seen as cool to be visibly drunk. Just as popular actors are now expected to do a nude scene, they were then expected to do a drunk scene, and most of the big names did so in one film or another. Drunkenness was cool because it was rebellious; it was a way of defying the prudes and scolds who disapproved of alcohol, the folks who supported Prohibition. And it wasn't enough to just enjoy a glass of wine; if others were going to be able to see and admire you, you had to be *visibly* drunk—in Southern parlance, "knee-walking, lamppost-talking" drunk. These scenes can be puzzling to today's audiences, and the famous actors appear unpleasant or even repulsive. But back then it was extremely hip.[23]

This remained fashionable for decades, even after the repeal of Prohibition made drinking no longer literally rebellious, and it was reconsidered only gradually. When the comedy "Arthur" came out in 1981, with a perpetually drunk lead character, there were some objections; some people could testify from family experience that alcoholism is not all that funny. Today "Arthur" is still enjoyable to watch, because of its excellent writing and cast. But the central premise, that someone bumbling around drunk is inherently hilarious, doesn't make sense anymore. Visible drunkenness has now been broadly rejected (except among college freshmen), and today you'd never see it portrayed as cool.

So something that was firmly embraced as hip and cool has now been just as firmly rejected. People changed their opinion about that, and changed for the better—spontaneously, it seems, without an ad campaign or nationwide revival.

That's good news. If behavior considered cool is actually causing pain, eventually people recognize that and, sometimes, turn away from it.

Something else that was thought thrilling and hip, even from the silent era, was male adultery. This was treated as something that should be taken for granted, that "boys will be boys," and a wife should ignore such misbehavior. A woman who did so was considered to be wise.

In "The Women" (1939), famous for its cast of 139 women and not a single man, the lead character discovers that her husband is having an affair with a saleswoman. She resolves to go to Reno for what was called a "quickie" divorce (Nevada then required only a six-week residency). But her mother counsels her to ignore her husband's escapade, saying that it's wrong for a wife to destroy her family for the sake of foolish pride. Note that it's the wife, not the wandering husband, who is destroying the family.

Visible drunkenness and male adultery are two values that were celebrated in film for most of the twentieth century, but are emphatically regarded in a negative way today. Those are just two of a list that could be much longer: cigarette-smoking, rough handling of women, and over-the-top racism. Once you start noticing such things, the examples are everywhere. We think, "Old movies uphold old-fashioned values," and they do; we just have no idea what those values were.

So the culture has changed for the good in a number of ways—but notice that it wasn't occasioned by widespread revival. It wasn't because someone designed an effective public relations campaign, or the right people got elected. Apparently, it just happened; the behavior entailed too many negative subsequent effects, and this became too obvious too ignore. I think one way this happens is when the generation who were children at the time, who saw how much these behaviors hurt their family, grow up and begin telling their own stories. As they present the damage done, others chime in, and the previously admired behavior is sometimes rejected very suddenly. It's like the rejection of the attitude was just waiting to happen, like the collapse of the Iron Curtain.

We are currently in a time, perhaps unprecedented, when talk about all kinds of sexual behavior is pervasive, even inescapable. And we Christians who value purity are very much on the outside, expressing beliefs that the culture can't even understand. There's little likelihood that, if we could only find the right way to say it, we'd win people over; I found that out with the pro-life issue. It's the beliefs themselves that they reject, and changing the words won't fool them.

It's still important to keep speaking out, of course; we have to plant our flag and stand by it, even if it attracts only jeering. Even more than that, it's important that we live up to our beliefs, which is the true test of our convictions. But we should expect to be ignored, or even hated and attacked, by those who can't resist that surge of malicious delight.

In fact, we should be prepared to find that standing up for our beliefs just turns us into lightning rods. Our opponents need a visible figure to nobly oppose; remember how excessive drinking became fashionable as a way of flouting people who opposed alcohol? Today there's the same kind of craving to find someone to cast in the role of oppressor, and discover some disapproving square to shock. It's not rebellion if no one is trying to stop you.

That's why people who do see the beauty in sexual purity, who try to practice it and encourage others, can find themselves unexpectedly cast as the bad guy in some stranger's personal drama. No wonder those who value purity tend to do so quietly, keeping their beliefs within the context of home, church, and community. Purity has become a deeply unpopular opinion, fit only for religious oddballs.

And yet, in other contexts, we all value purity. Don't we want purity to be top priority at the local dairy? On a stroll through Whole Foods, how many times do you see the word "Pure" on packaging? Dozens of magazines have "Pure" in their title, apparently believing that it sells magazines. About the only thing our fractured nation agrees on the necessity of guarding nature's purity.

Everyone understands the beauty of purity in other contexts. So why is sexual purity the exception? Why does it elicit a zesty, flavorful hate, and a desire to wound and sadden those who love it?

◆ ◆ ◆

Oddly enough, in the Orthodox Church we hold up as an example—literally, on our iconostasis—a man who was killed for denouncing sexual impurity. In his icon, St John the Baptist stands on a desert landscape, with a bowl at his feet displaying his severed head. A scroll tumbles open from his hand:

> O Word of God,
> See what they suffer,
> Those who censure the faults of the ungodly;
> Unable to bear rebuke,
> Behold, Herod has cut off my head,
> O Saviour.

King Herod was "unable to bear rebuke" for marrying his brother's wife; St John was unable to stop rebuking. We know how that story ends, for St John.

But, for King Herod, nothing changed. He did not find St John's words persuasive, and after John's execution he stayed married Herodias, right up till his death.

Might anything persuade people to honor sexual purity, if they don't instinctively sense its value? It's hard to find the words, and even attempting to find them makes us look like tasty targets. Meanwhile, the world keeps advertising the availability of everything anyone might desire. What could ever change this situation?

Well, to take the long view, there's the fact that it's false advertising. Wanting sex is not the same thing as having it. Every year, a fresh batch of twenty-year-olds rolls off the conveyor belt, and every year everyone else looks a year older. Time is relentless. Attractiveness is fleeting. Alongside the exalting of "free" sex, the two-faced world maintains a barrage of ads for snacky, fatty foods; these may be irresistibly comforting in the wake of rejection, but they affect the figure in ways that render it ever more rejectable.

Some years ago I noticed that there was a word that, if I said it during a speech, the audience would freeze. The word is "loneliness."[24] The freedom to have no obligations to anyone else means, conversely, that no one has any obligations to you. The personal repercussions of that disconnection grow more terrible with each accumulating year. Sexual liberation has set us free, like an astronaut cutting through his air hose. It's the freedom to be lost—completely lost and alone.

How much does it have to hurt, before people start saying, "This isn't fun anymore, I want something else"? How long till they say, "If the price of not being alone is being faithful and caring for someone else, I'm willing to accept it"?

The alternative to loneliness is not just marriage and family, but community. Those annoying prudes and scolds of earlier days had influence because they represented, not merely their own opinions, but their community's consensus. They vocalized the commonly held understanding of the bounds of acceptable behavior. The price of being in a community is reckoning with such commonly held expectations; the price of not being in a community is despair.

To imagine the re-establishment of community interdependence requires a very long view, and in the short term we're not likely to be any more successful than St John was. Even attempting to present the beauty of sexual purity is likely to attract only that mysterious malice. But we can continue to exhort and encourage each other, and in our private lives do our best not to let the team down. We can be watchful about the material we allow into our minds, because it's very hard to get it out again. We will find no better advice than St Paul's words: "Whatever things are true, whatever things are noble, whatever things are just, whatever things are pure, whatever things are lovely, whatever things are of good report, if there is any virtue, if there is anything praiseworthy— meditate on these things" (Philippians 4:8).

We can practice our convictions and support each other, but that's a long way from changing the culture. Are we fated to live in a time when Christians are becoming more and more irrelevant in the public arena?

All the early Christians could do in the public arena was die. But they did that with such grace that they gradually drew the whole world to Jesus Christ. We, their descendants, may not be able to win public influence, or transform cultural norms. But by doing faithfully what God has called us to do, we take our stand alongside those early martyrs, and all the rest of the "great cloud of witnesses" (Hebrews 12:1). With them, through the ages, we bear witness to the inexpressible beauty of purity, and the everlasting glory of the Kingdom of God.

# The Gnosticism of Modernity and the Quest for Radical Autonomy

Prof. Bruce Seraphim Foltz

## Introduction: The Two Worlds

A world is not primarily an aggregate of things. Rather, it is the way things themselves fit together into a whole. Let us then begin with an experiment in thought. Let us begin by envisioning two, very different worlds and comparing one with the other.

The first of them is deeply rooted in an unbounded goodness and infused with a beauty that radiates from unexpected places. Although sometimes surprising and even alarming, this world is interwoven with a harmonious order that lends itself to being trusted and known. And beyond this, it reveals to the innocent or to those with purified hearts, an inner graciousness that testifies to a loving Creator and Ruler. The soul can find a home in this world that everywhere beckons the faithful to a higher, truer, more beautiful order whose energies it reveals.

The second world is a harsh prison, dark and disorderly; it has been designed by evil powers to entrap the elusive spark that is buried within the soul. The deity itself is utterly remote from this baneful world—a world that offers within it no hint of anything transcendent at all—and this *deus absconditus*[25] is quite unconcerned with what happens far below. Therefore, bereft of transcendent grace, the alienated spirit-being who is cast into this alien world must rely on special knowledge to even know that a deity exists, much less to escape this deranged world order, as well as the hostile soul and body that even more deeply enchain it.

These are radically contrasting worlds, completely opposed to one another. But in reality, they are not two different worlds at all. They are two ways of understanding the one world, our own world, the only world there is. The first is the way of Orthodox Christianity, and the second is the way of Gnosticism, perhaps the most virulent and perennial of the ancient heresies, a way that still conceals itself in subtle and often surprising forms today. But our modern form of Gnosticism is typically masked by alluring promises, and its virulence is intensified by the very fact of its remaining incognito.

## The Cosmology of Modern Gnosticism

The philosophy of Kant, for example, might seem a most unlikely site for Gnostic teachings. And isn't modernity bright with hopes of progress, rather than affirming a darkened, Gnostic world? But beneath the dreams of enlightenment and progress lies a Gnostic worldview that precisely *epitomizes* modernity itself, a view of the world as cruel and indifferent to human aspirations. More than a century ago, Fr Pavel Florensky argued that this is perhaps most evident in Kant's twin doctrines of the autonomy of nature and the autonomy of humanity—both foundational for our modern understanding of the world. The human will, Kant insists, must be seen as radically free and autonomous, echoing a refrain that is already audible in Renaissance humanism and Protestant anthropology. And the physical universe, Kant continues, is also radically autonomous, operating on its own, much like a vast machine, and thus it is intelligible solely on its own terms. But in relation to what or whom, Florensky asks, are man and nature claimed to be autonomous?

Surely, he answers insightfully, it is against God that their autonomy is being asserted. Kant argues that nature must obey only its own laws, and indeed must conform to them if it is to be an object of human experience at all. We could not, that is, even experience an event that was not structured by the spatio-temporal-causal matrix, which must frame our reality like the bars of an epistemological prison. An angel could not enter such a world to announce salvation, nor could a Saviour ascend from it. Such a world, our modern world, is even more radically severed from any epiphany of a transcendent God than is the Gnostic world of the Bogomils,[26] to which Florensky compares the worldview of modern science.[27]

No depth of meaning and no breeze of transcendence would emanate from this godforsaken world, which presents itself only as a possible object of science. Conveniently, such a world offers no inner resistance to manipulation and control, presents no grain against which we ought not to cut. In Heidegger's words, it is a world that has become an inventory or resource (in German, *Bestand*) for technological control and consumption. Remote from God, and lacking an inner *logos* that commands our respect as a principle of meaning and order, it is entirely at our disposal to refashion as we please. For like the dark and hostile world of the earlier Gnostics, it has been fashioned by blind and random and indifferent forces, entitling and indeed obliging us to refashion it, to recreate it, to become its new creators.

And since both body and soul are part of this same, randomly generated world, it is up to us to refashion them as well, so that they might better serve the demands of the evanescent "spirit" that we sense within us. No longer am I a unity of body, soul, and spirit, for my body (formerly understood to be God-given) is now an alien shell, which I will change and reconfigure at will—for example, by covering it with tattoos or puncturing it with piercings, altering it through what we ironically call "cosmetic surgery," or trying to change its sexual constitution through hormones, enhancements, or surgical invasions. For the inner spirit with which I identify is seen to be trapped in its body as in an alien element, and this profound sense of alienation from my own embodiment—this dissonance "between the truth of the cosmos and the truth of existence"—suggests that I may be thrown into the wrong body altogether, perhaps even into the wrong species or onto the wrong planet.[28] One need only recall here the pervasive themes of alienation and estrangement in recent thought and literature, not to mention the sophomorically rebellious, adolescent rites of passage that today often continue for a lifetime, to glimpse the gnostic underpinnings of our contemporary worldview.

Hans Jonas, in the most important and influential recent work on Gnosticism, points to Pascal as prophet of this experience of the universe entailed by our modern Gnosticism. No longer is it *kosmos* or adornment in the ancient sense, nor is it *ktisis* or creation in the Christian sense, for it lacks both beauty and order. It possesses only magnitude and immensity: its signature feature is its infinity. "Cast into the infinite immensity of spaces of which I am ignorant, and which know me not, I am frightened," writes Pascal, an avowed Protestant Christian.[29] "I am frightened and amazed," he continues, "at finding myself here rather than there; for there is no reason whatever why here why here rather than there, why now rather than then."[30] For within this inconceivable immensity, there is only meaningless, indifferent, de-sacralized space, without plan or purpose. "Gone," comments Jonas, "is the *cosmos* with whose immanent *logos* my own [*logos*] can feel kinship, gone the order of the whole in which man has his place."[31] Meaning and order must instead be imported and imposed by humanity itself. And this nihilistic indifference of the world, Jonas argues, this eerie silence of empty spaces, is even more uncanny, even more inhuman than the overt hostility that characterized the universe of ancient Gnosticism. This is the cosmology of our own modern worldview, our modern Gnosticism.

**Social and Political Views of Modern Gnosticism**

But just as notable is the social and political theory of modern Gnosticism, most exhaustively studied by Jacob Taubes and Eric Voegelin. Both scholars see the pivotal figure in this development as a twelfth-century Italian monk named Joachim of Flora, who contested Augustine's understanding of history as divided into two epochs by the Incarnation of Christ. For Joachim, in contrast, there are three periods of history, that of the Father (from Abraham to Christ), that of the Son (from Christ to the twelfth century), and that of the Holy Spirit (beginning with the twelfth century). In this third epoch, the Church will become superfluous, for humanity will be led directly by the Holy Spirit, acting through a spiritual elect initially consisting of (we might have guessed) Monk Joachim and his fellow Franciscans, revitalizing the ancient notion of a Gnostic elite.[32] And here, as Voegelin emphasizes, for the first time the vaporous *eschaton* of Gnosticism—originally the mere hope of transcendent respite from the evils of this world—is projected as an immanent possibility for the existing world. As Taubes notes, the Gnostic God had previously been radically opposed to this world and utterly alien to it. Just as alien had been the kindred sparks or spirits imprisoned here below, whose only hope was to navigate all the obstacles and blind alleys the *archons* of this world have imposed to keep it in chains. Now, with this culminating third epoch of Joachim and his successors, the *eschaton* is to be realized within this world. The Gnostic elites no longer constitute a conspiracy of individuals planning a prison break that would free them into some empyrean realm, but a community of the elect divinely commissioned to bring heaven down to earth.[33] Significantly, Joachim's views here receive opposite valuations from Taubes—who sees them as the inception of the progressive and revolutionary spirit in modernity—and from Voegelin, who famously warns us moderns not to "immanentize the *eschaton*."

Modern-day Gnosticism robustly embraces the idea of inaugurating a third "new age," making it what Voegelin sees as the great heresy of modernity. It also generates a special pathology on the part of the utopians and revolutionaries who advance it. For like the ancient Gnostics, they too see the world as an alien place, created not by a beneficent God, but by hostile or indifferent forces, whether understood as evil deities, blind powers of nature, economic or racial groups, or social institutions. However, the lower world is no longer regarded merely a prison-house from which to take flight, but more like a poorly constructed, rundown building that needs rebuilding according to a different blueprint, that is, the *eschaton* revealed to the gnostic elect. This means, however, that every element of the "givenness" of creation—all that is given rather than made, *all that is natural*—must be demolished or denied. All must be leveled to prepare for the "dream world" of the Gnostic visionaries. For as Marx insisted, "a *being* regards itself as independent only when it stands on its own feet [through owing] its existence to itself alone," that is, its life must be its "own creation." Thus, the order of reality itself, within which man is, in fact, clearly dependent on nature, must be destroyed to make way for a speculative reality created by "human self-consciousness as the supreme deity." That is, Voegelin notes, the modern Gnostic seeks to "replace the reality of being with a second reality," the "dream-world" of its own creation.[34]

The pathology, Voegelin argues, lies not just in the Gnostic alienation from the existing world, but from the refusal to see its reality at all—a virtually psychotic "non-recognition of reality." For openness to the real would falsify the Gnostic dream order, casting light on actions that, in Voegelin's words, "in the real world would be considered morally insane."[35] The "transfigured dream world," a modern mutation of the ancient vision of a far-off realm surrounding a transcendent deity, must be further supported by a quarantine on any questioning of the Gnostic vision, for this would risk an awakening from the dream. Thereby, the dream world now displaces both the transcendent realm that once stood beyond our world, as well as worldly reality itself, whose vocabulary the dreamers appropriate, while radically changing its meaning.[36] Moreover, the creation of the new man requires the extermination of the old man, and therefore the murder of the God he once worshipped. The "death of God" becomes a central theme of the three great nineteenth-century Gnostics: Hegel, Marx, and Nietzsche.

Along with the positing of a dream world, the prohibition of questioning, and the "murder of God," a fourth element of the Gnostic vision is noted by Jonas, who shows how ancient Gnosticism rotated between an antinomian, and often libertine vision of morality, and on the other hand an extreme asceticism that condemns all earthy pleasures. And Gnostic sects since then have shown the same, strange oscillation, sometimes condemning all sexual activity (e.g., with the medieval Cathars, or as Florensky points out, with the bizarre condemnation of all sex in Tolstoy's *Kreuzer Sonata*) and sometimes advancing abandonment to dissoluteness.[37] Both of these, in fact, follow equally well from the Gnostic contempt for the earthly order, which can be combatted either by means of extreme, self-styled asceticism, or through the flagrantly libertine violation of all laws that govern this cursed realm, for these laws only help imprison us. Gnosis, then, can equally embrace (not uncommonly in concert) both the zealous English Puritan and the debauched libertine languishing in a French prison. But the path of debauchery seems to hold a special appeal. As Jonas puts it, the Gnostic can gain his freedom "by rendering to nature its own and exhausting its powers" that bind him. St Irenaeus, for example, reported that the Gnostic holds that "he shall not get free from the power of the [dark] angels that made the world . . . until he has committed every deed there is in the world, and only when nothing is still lacking will he be released to that [Gnostic deity] who is above the world-creating angels."[38] As Jonas comments: "Sin as the way to salvation, the theological inversion of the idea of sin itself—here is one of the antecedents of mediaeval Satanism; and again an archetype of the Faustian myth."

All this is neatly incorporated within the work of the Marquise de Sade, praised by Camus in *The Rebel*, where it is insisted that Sade is not an atheist, but a Gnostic who believes in "a criminal divinity who oppresses and denies mankind," and against whom rebellion is imperative.[39] The Enlightenment and its scientific worldview had already distanced themselves from God through the autonomy of nature and humanity. Politically, this had been implemented in the French Revolution and the destruction of the *ancien régime*. But Citizen Sade believed that this liberation was inadequate, for the idea of a Creator-God still lingered, if only in the imagination. Humanity must be freed from the Creator it has rejected by demolishing the very thought of God through revolutionary practice, which Sade saw as requiring not mere unbelief, but "a passion for sacrilege"—active blasphemy that would be profoundly offensive to the very idea of a Creator, while declaring war upon God's creation and all that is natural within it, seeking "to destroy what serves nature and to succor all that harms it; to insult it in all its works."[40] Significantly, he saw the most effective means of rebellion against the creator of this maleficent world as the blasphemous violation of every conceivable sexual prohibition, whether written or unwritten. Hence, those who dare to engage in and celebrate the most monstrous acts of sexual depravity—involving a panoply of unnatural horrors ranging from scatological indecency, to the violation of all bonds of kinship and friendship, to the outright murder of the sexual victim—become the Modern Gnostic's advance guard, the heroic shock troops inaugurating the reign of the "new man."

## Modern Gnosticism and the Autonomous Individual

But what of the individual who has embraced, however tacitly, this worldview of modern Gnosticism? An answer must begin with the radical character of the Cartesian *cogito* as entailing an ontological shift, a dislocation of our very sense of being from that of *substance* to that of *subject*. For Descartes' precise formula (and its logic) is not *cogito ergo sum* (I am conscious *therefore* I am) but simply *cogito sum* (*I am conscious: I am*). Within the consciousness of my own consciousness, and through this autonomous subjectivity alone, I am. For I am never merely conscious, but always simultaneously conscious of my own consciousness. That is, consciousness turns back upon itself by being aware of itself, thereby generating itself in the very act of self-consciousness. True consciousness is thus self-consciousness, producing itself through its very exercise. It creates itself, becomes its own foundation. Descartes thus recapitulates in philosophy the theological rebellion of his contemporary Luther, founding the modern worldview upon subjectivity. We are no longer in the world—rather the world is in our experience of it. Perhaps even more radically, he reverses the great affirmation of Exodus III: the "I AM" is not spoken, not given by the Creator, but accomplished by the creature, who by that fact becomes the new creator, the self-creator, the new *fundamentum inconcussum* or unshakeable foundation upon which all else is predicated, for whom all else is now an object.[41] And through this act of self-creation, consciousness asserts itself as radically autonomous from the world external to it, even if (as Descartes gnostically speculates) it has been created by an evil demon.

But alas, there are problems here. Hegel's celebrated master–slave dialectic showed that it is *recognition by another self* that allows self-consciousness to proceed beyond the empty, abstract formula of I=I, actualizing itself in the world.[42] This problem is further developed in Sartre's dilemma of the for-itself and the in-itself, where consciousness requires recognition by another consciousness, who meanwhile always threatens to objectify it, capture it within its own gaze, freeze it into an object that exists not *for itself* but *for another*. Radically free subjectivity, existing primarily through its own creation of itself, at the same time needs recognition by another self-consciousness to be more than an empty movement of pure reflexivity, that is, in order to have content, to *be something*. But when it is recognized *as* that something, it must immediately rebel against that objectification, negate it to insist on its own nothingness, which it mistakes for freedom. And back and forth, on and on. For Sartre, this is the unresolvable tragedy of the human condition. But, in fact, it is simply the agonized dilemma generated by the Gnostic self-creation of the autonomous individual in modernity.

It is also the anguish of identity politics. To ensure autonomy from an oppressive world of sinister origin, the individual must be self-defined, and indeed self-created—purified from the contamination of all that is merely given. If I am born into a certain social class, religious group, or above all "sexual identity," I must redefine, recreate myself in a way that conforms not to this lower world fashioned by nefarious powers—and it matters little whether these are seen as dark angels, social institutions, or sinister groups—but rather corresponds to the truer, higher world that the spiritual "spark" within me intuits. And there must be unlimited options open for this project of self-creation—not just two sexes, or two "sexual orientations," for example, but dozens, scores, hundreds that will allow for the discernment and realization of my higher "true" identity that his disordered world has obscured. Moreover, I must assume this new, self-created identity not just as something subsisting for my own eyes alone, but as something recognized by others—and not just for a few others, but as acknowledged by all others, who universally owe me this recognition. Why the importance of sexuality in particular? In Sartrean terms, it is because here I can pursue the ever-receding rainbow-end of being both pure subject for myself and pure object for another, lulling me into the deluded dream that I can be both at the same time. The Gnostic quest for radical autonomy, however, ends in a nightmarish oscillation between the exhilaration of liberation and the claustrophobia of objectification.

## Conclusion: The Two Paths

But this same dialectic was accurately diagnosed some two centuries ago by the Danish philosopher and theologian Søren Kierkegaard. In *The Sickness unto Death*, Kierkegaard maps the rotations and gyrations of the self that is trying to generate itself, trying to grasp itself in relation to others, trying to save itself. And he terms this agonizing exercise—through which self-consciousness twists and turns in order to be itself on its own terms—"*despair*" or more traditionally, as he notes, simply "*sin.*" Here, however, with the Christian Kierkegaard, in contrast to the figures just mentioned, there is a prescription for the ailment of despair: "the formula for the state in which there is no despair at all," he explains, is that state within which "in relating itself to itself and in willing to be itself, the self *rests transparently in the power that established it.*" The insane project of self-creation yields to the Creator and rests within His creating power. But there is more. For he immediately explains, "This formula in turn, as has been frequently pointed out, is the definition of *faith.*"[43]

More recently, both diagnosis and prescription have been eloquently reiterated by Geronda[44] Dionysios of Petra:

> When Satan, who was the first and highest angel, lo*oked away from God and turned his attention to himself*, there we had the first seed of an ego. He took his spiritual eyes [away] from the view of the Holy Trinity, the view of the Lord, and he looked at himself and started to think about himself . . . . That moment started the history, the reality, and the existence of the ego—which is not reality, but the refusal of reality. Ego is the flower that comes out from the death of love. When we kill love, the result is ego.[45]

More recently, the Greek Orthodox theologian Christos Yannaras has affirmed the patristic emphasis on *erōs* that culminates with St Maximus, and that reveals both why our salvation depends upon properly directed *erōs*, and why the Gnostic misdirection of sexuality is so toxic:

> The way of life, as Christians encounter it in the person of Christ, is the way of *erōs*: it is to *empty oneself* of any demand for individual self-existence, to draw existence and life not from our individual (and mortal) nature but from [a free] personal relationship . . . Not to claim anything but to share everything, in a frenzy of self-giving born of love. Love, the interpenetration of life that comes from *erōs*, is the mode of existence of God, the way that persons are made immortal—the way of true life.[46]

And so too, here we can see the danger posed by disruptions of *erōs* for our relations with God, especially as they are mediated through the dream reality of the ego.

Modern Gnosticism, like its ancient predecessor, is preoccupied with the self and its feelings of estrangement from the world, to which it responds either, like the ancient heresy, with an attempt at escape, or as is more typical in modernity, with a futile attempt to recreate the world according to its own dream-like illusions. In contrast, the perennial Orthodox alternative to the gnostic illness flows ecstatically in the opposite direction, toward God and the other person in a movement of love. Thus, not only are there two ways of viewing the world. There are also two paths within the world: on the one hand, the path of faith and life and love, and on the other hand, the path of hubristic world creation, desperate self-creation, and *libido dominando* or will to power. That is, there are the paths of Orthodox Christianity, and that of its heretical Gnostic distortion that has now become foundational for modernity itself.

# *Gnosis, Techne, Hedone* (Erudition, Technology, Pleasure): Secular Anthropological Assumptions Today

Rdr Gaelan Gilbert

## Introduction

This article is in part an exploration of the terms of its cryptic title, which names three overarching principles or assumptions at work in modern secular anthropology. It is within such an anthropology that gender and sexuality are elevated into meta-categories of human identity, or so I will argue. In our current moment, gender and sexuality have come to all but totalize public definitions of the contours of human experience and social relationship. This brief reflection offers some preliminary observations on these aspects of our culture's "social imaginary," the shared mind-set that lies behind progressive positions on gender and sexuality.

In the particular context of North Atlantic societies in the early twenty-first century, a secular cultural anthropology has certain recognizable characteristics. There are three I want to highlight: (1) it ideologically presumes to possess the enlightened prerogative on acceptable descriptions of human life and identity, monopolizing public discourse on this topic; I will refer to this as *gnosis*; (2) it assumes the positive and quasi-salvific role of technology and technique in redressing and improving human existence—*techne*; and (3) it assumes as the highest aim of human life the attainment and experience of pleasure and the concomitant avoidance and vilification of pain—*hedone*. Underneath all three of these lies a foundational emphasis on the individual will and the specifically modern concept of its uninhibited right to make self-defining choices. These three characteristics, and their relation to an overdetermined notion of individual volition, shall serve to organize our following analysis.

While in this chapter I will move through *gnosis, techne, hedone* in order so as to trace the symptoms to the source, their actual existential unfolding tends to move in the other direction. Starting with the search for pleasure (*hedone*) that self-love and self-will precipitates, one attempts to enable pleasure's artificial enhancement or to increase its frequency, which today typically involves the use of various technologies (*techne*), whether digital, social, contraceptive, or otherwise. Whether initially or only belatedly, the need then arises for an epistemology or framework of thought (*gnosis*) that can be deployed by the individual to justify the search for pleasure as definitive of a happy, individual life. But this progression from *hedone* to *techne* to *gnosis* is actually a recursive movement, establishing a vicious feedback loop of instant gratification, artificially assisted intensification, and ideological justification that is powered by the energy from its destructive effects.

These three aspects of a secular cultural anthropology are thus both instrumental in and symptomatic of the elevation of gender and sexuality to the existential level of identity. Arguably the most extreme form of this identitarian privileging of gender and sexuality occurs within the ideologized discourse surrounding transgenderism, and thus this discourse—*and not the actual character or experience of people themselves*—will serve as the objective focus of my critical reflections.

The italics above suggest that a disclaimer is in order, one vital to the spirit and purpose of this chapter. While the object of my critique are the ideological assumptions of transgender*ism* as a discursive phenomenon, I intend to utterly distinguish such a phenomenon from the value and personhood of the individuals suffering from gender dysphoria and its related psychological syndromes or conditions.[47] In other words, for purposes of this chapter, transgenderism refers to an anthropologically reductive and politicized discourse, which, even while sometimes deployed and adhered to by individual persons, must be distinguished from the complex of facts and findings that are denoted clinically by the term "gender dysphoria." The latter of which attempts to name, with objective criteria, a psychological condition actually experienced by individual human beings. What is more, the exigency motivating my analysis stems directly from the perception that, in speciously affirming the fashionable assumptions of a secular cultural anthropology, the ideologized discourse of transgender*ism* actually obstructs the genuine therapeutic process of self-acceptance and the attainment of psychological stability that can accompany a diagnosis and treatment plan for gender dysphoria, especially in youth. As the American College of Pediatricians puts it, "gender ideology harms children."[48]

In talking about transgenderism, then, I am speaking about a way of talking about the body and people's experiences of them that is woefully inadequate and distortive. As someone trained primarily in literary figuration, semantics, and rhetoric, I found my critique on attention to discourse, which is the vehicle for ideological (and nonideological) thought. At the same time, because words refer to the world, attention will also be extended to the nonlinguistic phenomena referred to with language.

### Gnosis, or E-rudition

So, first, *gnosis*. It is perhaps stating the obvious to reiterate that Gnosticism is a useful analogue for transgenderism. First, the bodily modification and transformation proposed by transgenderism as a part of social "transitioning" and justified with reference to an interior psychic experience of gender identity has an uncanny analogue with the ancient Gnostics' treatment of the body as an accessory inessential to the human person.[49] As inessential, the body for Gnosticism is seen as fundamentally separate from and inferior to the soul or self. The actions undertaken in the body can thus be held at a certain remove from the quality or purity of the soul, which remains in Gnosticism immune from any strong identification with embodied existence.[50] In transgenderism, the idea that a person can be "born into the wrong body" betrays a related assumption: namely, that the human person can be defined in opposition to his or her given sexed body, and that an existential grounding in the chromosomal objectivity of physical embodiment is ultimately, if one so decides, irrelevant to *who one is*.

Secondarily, there is an analogy insofar as certain Gnostics proposed a postmortem change from female to male that the souls of all enlightened, truly spiritual persons (esp. those of women), having shed their bodily shells, will undergo.[51] Gender transition, at least from female to male, was a part of how certain Gnostics imagined the experience of the afterlife.[52] The relation to transgenderism here is obvious.

The Orthodox Christian position on matters of sexuality, gender, and embodiment is at once far simpler, and also more nuanced than the Gnostic. According to Orthodox Christian teaching, people aim to loosen through God's grace our passionate attachment to the things and experiences of this world, and yet at the same time affirm the inherent and fundamental goodness of the material body and natural creation. This balance is grounded in both the *Genesis* accounts of creation, which repeatedly deploy *kalos*, the Greek term for goodness and beauty, to describe the material world (in clear contrast to Babylonian, Manichean, and Platonic creation myths). The life of Christ in the

Gospels likewise evinces the clear regard that Jesus has for the bodily welfare of others. The doctrine of the Incarnation, of course, provides the touchstone for a Christian emphasis on the worthiness of materiality for redemption. Not only did the Logos of God become incarnate in human flesh as Jesus Christ, but Christ himself, after overcoming death through his death and bodily resurrection, did not shed his incarnate flesh, rather bringing it up to the throne in heaven. In so ascending, He deified human nature, which is created in two complementary and enduring forms: male and female, patterned after the mysterious relationship between Christ and the Church, referred to in Pauline and Johannine literature as His Bride.[53]

But what of the connection in my title between the term *gnosis* and its English counterpart, erudition? Beyond a disdain for material creation and a contrived system of intermediary celestial agents and gendered personifications, the ancient heresy of Gnosticism also more fundamentally assumed possession of secret knowledge which the uninitiated inevitably lacked and were, therefore, held to be on a lower spiritual and even existential level. There is an inherent elitism within Gnosticism that is noticeably absent in the Apostolic witness.[54] The term "erudition" is a term that, while bearing some positive connotations, can be etymologically analyzed to imply a similarly elitist conception. To be erudite is to have come "out", implied by the prefix *ex-* or *e-* in Latin, from the condition of rudeness or ignorance, *rudis*. Erudition is thus meant to connote a sort of knowledge that, for Gnostics, distinguishes one from the common person, who is rude, crude, and ineluctably bound to the lower, embodied realm.

How different this is from the Apostolic emphasis on the simplicity and universality of the Gospel message. This simplicity was off-putting for some of the more educated theologians in the first centuries of the Faith. Various church fathers, educated in eloquent Greek and Latin rhetoric and philosophy, narrate their initial struggle with the seeming rudeness of the Scriptures. St Augustine's personal journey in *Confessions* is characteristic in this regard: he goes from a more erudite position to a humbling acceptance of the fact that God has "revealed [his wisdom] to babes" (Matthew 11:25), and that mere rhetorical adornment is no match for the profound depths of narrative truth in scriptural history, often expressed in the mundane agrarian, commercial, or nuptial imagery of the Psalms, Prophets, and Gospel parables.

Moreover, as a subjective attitudinal quality accompanying secret knowledge, elitist e-rudition is a mechanism or and symptom of schism. As Fr John Behr has argued, the catholic Christian witness in the early centuries always took the precariously balanced if capacious middle way, open to a range of positions as long as they did not compromise the central truths.[55] Heresy, on the other hand, deriving from the Greek noun, *haeresis,* or "choice," typically involves an emphasis on particular, chosen notions or passages to a degree that surpasses their proper place within the tradition. Heretical positions always insist that, despite not being evident to any but a small group, what *truly matters* is this or that point or fragmented idea or aspect. Thus erudition, in the negative sense we have been using it of *gnosis,* naturally accompanies theological heresy, almost as an instrument of self-justification and buttressing against dialogue. In claiming possession of knowledge that is arcane and inaccessible, gnostic erudition raises the status of *those who know* and renders those who do not know as inconsequential, with whom no dialogue is deemed desirable, or possible.

My claim is that there is a similar sort of gnostic exclusivism that pertains in the transgenderist position itself, though it need not be intentional or even consciously held. In fact, as with any ideologized position, it is often unrealized.[56] This is true on collective and individual levels. Collectively, there is the social atmosphere today in which the merest whisper of dissent to the accepted forms of reference to sexuality is slapped by the media with the label of bigotry, in which speakers who thus dissent are protested or assaulted on university campuses, and in which the heightened social prestige of victimhood becomes a status that one can appropriate and thereby emotively immunize oneself from the requirements of rationality and civility that otherwise apply to public discourse.[57]

In this context, the social capital of political correctness amounts to a sort of *gnosis,* rendering the holders of progressive positions functionally untouchable in their moral innocence and laden with fashionable terminology, whereas dissenters are vilified or ostracized. Ironically, as we've seen in the news over the past few years, this e-rudition can lead to divisions between homosexuality activists and transgender proponents. Lesbians, for example, tend to adhere to some form of feminism; but from the perspective of transgender theory, feminism is far too old-fashioned in its defense of only *biological* women. "Women" with male genitalia must not be excluded, is the absurd claim. Does this betray a lurking misogyny or double-standard? The recent controversies about males identifying as females in female athletic contests beg the question.[58]

The further irony is that transgender theory itself adheres to essentialized notions of gender which form the supposed basis for the need to "transition" from male to female, or vice versa. While purporting to defend "gender fluidity," in other words, transgenderism actually ascribes to inflexible notions of "maleness" or "femaleness" as an interiorly experienced condition utterly separable from biological embodiment. Such notions are used to justify bodily modification but miss the obvious point that stereotyped images of hyper-masculinity or objectified femininity do not exhaust what it means to be a man or woman.

It would be remiss to neglect, however, the ways in which conservative milieus likewise bolster themselves with irrationality and scare-mongering, and the sad reality of violence in both directions, whether from Antifa or neo-Nazism. The main point here is that in collective issues which hinge entirely on ideological positions, sides are inevitably taken, opponents are treated as deplorables, and in-fighting ensues as categories are repartitioned without any reference to first principles, common ground, or workable compromises. It is as if the e-rudition of ideology has raised sexuality to matters of religious, existential importance—which is precisely what has happened.[59]

On the level of the individual, the unquestionable practice of self-diagnosis when it comes to transgender identity has had the strange rhetorical effect of rendering taboo the possibility for any conversation with someone about his or her sense of gender identity. The dialogue is presumed to have always already taken place *inside* the individual, figured as an "internal struggle" that results in a "liberating realization" and decision to "come out." After this internal conversation, so to speak, to question or even talk at all with someone about his or her gender identity is understood to be a violation of the individual's freedom, and thus to be, well, rude. And not only rude, but even violent, in the sense of potentially stimulating emotional trauma. Thus someone can, through insistence on the experience of emotional duress as a result of others' non-recognition of a preferred gender identity, appropriate the status of a victim and its concomitant attribute of moral innocence, at least on the socio-rhetorical plane at which ideological discourse functions. At this point, all rational criticisms become taboo, and the conversation is shut down for fear of causing offense.

Another way of describing this is a withdrawal into what Charles Taylor calls "the buffered self" and there to stage a dialogue with oneself (helped often enough by celebrities on various digital media platforms). It is above all on social media where the new gnosticism of transgender ideology has been winning the day in the minds and souls of millennials and their Generation Z successors.[60] This ideologizing also afflicts conservative platforms and milieus, of course. The pathological influence of media (social and news), which treats transgenderism with all the respect of the latest fashion—that is, with frenetic attention—is a real contributing factor to the deepening impossibility of having open yet thick-skinned, respectful yet unsanctimonious conversations, at the very least because it is breeding a generation of hyper-sensitive individuals who have adolesced in echo-chambers of reified experience and self-defined meaning.[61] What is most problematic about the breakdown of open, informed conversation on these issues is the accompanying perpetuation of suffering, both social and psychological, by people genuinely struggling with gender dysphoria, who in the absence of a larger social discussion (rather than shouting match) are misled away from understanding the scientific and psychological complexities of their situation.

In sum, gnostic "e-rudition" operates as a basic assumption in transgenderist ideology in two ways: (1) in the assumed collective possession of an enlightened perspective and elite, politically correct jargon that renders all who disagree morally deficient or incorrigibly ignorant; and (2) by claiming that the experience of gender itself is an interior and unquestionable *qualia* disconnected with embodiment, and inaccessible to rational discourse. As such it must be given absolute prerogative as a basis for self-diagnosis and the subsequent process of transitioning. Unfortunately, it also tends to bring with it the requirement of altered speech and behavior in *other* people, for the most part bystanders whose emotions and beliefs are disregarded in the process.[62]

### *Techne,* or Technology

Next, onto *techne,* or technology. Jacques Ellul rightly described our society as a technological one, through and through, not just in the increasing presence of advancing technological devices, but in the fundamental mind-set of an approach to the material world and the betterment of human life through the former's manipulation, utilization, and in some cases exhaustion by mechanical or artificial means.[63] The material world includes our bodies. Thus, with the transgender movement, the technological approach of exerting human purposes over the natural world now includes the adaptation and transformation of human physiology.[64]

But let's pause to reflect a bit more deeply on how *techne* forms a second background element to the transgender movement and its discourse. First, let me be clear that technology has unparalleled benefits when it comes to the material standards of human life. The advances in medical technology alone are staggering, and the conveniences typical of daily life due to technology are not only ubiquitous but undeniable. This being said, there are obvious "externalities" as well, such as negative side effects of various new media technology on health, cognition, and psychological development, but in the context of a secular cultural anthropology these tend to get pushed under the rug in the face of how well technology both monetizes and increases the velocity of money.[65]

An ideological dimension also surfaces. The technological society, as Ellul calls it, or "technopolis," to use Neil Postman's neologism, is a world which sustains a belief that not only will technological advancement continue to make life better and more replete with convenience, but that the fundamental problems and challenges we face—whether ecological, medical, political, psychological, or even spiritual—can be solved through technological means, through technique, the manipulation of material elements.[66] People have come to put a sort of faith in technology.[67] And the use of materialist, technical approaches to all aspects of human life is now the norm. Naturally, then, the transgender movement looks to technological processes to solve what it sees as problems associated with biological embodiment. To see this, we can recall the three basic stages in the process of assuming a transgender identity: (1) social "transition"; (2) hormone treatment; (3) surgical modification.

The last two are, respectively, internal-chemical and external-surgical techniques for extirpating bodily aspects of reproductive development and sexual biology. Yet anatomical modification is not without its detractors, even in the transgender community, when it comes to youth and teens. The Witherspoon Institute has posted testimonials from parents of children claiming transgender identity and demanding treatment.[68] These parents lament their helplessness in the face of what is becoming accepted precedent and practice in legal, medical, and educational domains: supporting the child's demands even if they are below the age of consent.[69] The headlines earlier this year about a judge in Canada approving hormone treatment requested by a fourteen-year-old against parental opinion and consent is a chilling example—and it pertains to the enshrined status of the individual will that we'll look at more below.[70]

Other collaborative groups have emerged that provide articulate, first-hand reflections on the concerning dangers and social pathologies that can accompany what some call "the transgender narrative."[71] A well-researched set of findings in a letter from a parent group of more than 1,100 individuals named the Gender Critical Support Board, and who promote the *eventual* transitioning of youth to their preferred gender once puberty has passed, have been sent to the

American Pediatric Association in order to argue against hormone treatment in prepubescents and adolescents, for several reasons.[72] Chief among these reasons are (1) the tendency for a sense of gender identity to fluctuate prior to the attainment of sexual, physiological and psychological maturity; (2) the resulting permanent sterility and the other side effects that come from hormone treatment; and (3) the irreversible nature of certain surgical procedures. Such letters and other publications indicate that there is a well-informed, growing resistance to technologically enabled practices of hormone treatment and surgeries in the field of pediatric medicine, at least.[73]

In the turn to hormone treatment and surgery that defines the final stage of attaining a transgender identity, the human body is subject to technological procedures that "correct" it, according to the individual will of the subject who happens to be "inhabiting" it.

### The Will

A crude Cartesian philosophy of the "ghost in the machine," in which the soul is separate from and merely inhabiting the body, naturally accompanies the technological worldview. Such an idea is ironically similar to Gnosticism, but very far from Orthodox anthropological teachings. We must remember that the primary human attribute in relation to *techne* is the will. More specifically, what Friedrich Nietzsche calls "the will to power."[74] As the philosopher Martin Heidegger explores in his essay on the subject, technology can even be defined as the artificial extension of the power of the will. To use philosophical jargon, the ontology of technology is a voluntarist, or volition-based, ontology.

In our twenty-first century, the individual will and its choices have been emptied of their substantial relationship to God or the orienting transcendental predicates of Being: Goodness, Truth, and Beauty. The will has itself replaced these standards with its own transcendent ideal: choice. When one is able to do and choose what one wills, at any given moment, one is considered free. No consideration is given in this impoverished perspective to the enslavement of the will itself to the passions. Such an oversight exposes this limited definition of freedom to be perhaps the least free, because *internally* bound. David Bentley Hart offers a synopsis of the modern predominance of the will in his essay, "Christ and Nothing (No Other God)":

[W]e live in an age whose chief moral value has been determined, by overwhelming consensus, to be the absolute liberty of personal volition, the power of each of us to choose what he or she believes, wants, needs, or must possess; our culturally most persuasive models of human freedom are unambiguously voluntarist and, in a rather debased and degraded way, Promethean; the will, we believe, is sovereign because unpremised, free because spontaneous, and this is the highest good. And a society that believes this must, at least implicitly, embrace and subtly advocate a very particular moral metaphysics: the unreality of any value higher than choice, or of any transcendent Good ordering desire towards a higher end. Desire is free to propose, seize, accept or reject, want or not want—but not to obey. Thus society must be secured against the intrusions of the Good, or of God, so that its citizens may determine their own lives by the choices they make from a universe of morally indifferent but variably desirable ends unencumbered by any prior grammar of obligation or value []. Thus the liberties that permit one to purchase lavender bed clothes, to enjoy pornography, to become a Unitarian, to market popular celebrations of brutal violence, or to destroy one's unborn child are all equally intrinsically good because all are expressions of an inalienable freedom of choice."[75]

One could easily imagine added to this list the choice to dress like the opposite sex, take hormones, and surgically alter one's genitalia, which, if it meets the minimum sufficient criteria for a voluntary act, would thus be affirmed as an expression of the human pursuit of happiness that is as equally valid as any other. Such stunning logic, which is being exported rapidly through globalization, lends insight into what the late Fr Thomas Hopko may have meant in his famous comment about living in America; it is both the best and the worst or most dangerous place to be an Orthodox Christian. Far more dangerous than overt persecution, in other words, are the cultural perspectives that eat away personal faith from the inside and replace God with the individual will on the throne of the human heart.[76]

In the situation Hart describes, anything perceived as an attempt to keep someone from pursuing his or her choices is understood as an evil that must be opposed, unless those choices can be shown to be keeping someone else from pursuing *their* choices—the litmus test of classical liberalism. But beneath liberalism lurks a deeper, older philosophical exaltation of the will, that of voluntarism. Voluntarism, expressed most succinctly as the principle that an action is morally good simply because it was freely willed, grew from a deviation in the traditional understanding of God, and can be traced historically to the fourteenth-century doctrine of divine voluntarism propounded by John Duns Scotus and William of Ockham in western Europe.[77]

Today, as Hart suggests, voluntarism is all but enshrined in our secular cultural anthropology. The bifurcation of social life into public and private spheres, the Enlightenment philosophies of liberty and subjective rights, the rise of both absolutist and democratic political forms, and the rapid expansion of a consumerist global capitalism in the twentieth century all contribute in differing ways to the prevalence of voluntarism, in which choice by default determines the good *What* one chooses becomes, in fact, irrelevant. *That* one chooses is all that matters. Voluntarism flattens all value and meaning by reducing everything to the unstable judgement of the human will.

This enshrinement of individual choice is, quite obviously, an important premise of the transgender narrative, which elevates the will of the individual subject over and above all other considerations, whether biochemistry, embodiment, social belonging, or even emotional and psychological well-being, contrary to how that sounds.[78] What is more, voluntarism is a sort of universal acid, which, by magically rendering something good simply through choice, expedites the corrosive influence of progressivism on longstanding cultural and social norms. The suggested policy guidelines in the Gay, Lesbian & Straight Education Network (GLSEN)'s "Model District Policy on Transgender and Gender Nonconforming Students" provide an instructive case in point.[79] While there is not space here to go into the voluntarist emotivism that underpins this document's definition of "gender identity," we can let that definition speak for itself.

The GLSEN document defines gender identity as "a person's deeply held sense or psychological knowledge of their own gender," and proceeds to build a top-heavy edifice of safeguards and protections upon a concept that is supposedly impossible to diagnose by anyone *other than* the individual in question. In possessing privileged access to a self-understanding that has no rational (i.e., falsifiable) basis, individuals claiming a transgender identity are then treated by the document as sacrosanct. To their *self-defined* emotional well-being, others are soon beholden; the document insists on a string of constraints upon the speech and behavior of other people in the name of guarding the subjective "sense" of gender identity that is "deeply held" by a single individual.

Such recommendations evince one of the key strategies of policy documents such as this; namely, to simplify and normalize as a free expression of the will what is in fact a debilitating psychological condition.[80] The transgender narrative subordinates language of mental illness in favor of recommending biotechnological treatments that obstruct the biochemical processes of the reproductive and endocrine systems, sacrificing both fertility and natural hormonal development to an ideological position without philosophical and scientific coherence. In clinical diagnoses of gender dysphoria, on the other hand, psychosomatic complexity is acknowledged and followed by the recognition, initially upsetting though it may be, that someone who has a "deeply held sense" of alienation from their sexual biology is likely afflicted by a treatable form of mental illness.

To presume that the act of affirming forms of mental illness as normal is a legitimate form of treatment is not only incoherent; it also does more harm than good. Yet such normalization is how the ideology of progressivism, for better or ill, responds to social pathologies—it embraces them as expressions of individual volition, and pretends there is no harm done. Yet there is harm done. It is those who struggle with gender dysphoria who suffer most in the aftermath of transgender ideology's recommendations. Among those who, after undergoing a gender transition and then, years later, regret it and realize it was a mistake, the most common statement one hears is "why didn't anyone try to dissuade me?"[81] This statement suggests that the manner in which such issues are increasingly handled by professional practitioners, as well as friends and family, must be revisited, despite a social climate saturated with litigation and accusations of intolerance or bigotry.[82] The more the enforced acceptance and "celebration" of aberrant psychological conditions or immoral socio-ethical positions becomes entrenched in the institutional structures of daily life, the more the approach of normalization will be recharacterized as loving, despite, in this case, the negative impact on the individuals genuinely struggling with accepting their biologically grounded gender. Given the often serious social and work-related repercussions for being even perceived as dissenting from politically acceptable positions in sexuality and gender, people are increasingly inclining to a position of simply "live and let live," even if that means surrendering loved ones to technological procedures that cause irreparable self-harm. The dissolution of practices of and spaces for genuine, care-full conversation accelerates this inclination.

And so we must ask: where does self-love, in the facilitating context of *gnosis* and *techne,* tend to direct the will, and thus the human person? This question brings us to our final and third term: *hedone.*

### *Hedone,* or Pleasure

Lastly—but actually moving backward to the originating element—*hedone,* or pleasure. According to Orthodox patristics scholar Jean-Claude Larchet, the "pleasure-displeasure principle" is the "source of all passions," having become a predominant factor of human anthropology as a result of the Fall.[83] For the Church Fathers whose position Larchet is enunciating, the Fall describes a shift in which "we consider the reality of the world, and especially our own body [...] no longer according to the contemplative activity of the spirit, but through our senses alone, to which our intelligence and our other faculties are henceforth subordinate. The pleasure and pain that we experience in our own body become, as a consequence, the main criteria by which we judge the value of things."[84]

Larchet goes on to explore St Maximus the Confessor's treatment of humanity's "impassioned" state as *philautia,* or self-love, in which "one group of passions stems from the search for pleasure," and "a second from the avoidance of pain," and a third from their combination.[85] If our modern age exalts the individual will and choice as foundational values, it is because individual, sensual pleasure has become the ultimate good. I am not suggesting that people espousing a transgender identity are sex addicts or obsessed with pleasure; rather, I am calling attention to the pleasure principle as a cultural assumption of the secular anthropology within which a position like transgenderism becomes intelligible. Today, when happiness has arguably been redefined along voluntarist-hedonist lines, and its pursuit enshrined as a basic right, an acknowledgement of the originary importance and contemporary significance and shape of pleasure-seeking is worth making, however cursory.

When it was philosophically proposed as the highest good of human life, whether by the Epicureans in ancient Greece or the Utilitarians in Victorian England, pleasure often meant the enjoyment of and taste for refined aesthetic, culinary, or ideational experiences. But both Epicurus and John Stuart Mill would be appalled at where the pursuit of pleasure (or maximized rational utility) has brought us today: not only the wasteland of popular culture and internet instant gratification, but also a string of epidemics involving addiction to dopamine-flooding technologies: slot machines and online gambling addiction (Americans spent 117 billion dollars on gambling in 2016 alone, with 85 percent of that revenue coming through slot machines)[86]; sex addiction through the consumption of pornography (America's second largest international export, after military armaments)[87]; unprecedented increases in screen time, especially in children (with dire cognitive and psychological impacts)[88]; and ongoing substance addiction crises, particularly with opioids, which killed upwards of 65,000 people in the United States *in 2016 alone.*[89] Gambling (esp. slot machines), drugs (esp. opioids), and screens all work similarly in their effect on the human brain and its pleasure-receptors.[90] In this regard, one has a basis for saying that the pursuit of and addiction to cheap, instant, repeatable pleasure is literally killing society.

But how does this relate to the identitarian sexuality of transgenderism? It's multifaceted, and so worth widening our scope to sketch a broader picture. Essentially, people are becoming ever more poorly equipped to resist the temptations available in modern life. Partly due to the ubiquitous presence of digital media, people are increasingly beholden to a narrow "social imaginary" regarding the contours of a happy life. Omnipresent screens consistently portray happiness as the frequent attainment and sustenance of pleasure. This understanding of happiness, in its adherence to purely immanent or materialist visions of human flourishing, tends to devolve into various forms of addiction, at both the highest and lowest social strata.[91] In a globalized, consumerist, media-saturated society, those who do not attain material success are more prone either toward self-medication and other coping mechanisms or to the surrender of critical self-knowledge in politicized enclaves which offer a basis for meaning beyond pleasure. The withering of faith and a sense of the transcendent orientation of life, along with the decline of historically perdurable social institutions such as family, school, and church, leaves individuals without nonpolitical communities of substantial, accountable belonging or a deeper sense of purpose that would enable resistance to the pursuits of hedonism and their assumed anthropology, which is an impoverished vision of human existence.[92]

Within this anthropology, the human will, when enabled to gain access to voluntarily sought pleasure, and in the absence of good (read: freely chosen) reasons to resist this pleasure, should seek such pleasure. Within this meagre concept of human purpose, it then becomes not just possible but logical to define the individual primarily as a sexual being; doing so subordinates the body to the pleasure principle, as Larchet suggest above. This is the primary significance of *hedone* and hedonism as a secular anthropological assumption of transgenderism: it is the illusory, immanent *telos* without which the sexualization of human identity, whether toward heterosexuality or any of the LGBTQ+ forms as reified reductions of human desire would not be possible, or even thinkable.

The sexualization of human existence carries with it the assumptions of *gnosis* and *techne* discussed above and presumes the normality of a secular anthropology. It is a vicious feedback loop, which can only be disrupted or exited through a recognition of and entrance into an alternative vision of human purpose. Such a vision is offered by the historic Church. From a perspective informed by the patristic theology and ascetic, liturgical spirituality of Orthodox Christianity, the entire secular anthropological nexus and its hyper-valuation of pleasure is not only contradictory, but tragically naïve. From an Orthodox Christian perspective, a life lived under the aegis of the (self-)will to power (toward pleasure) is one that quickly becomes enslaved to the passions, losing freedom through its misdirected use. The tragic irony here is that exaltation of pleasure, which for secular modernity is human freedom's highest goal, is for Orthodoxy a proof of our fallen condition, as Larchet following the patristic tradition suggests. To adapt a phrase from Jean-Jacques Rousseau, one could say about any context within which a secular anthropology reigns, that "man is *called* free; but is everywhere in chains."

### Conclusion

Together, *gnosis, techne,* and *hedone* constitute a threefold assumption of the secular anthropology within which the phenomenon of transgenderism becomes culturally intelligible. It is to the critical dismantlement of this ideological discourse that we must, among other things, turn our attention, if we are to advance the discussion regarding the interrelationship of humankind's transcendent horizons in Christ and the good place of sexuality in human life. Doing so is actually a part of laboring to help alleviate the suffering of those afflicted with gender dysphoria, in two ways: first, by insisting that the accurate diagnosis of a debilitating condition—with humility and compassion—is the first step in receiving healing; and second, by presenting faithfully the profound vision of human personhood and purpose in Christ—one of unending *epektasis,* no less—that is put forward within the spiritual anthropology of the Orthodox Church.

The faithful presentation of this vision, so to speak, is not primarily an intellectual or academic enterprise. It involves dying to self—the death of self-love—for love of God and neighbor. God in His wisdom has given humankind the means to participate in the life-giving death and resurrection of Jesus Christ: and that means is the ascetic spirituality and sacramental liturgical worship of the Church, which assume the goodness and beauty of material creation and orient us toward the purification and healing of the human soul *and* body, as we pray in the office of Preparation for Communion.

As Orthodox Christians, we must remember that all are in need of healing, and that we are each liable to surrender on a daily basis to our particular passions, whatever they may be. Because of that, we must attend, through God's grace, first of all to the plank in our own eyes, heeding the Apostle Paul's injunction: always "in lowliness of mind let each esteem others better than himself" (Philippians 2:3). Thus we may learn to love others truly, receiving and sharing in the love that God pours out on all. In this process, we can learn from those who struggle with physical afflictions about what it means to truly accept our finitude and take up our crosses to follow the Lord. For in following Him, we are "always carrying about in the body the dying of the Lord Jesus, that the life of Jesus also may be manifested in our body. For we who live are always delivered to death for Jesus' sake, that the life of Jesus also may be manifested in our mortal flesh" (2 Corinthians 4:10–11).

# Orthodox Christian Bioethics versus Secular Bioethics: A Conceptual Geography

Prof. Mark J. Cherry

## Introduction

> The most disturbing truth for an intellectual, is that good arguments and well-crafted books do not save; only true repentance, achieved through grace in a ceaseless prayer of repentance, can bring one to salvation.
>
> —Engelhardt, 2017, 30

Orthodox Christianity is not rightly appreciated as an academic discussion or the results of discursive philosophical argument. Christianity's knowledge of rightly oriented moral decision-making is not found in the search for the guidelines for human conduct in the general tendencies of nature, nor does it attempt to justify principles open to all through sound rational argument. Indeed, such a rationalistic project is fundamentally misguided in its hopes to establish a universal set of canonical moral norms (see Engelhardt, 1996, chapters 1–4). The Gospel's admonition to convert the world, "Go therefore and make disciples of all the nations, baptizing them in the name of the Father and of the Son and of the Holy Spirit, teaching them to observe all things that I have commanded you" (Matthew 28:19–20), is not a request for more and better scholarly arguments. It is neither the rallying cry for a progressive political campaign to establish egalitarian social justice nor a set of moral sentiments. We are commanded to enter into the mystical experience of God that is central to the lifeworld of Orthodox Christianity, learning to pray properly and submitting to God in all things. Orthodox Christians must internalize the truth of the fourth-century adage: "if you are a theologian, you will pray truly. And if you pray truly, you are a theologian" (Evagrios, 1988, 62). This means that properly to understand the right, the good, the virtuous and the just, and thus appropriately to capture Christian

46

bioethics, one must first turn to God and come to know Him; and with love convert others as well.

This essay develops a conceptual geography of the collision between Orthodox Christian bioethics, grounded in traditional Christianity's experience of God, and the ideologically driven nature of its secular counterpart. For the secular world, Orthodox Christian bioethics is scandalous. After all, Orthodox Christianity knows the sinfulness of abortion, embryonic stem-cell research, sexual activity outside of the monogamous heterosexual marriage of husband and wife, surrogate motherhood, euthanasia, and physician-assisted suicide. Secular bioethics, with its emphasis on personal autonomy as self-sovereignty, has deflated the moral importance of such significant choices to mere lifestyle and death-style preferences. Even for many self-confessed Christians, medical decision-making proceeds without adequate appreciation of traditional Christian understandings regarding sexuality, reproduction, and end-of-life concerns. Bioethical decision-making is too often located within a pastoral discourse that simply affirms modern medicine and autonomous choice, while underscoring progressive egalitarian political interests. In such circumstances, there is a failure to recognize the importance of placing medical decision-making within a fully Christian context. Submitting to God's commands and seeking proper orientation toward Him for many have ceased to be important undertakings.

As this essay explores, Christianity, and thus Christian bioethics, must remain overtly true to its own teachings if it is to sustain an authentic and distinctly Christian culture. It must maintain a bioethics that advances the Gospel of Christ, so as to bring people to Christ. An authentic Christian bioethics will not be philosophical in the sense of relying primarily on discursive rational analysis. Christian bioethics is not merely one scholarly discipline among many. Christianity is first and foremost a practical spiritual enterprise: humans are created to worship God and to come to know Him. This central reality must frame all of one's life, including medical decision-making. Consequently, if the next generation is to remain Orthodox, Christians must be deeply and openly counter-cultural. Morality, and thus bioethics, simply cannot be rightly understood within the immanent horizon of human needs, interests, and personal or political passions. If we are to maintain authentic Orthodox Christian bioethics as a core component of a Christian culture, medical interventions cannot be properly understood if one only regards human needs and interests within an immanent horizon. A transcendent focus is essential: "For what will it profit a man, if he gains the whole world, and loses his own soul" (Mark 8:36).

## Christian Bioethics: Why a Transcendent Focus Is Essential

> The perfection of man does not consist in that which assimilates him
> to the whole of creation, but in that which distinguishes him from the
> created order and assimilates him to his Creator.
>
> —Lossky, 1957, 114

Orthodox Christianity has long appreciated that medicine is permissible, indeed to be encouraged, provided that it does not involve sinful actions, or otherwise impede one's relationship with God. Saint Basil the Great (AD 329–379), for example, reminds us that medicine is one of God's gifts to the world. It is to be used appropriately to benefit mankind:

> Each of the arts is God's gift to us, remedying the deficiencies of nature. . . .
> And, when we were commanded to return to the earth whence we
> had been taken and were united with the pain-ridden flesh doomed to
> destruction because of sin and, for the same reason, also subject to dis-
> ease, the medical art was given to us to relieve the sick, in some degree at
> least. (St. Basil, 1962, 330–1)

Medicine, however, must not involve sinful choices or actions, nor should it become an all-consuming endeavor. As St Maximus reminds us, it is often the distortion of human goods, rather than the goods themselves, which is sinful. "It is not food that is evil, but gluttony, not the begetting of children but unchastity, not material things but avarice, not esteem but self-esteem. This being so, it is only the misuse of things that is evil" (St Maximus, 1981, 83). As St Basil warns: "To place that hope of one's health in the hands of the doctor is the act of an irrational animal" (St Basil, 1962, 331). Christians must refuse illicit, sinful, or obsessive practices, never losing sight of the fact that medicine should not replace faith in God and submission to Him.

Medical interventions, such as vaccines, preventative and curative care, as well as surgery, to preserve and protect ourselves and our children are typically appropriate. Saint Basil, however, forbids "whatever requires an undue amount of thought or trouble or involves a large expenditure of effort and causes our whole life to revolve, as it were, around solicitude for the flesh" (St Basil 1962, 331). Applying such a standard requires careful spiritual guidance. For example, there are permissible uses of plastic surgery (such as fixing a cleft pallet, facial reformation after an accident, or breast reconstruction after radical mastectomy for cancer treatment), but cosmetic surgery in search of the "perfect figure" or the "most attractive nose" may lead one to focus on the wrong things. Medical assistance with reproduction that avoids impermissible practices, such as abortion, surrogate motherhood, or use of third-party gametes, can assist couples who are having difficulty conceiving a child, but an excessive focus on conception may lead the couple away from each other and from God. It is typically appropriate to expend time and resources endeavoring to save life, but refusing to recognize that life is finite and not of ultimate value may turn life itself into an idol. The risk at stake is not dying; it is dying unrepentant and unprepared for the dread judgment seat of Christ. Similarly, when appropriately turned toward God, suffering can help us to learn to control our passions, to love others unselfishly, and to love God above all else. However, St Basil concludes that even control of pain can be an important good: "with mandrake doctors give us sleep; with opium they lull violent pain." Again, it is the distortion of such goods, not the goods themselves, which can be sinful.

An overwhelming focus on medicine, whether in one's personal life or as part of a political campaign, can lead one astray from one's primary focus on God. Outside of a proper orientation toward God, even pursuit of the Christian virtues may disorient. Saint Maximus writes:

> There are many people in the world who are poor in spirit, but not in the way that they should be; there are many who mourn . . . many are gentle, but towards unclean passions; many hunger and thirst, but only to seize what does not belong to them and to profit from injustice; many are merciful, but towards their bodies and the things that serve the body; many are pure in heart, but for the sake of self-esteem; many are peace-makers, but by making the soul submit to the flesh; many are persecuted, but as wrongdoers; many are reviled, but for shameful sins. Only those are blessed who do or suffer these things for the sake of Christ and after His example. (St Maximus, 1981, 90)

Virtuous action and charitable concern for others must always be framed carefully through our struggle to know God. Similarly, taking care of the poor is good, but one must care for the poor out of love for and submission to God, not out of secular concerns for social justice. As the Gospel of John 13: 34–35 makes clear: "A new commandment I give to you, that you love one another; as I have loved you, that you also love one another. By this all will know that you are My disciples, if you have love for one another." A focus on social justice misses this central relationship with Christ. Those who reject Christ may also act in ways that are believed to benefit the poor.[93] As H. Tristram Engelhardt (1941–2018) notes:

> Jesus said, "If you want to be perfect, go, sell what you have and give to the poor . . . and you will have treasure in heaven; and come, follow Me" (Matthew 19:21). There is no evidence that He said, "If you would be perfect, become a political activist on behalf of the poor, establish a progressive redistributive tax system, and use state force to be sure all support a welfare program." Being committed to aiding the poor is not equivalent to being committed to using state force to compel nonbelievers to be charitable. Moreover, the final emphasis is on following Jesus. (1996, 406)

Jesus did not come into the world preaching the gospel of egalitarian access to health care.

### Christianity as Moral Sentiment: Weakening Christian Bioethics

Unfortunately, many have come to approach Christianity more like a set of moral sentiments and political commitments, rather than as an encounter with a personal God.[94] There has been a hope for a unity grounded in philosophical reason, which would guide moral content and rational choice, while also avoiding the sectarianism that would accompany a Christian morality grounded on God as lawgiver[95] or dependent on theologians as mystics, who encounter God Himself. As a result, even many supposedly Christian ethicists have stepped back from the mystical grounding that is central to the experience of God in the lifeworld of Orthodox Christianity to recast "Christian" ethics and bioethics in much more secular terms.[96]

The implications of this shift are significant. Even among many purportedly Christian scholars, philosophical analysis and political goals have come to be seen as more important than an encounter with the living God. Consider, for example, Richard McCormick (1922–2000), who played a foundational role in crafting bioethics as a field of scholarly inquiry. While his scholarship, at times, mentioned Christ, it judged human reason sufficient to defend moral and political analysis. As Peter Clark summarizes McCormick's position: "[h]uman reason, unaided by faith, can come to the same judgments about rightness and wrongness" (2008, 249). Moreover, "For McCormick, Christian commitment shapes human perspectives, motivation, and processes of reasoning, but only in a general way" (Clark, 2008, 249). Consequently, McCormick emphasized that "a Christian's conclusions will not be substantially different from those yielded by objective and reasonable but nonreligious analysis" (Clark, 2008, 249). McCormick concluded that Christianity does not yield "moral norms and rules for decision-making, nor do they conduce to concrete answers unique to that tradition" (Clark, 2008, 249). On this point, one might also consider James Walter, who held that "It has been my contention that there is neither anything distinctive nor specific to Christian ethics at the level of ground of ethics" (1980, 107). Or, Joseph Fuchs: "If, therefore, our church and other human communities do not always reach the same conclusions, this is not due to the fact that there exists a different morality for Christians from that for non-Christians" (Fuchs 1980, 11).[97] Or even Charles Curran: "Christian and the explicitly non-Christian can and do arrive at the same ethical conclusions and can and do share the same general ethical attitudes" (1976, 20).[98] While such prominent scholars may not have fully realized the implications of their analyses, or that secular bioethics would soon affirm abortion, euthanasia,[99] and gender reassignment surgery, their moral-theological reflections generally identified the material content of Christian morality with the ethics resulting from rational philosophical reflection (see Engelhardt, 2000, 15).[100]

In short, they ceased to underscore the gulf separating Christianity from the surrounding secular culture (Engelhardt, 2014, 147). There was a general unwillingness to recognize the obvious differences separating the various Christian religions (Engelhardt, 2014, 147). Commentators often even failed to accentuate the divergence between Christianity and other religions or cultural worldviews. If what matters is not submission to a living God and His commands, but living a moral life, and if the terms of such a life are available through philosophy, then God is extraneous and distinctively Christian bioethics unwanted. As a result, such "Christian" scholarship was essentially indistinguishable from its progressive secular counterpart (Engelhardt, 2014, 153–4).

Moreover, insofar as the Gospel of Christ is just a source of moral inspiration, a set of "gospel values" it is subject to philosophical reevaluation. This would mean that Christian bioethics would always be open for reinterpretation in light of reason's grasp of changing personal, social, or political circumstances.[101] As Immanuel Kant argued, for example, Biblical commands, such as "but I say unto you, love your enemies; bless them that curse you," should be appreciated as open to reinterpretation in the light of reason. Kant stated that he would seek to determine if such commands "can be adapted and accommodated to my existing moral principles" (1838, 141). Or, as McCormick put it: this requires "taking our culture seriously as soil for the 'sign of the times', as framer of our self-awareness. That means a fresh look at how Christian perspectives ought to read the modern world so that our practices are the best possible mediation of gospel values in the contemporary world" (McCormick, 1989; quoted in Clark, 2008, 246). Read in this way, even central Christian truths become culturally and historically relative, and subject to philosophical reevaluation in light of contemporary human interests.

## Secular Bioethics Is Not Christian Bioethics

Christians need to recognize that much of the "good" of which secular bio-ethics approves is perverse. Consider, for example, how such a secularization of Christianity has been used to re-conceptualize traditional Christian concepts, such as "holiness," "saint," ministry, and "the Lord's work," in support of currently popular secular assertions. Abortion, for example, has been embraced as central to the social equality of women, with abortionists often held in high esteem. Colleagues described George Tiller, a professional abortionist, as a "highly spiritual person," and referred to his abortion clinic as a "ministry" (Joffe, 2011, 203). Apologists have described the abortion procedure in very religious terms:

> "I felt I was doing the Lord's work," said the staff member charged with readying the stillborn babies to be seen by their parents. In almost identical terms, the woman who prepared the babies' bodies for cremation said, "God put me here to do this work." And the clinic chaplain, referring to the comfort she tried to give to grieving parents, recounted, "This was holy work we were doing here." (Joffe, 2011, 203)

Consider also this depiction of an abortion nurse as an angel:

> During her abortion procedure, the patient turned to Claudia, a fifty-year-old Latina licensed vocational nurse who sat beside her . . . Claudia perched forward on her stool to get closer to the patient and suddenly the patient grasped the crucifix that dangled from Claudia's necklace. . . . The patient was very focused on the crucifix and seemed to stop paying attention to what was going on in the room. . . . At the end, Claudia recalled, "I said to her, 'Mi hija, it's over.' And she said, 'It is?'" And then the patient took Claudia's hand, kissed it, and said, "You're an Angel." (Freedman, 2014, 6)

Abortion has even been described as a "sacred choice" (Maguire, 2001).

Note the intentional distortion of traditional Christianity. The abortion nurse is described as wearing a crucifix, rhetorically signifying Christian sanctity and holiness. The woman kisses the nurse's hand, as one might kiss the hand of a priest or nun. Such deformation of Christian language and practice is designed to propagate very secular understandings so as to reshape the background culture. Whereas St John Chrysostom reminds us that all things done by the angels are of Christ: "So that the things also done through Angels are of Him" (Chrysostom, Homily III on Colossians, 2004, 271), such distortions encourage us to treat as "saints," "martyrs," and angels those who have rejected Christ and His Church.

Consider also the example of sexual activity. The dominant secular culture of the West rejects the unbroken understanding of Christianity which places all carnal sexual activity within the relationship of husband and wife. The moral significance of such choices has been deflated. There is a presumption in favor of sexual freedom, the pursuit of self-satisfaction, separated from the biological norms of reproduction. This secular worldview is characterized as supporting equality for persons who prefer sexual relationships outside of the marriage of man and woman. Decisions about sexual practices are held to be "private" and largely beyond moral judgment. Decisions to engage in consensual fornication, sexual experimentation, and alternative sexual lifestyles are judged morally neutral. The secular world has replaced the Christian obligation to preserve the body in holiness with the pursuit of pleasure and self-satisfaction.

Advocates have sought to recast Christianity in such terms. Jillian Cox argues, for example, that homosexual acts should be understood in terms of "a contemporary notion of committed, egalitarian, lesbian and gay relationships" (2013, 369). Cox asserts: "Queer theologies expose the fact that much Christian theology has been based upon the assumption of a particular kind of love and sexual expression as universally normative" (2013, 370).[102] Homosexual acts, advocates conclude, should not be understood as sinful. Cox urges Christians to embrace "an understanding of sin that recognizes individual agency and exposes homophobic ideologies as sinful" (Cox, 2013, 369). Kathryn Reinhard similarly urges members of the Anglican Communion to reevaluate homosexual acts: "Rather than understanding homosexuality as a matter of 'sin,' the churches of the Anglican Communion would be better served by considering it as a matter of 'conscience'" (Reinhard, 2012, 425). The traditional Christian condemnation of fornication has been philosophically reassessed, judged an unenlightened prejudice, and set aside. "Sin" is attached to those who refuse to affirm the virtue of sex outside of the monogamous marital union of husband and wife.

It is worth noting that an increase in the number of children born to single mothers[103] and significant annual financial expenditures (some 17–23 billion dollars annually in the United States alone) on the direct medical costs of sexually transmitted disease are only two of the more predictable outcomes of this cultural shift.[104] Moreover, when persons finally decide to have children, regardless of whether they marry, important other interests routinely interfere. There is considerable pressure, for example, to ensure that offspring are free from mental or physical disabilities. Disabled children, after all, impact on career, lifestyle, and financial goals. This desire to give birth to a perfect and healthy child, who fulfills our expectations, has pushed the boundaries of medicine and permissible social choice:

- Abortion has become foundational for this cultural milieu. In part, easy access to abortion is judged essential, since men and women are willing to have sexual intercourse with others with whom they are not willing to raise children, and at a time when a child would be inconvenient for career or lifestyle. Since no method of artificial birth control is perfect, abortion is appreciated as a fail-safe. Similarly, prenatal diagnosis and selective killing in utero of children with a likelihood of significant disabilities have become a fairly routine part of reproductive medicine. Denmark, for example, instituted customary prenatal screening for Down's syndrome in 2006 as a public health initiative; other European countries, including France and Switzerland, followed. The data demonstrate that this policy has reduced the number of children born with Down's syndrome. However, there is no medical cure for Down's syndrome: to remove it from the population one must abort all children who test positive (Lindeman, 2015; see also Mansfield et al., 1999; Natoli et al., 2012).[105]

- Research teams have manipulated human embryos so as to substitute the original mother's mitochondrial DNA with a donor female's mitochondrial DNA. The goal is to generate human babies without mitochondrial defects, which are implicated in diseases such as multiple sclerosis and Parkinson's disease (Tachibana, Amato, Sparman et al., 2013; Tavare, 2012). A child is created with two mothers and one father. The mother who provides the ovum, the mother who provides the donor mitochondria, and the father who provides the sperm.

- Assisted reproduction is commonplace. Secular bioethics judges access to assisted reproductive services, often at tax-payer expense, central to civil rights and moral equality.[106]
- Surrogate motherhood has become more socially acceptable. Couples are paying women to gestate and give birth to children on their behalf. Surrogacy contracts create different types of arrangements for the production of children, such as (a) for the surrogate mother to be impregnated with the husband's sperm; (b) gestational surrogacy, in which the husband and wife create an embryo with their own sperm and ovum, but hire another woman to carry the child to term; (c) the use of donated embryos, or (d) the use of donor ova or donor sperm, and so forth. Surrogacy clinics have been established to assist homosexual men to become parents.[107]
- In a growing number of cases, parents have had their children, including very young children and teens, medically or surgically altered so that the child's phenotype, personal attributes, as well as potential or actual sexual behavior maps onto the child's (or the parents') current gender preference (Turner, 2017).[108]

Lost in this secular context is the Christian recognition that the union of husband and wife is the uniquely appropriate locus for reproduction. The purchase of gestational services for the delivery of a healthy baby sets aside the bonds of Christian marriage so as to reproduce in accordance with one's own passions. Extramarital partners, such as gamete and embryo donors or gestational carriers, should not be invited into the intimate relationship of husband and wife. To do so involves a form of reproductive adultery (see Engelhardt, 2000, 251–2). Moreover, it is not permissible to eliminate children from the family, when, through prenatal diagnosis, they are found to be imperfect; nor are we to deny the goodness of the body that God has provided through inappropriate surgical or medical alteration.[109] Everything, including the sexual union of husband and wife, the conceiving and raising of children, as well as how we utilize the human body, is to be done in a way that is compatible with approaching holiness (Engelhardt, 2000, 235).

In summary, the strategy of recasting the Christian experience of God in terms of secular philosophy and contemporary moral sentiment has had significant impact. Moral norms that follow the commands of God, but which are not justified in terms of secular rationality, have been critically brought into question. If Christianity is no more than a set of moral sentiments, ungrounded in God's revelation and the Church's mystical experience of Him, then it can easily be distorted in support of non-Christian conclusions or dismissed entirely as a set of old-fashioned moral claims. Indeed, the narrative that there is nothing distinctive about Christian morality, that all persons "can and do share the same general ethical attitudes" (Curran, 1976, 20), has been taken to mean that secular moral analysis is sufficient to secure bioethics. The significant dissonance between secular bioethics and traditional Christian bioethics has come to be appreciated as impeaching religious, rather than secular, claims.

**Secular Bioethics Cannot Secure Its Moral Judgments**

All of morality must be appreciated in terms of our relationship with God; every other attempt will always fall short of the mark. Without God to secure a definitive understanding of reality, together with a uniquely true ethical standpoint, moral claims represent no more than the subjective expressions of particular social, historical, and culturally conditioned perspectives. As philosopher Thomas Nagel situates the epistemic concerns: "If there were a god who was responsible for the existence of the universe and our place in it, the sense of everything would depend on him, but if there is no god, there is nothing by reference to which the universe can either have or lack sense" (2009, 7). Absent God, there is no way to step outside of one's own particular experience to know reality in itself. As a result, there is no way to talk about an unconditioned perspective on reality or the morality that such a perspective would secure. Without God, all moral claims are set within one's own personal intuitions, cultural interests, or political objectives, each of which is also always socially, culturally, and historically conditioned. Morality is necessarily fragmented into numerous perspectives with no in principle method for choosing among the various possible alternatives. As Richard Rorty summarized: "in such circumstances . . . morality is not a matter of unconditional obligations imposed by a divine or quasi-divine authority but rather is something cobbled together by a group of people trying to adjust to their circumstances and achieve their goals by cooperative efforts" (Rorty, 2004, xviii).

Without the ability to appeal to unconditioned moral meaning or to an unconditioned absolute perspective on reality to secure a canonical moral perspective, there can be no moral truth per se. The right, the good, and the virtuous are no longer appreciated as flowing from God's command but have been reduced to the idiosyncratic and socially influenced choices of particular persons and historically conditioned communities. There are only the particular moral intuitions that different persons affirm. This is why, for example, secular bioethics no longer appreciates choices such as abortion, voluntary euthanasia, and gender reassignment surgery, as serious matters. Each has been demoralized into particular lifestyle and death-style choices.

The same is true with regard to appeals to one's conscience. While affirmation of one's "deeply held moral beliefs" has come to represent independent access to moral and theological truth, there is the real danger that one will be misled by one's passions, or a corrupt underlying intellectual and moral culture. Yet, Pope Francis in his *Evangelii Gaudium* stated that "Non-Christians, by God's gracious initiative, when they are faithful to their own consciences, can live 'justified by the grace of God,' and thus be associated to the paschal mystery of Jesus Christ" (Francis 2013, 189, #254). Pope Francis did not note the need for an objective standard through which to judge the propriety of one's choices, or that one must repent for having followed one's conscience to sinful ends. Much of the "good" which the secular world uses to guide individual conscientious choice, Christianity knows to be sinful. As illustrated, the background culture of the Western world affirms lifestyles that sustain inappropriate human passions, darkening the intellect and our capacity to know truly. Within a fallen and broken culture, it can be difficult to discern appropriate choices undistorted by one's desires.

It is not enough to reason well or to act with a clear conscience. Without first knowing God, our concerns to act rightly, to create the good, or to enact social justice, will be distorted by human passions. Accounts of the moral life that do not properly recognize our relationship with the Creator will always be at best one-sided and incomplete, if not substantially misguided. The essential priority of first knowing God is reflected in the order of the two great commandments. "You shall love the Lord your God with all of your heart, with all your soul, and with all your mind" (Matt 22:37). This first commandment requires that we turn initially to God, in part for no reason other than that He is God, but also because it is only in terms of this foundational orientation that the truth of any other choice can be correctly determined. If we don't first love God rightly, we will not know what it means non-perversely to "love your neighbor as yourself" (Matt 22:39). To place our interests in the concerns of this world, such as passionate claims regarding equality and social justice, is to ignore the Pauline warning about the consequences of worshipping "the creature rather than the Creator" (Romans 1:25). Love of one's neighbor without properly loving God will always to some extent be deviant (see Romans 1:20). We may simply encourage our neighbors toward sin.

## Conclusion

Knowledge of God and His commands, including understanding our moral obligations, requires us to change. The role of the traditional ascetic disciplines (e.g., prayer, fasting, alms-giving, frequent confession, and repentance) is to aid in the development of spiritual discipline, as one learns to set aside one's own passions and desires so as to acquire a will in union with God. Rightly oriented and guided, such practices can be spiritually therapeutic: engaging in action which changes oneself and leads one closer to God, treats the soul and cures the effects of sin so that one can learn to judge rightly. As St Maximus put it: "Afflict your flesh with hunger and vigils and apply yourself tirelessly to psalmody and prayer; then the sanctifying gift of self-restraint will descend upon you and bring you love" (St Maximus the Confessor, 1981, 57).[110] For our salvation, we must come into union with God, which does not require living a morally upright life, but a life transformed by God. Secular morality will always fail in this regard.

Orthodox Christianity is neither a philosophical system nor a set of personal values or moral sentiments. As Engelhardt has noted: "'Christ came not preaching a philosophy, but inviting a very specific confession of Him as the Messiah of Israel and the Son of the living God' ([see] Matt 16:16)." (Engelhardt, 2014, 160). Orthodox Christianity "[D]oes not recognize the jurisdiction of an independent moral perspective that can critically bring into question the norms of behavior supported by a rightly ordered religious life."[111] If the next generation is to be Orthodox, we must take seriously the presence of God in the world; His commands and the Church's experience of His revelation. We must neither talk nor act as if Orthodox Christian bioethics is merely one more idiosyncratic and culturally embedded worldview. Rather, Orthodox Christian bioethics must of necessity challenge the nature, substance, and content of secular bioethics and secular culture. It is true that such a Christian bioethics will drive a wedge between Christians and non-Christians; it will also divide the various Christian religions from each other. It will not be ecumenical. As noted, it will be scandalous in the eyes of the world. But, as Engelhardt concluded, "should the moral requirements of the religious life offend 'ordinary,' that is secular, moral intuitions, sentiments, and settled judgments, then so much the worse for ordinary morality" (Engelhardt, 2007, 117). Such an authentic Christian bioethics will, however, permit us better to appreciate how and why one ought to live a fully Christian life. Such a Christian bioethics ought to help one navigate the narrow path toward God.

# Hierarchy, Inequality, and the Mystery of Male and Female

### Prof. Mary S. Ford

This brief reflection sketches out some background ideas concerning hierarchy, equality/inequality (and thus, discrimination), including a little about why we have trouble even discussing these kinds of topics in our culture, why there is so much strong emotion—and misunderstanding—about them, and then some other ways to consider thinking about a few aspects of this topic from a traditional Orthodox Christian perspective.

As the well-known sociologist René Girard has said, "All discourses on exclusion, discrimination, racism, etc., will remain superficial as long as they don't address the *religious* foundations of the problems that besiege our society."[112] Indeed, more specifically from an Orthodox Christian perspective, one problem we have in our culture is not starting with the revelation of Jesus Christ. One key we learn from His revelation is that everything is created by, or through, the Logos ("all things came into being through Him"—John 1:3 (NASB)). And this was commonly understood to mean not only that everything only exists in participation *with* God—through the *logoi*—but also that everything is a kind of communication *from* God, that all of reality has a meaning beyond itself, partly because it points to God (and/or spiritual realities) and/or makes Him (or them) present in some way. Some people indicate this by describing the world as "iconic," or they describe the world as a *sacrament*.

In the past, it was generally understood in cultures shaped by the Judeo-Christian worldview that God gave humanity two books: Holy Scripture, and the book of the world, or nature—material reality. As a clear example of this in the New Testament, St Paul says in Romans 1:20: "For . . . His invisible attributes are clearly seen, being understood by the things that are made." Saint Basil the Great (fourth century) quotes this verse from St Paul and then elaborates on it, explaining:

You will finally discover that the world was not conceived by chance and without reason, but for a useful end and for the great advantage of all beings, since it is really a school where reasonable souls exercise themselves, the training ground where they learn to know God: *since by the sight of visible and sensible things the mind is led, as by a hand, to the contemplation of invisible things.*[113]

Saint Maximus the Confessor (seventh century) also conveys this understanding when he says, "To those who have eyes to see, all the invisible (spiritual) world is mysteriously presented in symbols of the visible world."[114] Finally, from the twentieth century, St Nikolai of Zicha compares those who don't see the spiritual meanings of the material world to children who recognize the letters of the alphabet, but don't know how to read:

It is clear from this that whoever reads the natural without knowing the spiritual content and significance of what he has read, reads death. . . . Also, whoever considers visible nature as the only reality and not as a riddle in the mirror of the spirit, does not know more than the child who may recognize letters but is far from understanding written words.[115]

Furthermore, St Maximus even says elsewhere that "traces of God's own majesty are intermingled with sensible things. . . . These traces of God's majesty are able to transport the human mind, which uses them as a vehicle."[116] Thus, this is not just human imagination or human projections of itself, making God after our own images. Rather, it's that God has *created* reality so that through the visible creation, people can really know Him, and know about Him, and can know what are the foundational spiritual laws/patterns/realities that we should align ourselves with, and how they operate. In other words, we can learn through creation how reality really works.

Hence, material reality is not just "itself": it is also a communication about spiritual realities. But it can only teach us about spiritual realities *if* we know how to read it.

However, in a secular worldview, like that of our current culture, the material world *is* thought to be "just itself." Clearly, that would mean that it does *not* participate in, or communicate, or point to, any other reality. Rather, in this view, the way material things are is considered to be the result of random chance; and thus, they can have no meaning beyond their own random physical existence. This obviously implies that the world cannot be a "book." And if everything is the result of random chance, this also means that God—if there even is a God—is not the good God Who loves mankind, Who does everything for our benefit (as the Fathers say). That He *is* the good God Who loves mankind, doing everything for our benefit can, I think, rightly be called the foundational belief of traditional Christianity (having its roots in the Jewish tradition). So it's clear that the secular and the Judeo-Christian worldviews are fundamentally incompatible.

It seems to me that it is essential, for many reasons, to make clear to people in our culture what the true alternative to secularism is, as well as why the secular/basically gnostic or dualistic worldview is not only wrong, but also at best unhelpful—and generally even damaging in many ways.

At a fundamental level, and probably in an unavoidable way, people think analogically: we understand one thing in terms of another. Even those with a secular worldview cannot avoid this! So, as I explored in my doctoral dissertation many years ago,[117] people think of the relationship between the body and soul (however conceived of) in a way generally parallel to how they think about many twofold relationships that can in some way be seen as form and content, including the relationship between words (also, larger units of text) and their meaning.

For example, in a "gnostic" worldview, the material world is not a communication from God; it doesn't point to Him, it can't make Him present, it's not a sacrament, and it's not inherently good. The key gnostic pattern for form/content relationships can be compared to a cardboard box holding a pizza: the box has no intrinsic connection to the pizza, it has no value once it has conveyed the pizza to your house—it has served its purpose and can be thrown away. Or you could say it's like a box holding a valuable jewel, but even if it's a pretty box, the container is not really important. Similarly, for the gnostic, the body is understood to be a dispensable container for all that really matters—the soul.

The gnostic use of allegorical interpretation reflects this understanding: meanings are arbitrarily, randomly assigned, there's no logical connection, there's no natural or religious symbolism being used, there's no consideration of how the images are used elsewhere in the text, and so on. This is in direct contrast to what we find in the mainstream patristic authors when they use allegorical interpretation (which has been helpfully described as "incarnational" allegory[118]).

One key aspect of secularism is also a denial of the sacramental worldview and of the Incarnation properly understood, because instead of starting with the Incarnation and letting that inform us about what is possible, what the inherent patterns of reality are, or can be, the starting point rather seems to be the belief that a thing can only be itself.[119] Therefore, a form can't communicate a meaning or convey any kind of content if it is to be truly valued. So, for example, a commonly held idea by those who do biblical studies and/or theology who also espouse a secular worldview is that the Fathers "made" Jesus divine, and we have never been able to truly value his humanity ever since.

Those who deny that the world is a "book," that all these forms of the material world have a content, still think analogically, however. This means that in a secular worldview, all form/content relationships are understood in a kind of "gnostic," or dualistic, way: either things are just forms (or just contents); or the form is not really important, it's just a dispensable container—not co-inhering with the "content." In contrast, in a holistic and incarnational worldview. the form does co-inhere with the content, and so it is indispensable.

To emphasize again, in secularism, the world cannot be a book, and God cannot be the good God Who does everything for our benefit. For the way things are is rather understood to be the result of random chance, so the material realm can't communicate anything beyond its own random physical existence.

Now we should add to the secular understanding sketched above, René Descartes' related ideas—essentially having the same gnostic pattern, only mechanized. For he emphasized that the human body is essentially a machine that contains my "I"—my thinking, real self, which is the content part, the only part that's really important. The body is just a pizza-holding, or a jewel-holding, machine.

Again, to emphasize the point, those who deny that the world is a "book," that all the forms of material reality have a content, still think analogically. Hence, one can accurately say that instead of accepting that the meaning of the "text" of the material world is written in reality, they are asserting that any supposed "meaning" of reality was simply what people created in the past, and now they want to create new "meanings" that are more to their liking.

Being male or female certainly has to do with our bodies, and thus includes the relationship of our bodies with our souls—or we could say, with our "true selves," who we "really are." And since we all think analogically, how we think about the relationship between the material world and its meaning (or lack of meaning) will directly shape how we think about the relationship between our bodies and our souls/"true selves," and thus how we think about being male and female.

Within the secular worldview, because being male or female has no meaning and no importance for who I truly am, and because in this view being male or female does not reflect anything about spiritual realities (for the world is not a sacrament, not a communication from God, having no meaning beyond just its material properties), this means that being male or female can't reveal anything important about any aspect of reality, and cannot make any transcendent reality present. Remember, in this perspective, if the material world had a meaning beyond just its physical properties, it wouldn't be valued/valuable, because a thing can only be valued if it is just itself. That is, if it conveys a meaning, or anything spiritual/divine, it loses its own value, or even its own reality in some sense.

In light of the above, one can see that it's a very small step to say that since the body is an ultimately unimportant, machine-like container for "the real me," with no meaning transcending its own physical existence, why should it matter what I do with it? Why should fornication or adultery be a problem? Or, since my male or female body is nothing to do with the "real me," why shouldn't I change my body through technology to be whatever I want it to be? Why shouldn't I create a new meaning for this "text"—or a new "text" for my true meaning? These are actual logical conclusions to be drawn from this secular world view.

And as many have pointed out—including Fr Alexander Schmemann in *For the Life of the World*—this view, in effect, reflects the medieval Roman Catholic doctrine of transubstantiation: the bread and wine cease to be bread and wine in order to communicate the Body and Blood of Christ, rather than becoming more truly bread and wine by fulfilling their true, originally intended purpose of being a means of real communion with God.[120] Likewise, our humanity is not devalued, or even eliminated, but rather fulfilled by being in communion with, and communicating, the divine—as the Incarnation properly understood indicates.

It seems to me, in light of all this, that we as Orthodox Christians can say, and need to say, that our bodies—which are always either male or female—these material forms, are truly *meaningful.* Not only is our maleness or femaleness an inseparable part of who we are (it's part of every cell in our bodies, as we now know through contemporary science),[121] but also these realities reflect and communicate something important about the underlying spiritual laws or patterns of reality (as, for example, St Paul indicates when in Ephesians 5 he makes an analogy between the relationship between a man and a woman in marriage to Christ and the Church).

In that case, why has it become so important to people who espouse a secular worldview—and sadly, many Christians as well—that being male or female *not* communicate any spiritual realities, and not even be an important fixed part of our identity? This false idea is held so strongly that all the recent science showing that being male or female *is* an important fixed part of our identity—such as the fact that even isolated human cells grown in cultures in a lab respond differently to medicines depending on whether the cells are taken from males or females[122]—all this kind of evidence is ignored.

There is more to this than the secular rejection of the traditional beliefs just mentioned (the sacramental worldview, and the rejection of the idea that God is the good God Who loves mankind, and Who has created reality in such a way that we can learn about spiritual realities and about Him—and even participate in His grace—through material realities), though all that is part of it.

Richard Weaver suggests, I think rightly, that "surmounting all [specific beliefs] is an intuitive *feeling* about the *immanent nature of reality*, and this is the sanction to which both ideas and beliefs are ultimately referred for verification."[123] People who want to say that being male or female is not a fixed, important part of who we are, and does not reveal spiritual realities—and all that goes with the "new thinking," such as the normalization of homosexuality—have accepted at least some key aspects of what is often called a "Postmodernist"[124] view of the world.

For Postmodernists, this "intuitive feeling about the immanent nature of reality," the key "perception" woven through so many areas of understanding, is that much of reality, including the relationship between the self and the other/Other, is set up as binary opposites in a hierarchy in which you always have an oppressor and the oppressed. In addition, the opposite entities in each binary must be in ongoing conflict and struggle—until the oppressed overthrows the oppressor (perhaps through revolution, or through softer legal means). Then a synthesis is supposed to occur; or, one could say, "equality" is achieved. What this means, though this is not usually pointed out, is that at the heart of reality in this secular view is a *conflict created by inequality and difference*, because inequality/difference leads to hierarchy, which is imagined to be *always* oppressive—always leading to, and even necessitating, rebellion by the oppressed.

This underlying principle has been used to "frame" the relationship between humanity and God—from Karl Marx's choosing Prometheus as an ideal model instead of Christ; to Marx's pitting the "bourgeoisie" against the workers; to Simon de Beauvoir, the mother of radical feminism, pitting men in an oppressive hierarchy over and against women; to, more recently, Judith Butler's attempts not only to eliminate the oppression which de Beauvoir assumes is always present between men and women, but also to abolish the conflict/inequality/hierarchy between the "oppressive" heterosexuals and the "oppressed" homosexuals and transgender people, by eliminating—or at least, radically altering—the language that describes them, in an effort to eliminate the realities which the language describes. This is because she, and many others influenced by Postmodernism, believes that *language creates reality* (in a kind of modern version of late medieval Nominalism). (By the way, heterosexuals are held to be oppressive simply because they are the vast majority, due to the "dictatorship of nature."[125])

This "intuition" about conflict and oppression being at the heart of reality has also been used as an alternative to Christianity's understanding of the Fall. The alienation and unhappiness people feel—indeed, most of the problems of the world—are said to be the result of different kinds of inequality and oppression, such as oppression by an economic system, by white people, by men, by heterosexuals, by the idea of "normal and abnormal" or of "natural and unnatural," and even by those in the Church teaching that abortion, or an active homosexual lifestyle, is sinful. Many will even openly claim that in their view, abortion is necessary, because they feel it's the "best" way to ensure "equality" between men and women—taking away the consequence of sexual relations that in its fullness is only borne by women.

As others have pointed out, as soon as you have any differences, especially fixed differences as we're saying being male or female are, then you will have inequality and some kind of hierarchy. So the idea that differences/distinctions always lead to "inequality" is true; and the idea that inequality always leads to some kind of hierarchy is also true. But this entire Postmodern way of looking at the world, this meta-narrative that claims to "deconstruct" and to be against all meta-narratives,[126] hangs on the belief in a key falsehood: that any and every kind of hierarchy is *always* oppressive, and thus bad. And since hierarchy is always oppressive and bad, the only good system, especially for the historically oppressed groups, is one in which everyone is equal—not just in the sense of being equal under the law, or equally valued because made in the image of God, but equal in the sense of being *the same*, or at least interchangeable.

This understanding has led to rampant "equalitarianism,"[127] which is believed to be the solution to end all oppression. And in this view, oppression, especially from any kind of hierarchical system, seems to be what must be avoided at all costs—even to the point of the heavily funded, praised, and promoted Judith Butler[128] saying that "male" and "female," "father" and "mother," are not words that *reflect,* or point to, realities, but that such words have *created* those realities (again, in this view, language creates reality). And since she believes those realities have been and are *always* inevitably oppressive, she also believes that the words themselves must be radically changed—or better, eliminated, in order to destroy the oppressive "realities" which the language has created. *This* radical kind of thinking is the real, underlying reason why people are being told they have to use whatever pronoun someone else wants, and the other "politically correct" linguistic changes that are being demanded—and not simply a sympathetic concern for the feelings of others.

There is a lot that can be said about this, but just to mention: this negative and false understanding of hierarchy, at least partly, if not largely, comes from a Marxist reading of the philosopher Hegel (d. 1831) and his understanding of the key inherent pattern of history/reality as binaries in conflict—as in a master–slave, oppressor/oppressed relationship. And, he claimed, this relationship necessitates the struggle of the oppressed to get free from the oppressors (as the only way to be authentic).[129]

This is, then, the key inherent pattern for history/reality that's picked up (usually directly from Hegel) by nearly all the revolutionary thinkers from Karl Marx to Judith Butler. And, it seems to me, that Hegel's thought, and its deep resonance for Marx and many others, at least partly goes back to the Protestant Reformers such as Luther, who saw so much of reality in terms of conflicting binaries: Scripture, not Tradition; faith, not works; grace, not free will, and so on; and the rejection of many key antinomies of the Faith: that is, binaries in which the two components seem to be contradictory, or mutually incompatible, but are actually *both true at the same time.* This goes right back to the necessity for a proper understanding of the Incarnation and the fact that Christ is truly *both* God and man. Saint Gregory Palamas (fourteenth century) could even say, "The antinomy is the criterion of Orthodoxy."

As we've observed, Marx and the others influenced by him believe that the key pattern for history/reality is hierarchies/differences/inequalities that always result in oppression. And who wants oppression? So they insist that we should try to eliminate oppression by either eliminating differences, or *neutralizing* the differences by claiming that both elements in the binaries are not simply equally good, or equally valuable, but that they can and should be even *interchangeable,* since they are believed to be *essentially the same.* Hence, we have multi-culturalism, with the concomitant claim that "truth is relative"—you have your truth, I have mine—which directly leads to ethical relativism, and all the problems this has created.

In the Marxist view, oppression doesn't come primarily from human sin but from the way things are set up—from certain people who are oppressors, and from the dictatorship of nature, or reality. There seems to be a connection here going back at least to Luther and the Reformers again, whose approach at least implied that the main problems in the Roman Catholic Church of their day were not *primarily* the result of human sin (in which case, one would work to reform the church while staying within it), but from *the institution of the church itself*—that is, the way things have been set up. Something external to people is held to be the central problem, so the way things are set up is the primary thing that has to be changed or even destroyed, and a new system set up. Then the very naïve assumption is that everything will be fine. This is not to say that some systems aren't better than others—obviously they are! But it's a question of putting the focus in the wrong place.

Postmodernists have the same basic thought: the primary problem is not human sin, to be solved by personal repentance for sin, and by the ascetic and sacramental life of the Church, and so on. Rather, the primary problem, the cause of oppression, is the way things are set up. Only this time, it's not just the Church as an institution that's seen as the problem. Rather, it's how society as whole has been set up, and even how reality itself is set up, including all people being male or female—and for some, like Judith Butler, heterosexuality as being normative, and all such differences/hierarchies.

Perhaps just as important is the ultimate goal in the Postmodern world-view: all should be free, in the sense of the medieval Nominalists' view of God's freedom—being omnipotent, meaning doing whatever one wishes, with no constraints of consistency, goodness, moral standards, or limitations "imposed" by the way reality is "set up." So really, I think it can be said that people who are promoting and accepting these Postmodern ideas unconsciously are making themselves in the image of the medieval Nominalist God—who is much more like a vindictive pagan god—instead of trying to be like, and living in communion with, Jesus Christ, and living according to what He reveals about the true God.

It's critical, then, to take a look at hierarchy as understood within our Tradition—at the fact that, as St Nikolai of Zicha (twentieth century), in an incredibly brilliant sermon on the parable of the Talents, says:

*God creates inequality*; men grumble at it. Are men wiser than God? When God creates inequality, it means that inequality is wiser and better than equality. God creates inequality for man's good, but men cannot see the good in their inequality.... God creates inequality out of love, which is aroused and sustained by inequality, but man can see no love in it.[130]

So God's intention in creating inequalities is to "arouse and sustain" love. How can this be? Inequalities provide opportunities to show love, to give, and to serve others in need. When this doesn't happen, again, the root problem is sin, and not the inequality.

This is why everything will not automatically become better if we have some different system, some supposedly perfect system—or if we only change what is *external* to the human heart. It's fascinating to note here the key difference between these two views: traditional Christianity is very positive about God and reality (how things are is ultimately for our spiritual benefit), and clear that when people follow their own agenda, things will not work out well; while the Postmodernists and secularists are very negative about God and reality (they don't like how things are "set up"), and they are very confident that people can do better if they follow their own agenda and ignore how reality is "set up."[131]

Jesus Christ, the Creator of this world—Who, as St John Chrysostom says, does everything for our benefit—confirms that inequalities and hierarchy are built into reality. It's a utopian fantasy to imagine that we can get rid of differences, inequalities, or hierarchy. You are fighting against reality, the way things are created, if you try—and as one medical doctor said in another context, if you do that, "welcome to hell."

We ought to add that the reason hierarchy can easily be believed by so many to be so negative is also because of sin—because of oppressive, or "gentile" hierarchies like Jesus describes in Matt. 20:25–28:

> You know that the rulers of the Gentiles lord it over them, and those who are great exercise authority over them. Yet it shall *not* be so among you: but whoever desires to become great among you, let him be your servant. And whoever desires to be first among you, let him be your slave—just as the Son of Man did not come to be served, but to serve, and to give His life a ransom for many.

Christ reveals the pattern for hierarchy that God intended. This is the necessary pattern to follow to eliminate oppression, to promote harmony and human flourishing. We can't avoid hierarchy, so Christ reveals the *only* way of having hierarchy that will really work long term to eliminate oppression—and that is for those in the higher positions of any hierarchy to be inspired to *voluntarily serve*, out of love, those who are lower.

The term "hierarchy" was actually coined by the saint known as Dionysius the Areopagite (probably in the sixth century).[132] How did St Dionysius explain this term himself? He states, "Hierarchy, in my opinion, is a sacred order, and knowledge, and activity, assimilated, so far as possible, to the divine likeness, and led up in due degree to the illuminations given it from God for the imitation of God."[133]

It's important for our discussion to see that in a traditional Christian context, hierarchy is not understood to be, nor is it intended to be, a "one-way" structure—with those higher dominating those lower. Christ Himself made that crystal clear, both in His words and especially in His actions. Rather, as Bishop Alexander (Golitzin), in his book about Dionysius's works, explains, "It is the point in the *cycle of love* . . . at which the descent of God's *dynameis* [energies] into creation becomes the ascent of the creation into God."[134]

Hierarchy is, thus, meant to be a "cycle of love," in which the higher gives beneficent love to the lower, and the lower gives grateful love back to the higher—in a kind of dance or harmony of love starting with God in His relationship to His creation. The real purpose of the hierarchy is to bring about the unity of all—that *all* be "led up in due degree to the illuminations given . . . from God for the imitation of God" or the *communion* of *all*, in God.

So proper hierarchy leads to union, and to a kind of *conciliarity*, or a kind of "equality," we could say, as the pattern seen in the Holy Trinity, which is *both* hierarchical and conciliar. For the Holy Trinity is three distinct Persons in a hierarchical relationship, with the Father being the source, or "Fountainhead," of the Son and the Spirit, and also a conciliar unity because of the oneness of the divine nature equally shared by all three of the Persons.

We see this view of hierarchy reflected throughout the Divine Liturgy as well: for example, the Bishop/priest say "Peace be to you all" and the laity reply "and to thy spirit"—and so on, until the primary purpose for the liturgy is reached—when the priest comes down, often literally, and gives holy communion to the faithful. At this point he is literally *serving* the people, so that all are united in Christ in a union without confusion, yet without any loss of hierarchy and difference.

The key point is not about which role you play in this cosmic, harmonious dance. Rather, the focus is union with Christ, and with all the members of His Body. And this is possible from any point in the hierarchy, whether one is an illiterate peasant woman or a patriarch.

Thus, hierarchy is intended to be *not* about power but about enabling this harmonious dance—reflecting, or in alignment with, the way the cosmos was intended to function, as Christ reveals and as we see in many places in Scripture. For example, in Genesis, God creates, that is, He separates and distinguishes light and dark, heaven and earth, animals and people, Adam and Eve—and hence, male and female.

So there are many binaries, but the components of each one are separated in order for them ultimately to be unified in a harmonious *union without confusion*, with all ultimately returning to communion with God. This was the role Adam and Eve were supposed to play—to expand the "temple," the special place of God's presence that the garden of Eden was, and to lead the creation back to union with the Creator. Instead, they subverted all the hierarchies (Eve letting a lower animal dominate her, etc.), rejecting God's beneficent love, and failing to give back grateful love, which all led to fragmentation and alienation.

Saint Nikolai concludes his homily on inequality by saying, "Thus inequality is placed in the very foundations of the created world. We must rejoice at this inequality, and not rebel against it, for it is placed there by Love, not by hatred; and by Understanding, not by folly. *Human life is not made ugly by the absence of equality, but by the absence of love and spiritual understanding in men.* Let us have more divine love and spiritual understanding of life, and we shall see that twice as much inequality would in no way lessen the blessedness given to men."[135]

This is, then, the key pattern that Christ reveals: there is no way to avoid hierarchy; but Christian hierarchy means voluntary, loving service of the higher to the lower, with the lower responding by giving back grateful love, in order for all to be united in a loving union without confusion. The solution to bad, or oppressive, hierarchy isn't to try to eliminate hierarchy, as our culture is claiming—that's a utopian fantasy. Rather, the solution is having good, healthy, loving hierarchy, as revealed by Christ. Just as the solution to "toxic masculinity"—or femininity—is not trying to eliminate masculinity, or to erase the differences between the masculine and the feminine, but rather to have good, healthy masculinity and femininity.

In conclusion, we have a clear choice: we can align ourselves with reality as God created it to be, as it has been revealed most fully in and by Jesus Christ, or we can try to make our own, "better," easier, more "equal"/"fair" version or path to the highest good and best flourishing. But we have been given examples of the "do it my way" approach multiple times in Scripture, and we should take note that choosing that approach did not work well for anyone, from Adam and Eve, to Judas. We've also seen multiple examples in recent history of the horrors to which the Marxist-inspired efforts to force a "better," "more egalitarian" system on whole nations have led.

Aligning ourselves with the harmonious patterns inherent in reality should be easier for Christians, because Christ has revealed them to us. Accepting the patterns He has revealed is what will lead to harmony and peace and elimination of oppression—in individuals, churches, and societies.

The more we align ourselves with the many God-given patterns in reality, the more harmony and peace and flourishing there will be—and it will be a flourishing that is sustainable. This approach, working *with* nature, works best also when you are growing crops. You can get away with working against nature, or ignoring how reality actually works, for a while, but there is always a high price to pay for that in the end.

Surely many would be helped and even inspired if we present in a clearer, fuller way, both in theory *and in practice*, a true Christian understanding of hierarchy (as well as other related areas, such as submission/obedience) in order to have a better understanding of the mystery of male and female. With God's help, surely that would go a long way toward effectively reaching with the life-transforming Truth the many people caught up in today's Postmodern worldview, with its completely false understanding of the key patterns, or underlying laws, inherent in reality.

# The Mystery of Male and Female, Masculine and Feminine: Whys, Wherefores, and Warnings

## Prof. Edith M. Humphrey

In past ages, the Church has met various challenges to her central teachings, particularly in the patristic era, when the mystery of the Incarnation, the sublime interrelationships of the Persons of the Holy Trinity, and the personhood of the Holy Spirit were misunderstood by significant teachers, who misled not a few. Centuries later, the matter of holy icons and their integral connection with the Incarnation came under review. Hundreds more years passed after this before St Gregory Palamas thoroughly countered the Calabrian monk Barlaam, who was giving voice to Western skepticism regarding the possibility of seeing the uncreated energies in this life, and thus undergoing theosis. Even later, the Eastern Church, though somewhat removed (in a day of less easy communication) from the battles of the Reformation and Counter-Reformation, was not insensible to the disputes that embroiled Western Christians. Of course, the Orthodox peoples had their own struggles, but these appear to have been more socially driven than theological. Nevertheless, the division between culture and theology is hardly impermeable, as Fr Georges Florovsky compellingly demonstrated in his discussion of the "captivity" of the Church and the danger of attendant pseudomorphosis.[136]

Today, it would seem, there are two main subjects of contention among those who take the name of Christ: the nature of the Church (ecclesiology) and the nature of humanity (theological anthropology). The first question is one that is both implicitly and explicitly raised in various different Christian contexts, from the doomed ecumenist dialogues that have become common among revisionist circles (which seek the lowest common denominator in minimizing serious differences) to more substantive discussions joined by conservative Protestants who are seeking their ancient roots, Catholics who sense (with Pope John Paul II) that they have lost one of their theological "lungs," and Orthodox who seek to be light and life to believers who are removed from the apostolic Church. The second question, that of theological anthropology,

72

is a ubiquitous theme today, sounded not only among those who call themselves Christians but also among many outside the boundaries of the Church—
though, of course, the adjective "theological" is less seldom attached to outside
discussions.

Indeed, the last hundred years have seen an onslaught against common, but
(sadly) unexamined assumptions regarding male and female, which our culture inherited mostly from its Christian past. During the twentieth century in
the West, the concepts of human sexuality and gender first have been subjected
to scientific and cultural rationalization and now are being described in terms
of personal subjective preference. In all this, we have met a clear and destructive challenge to dominical teaching: both non-Christians and (astonishingly)
some who name Christ presume that Jesus was simply bound by His culture
when He declared, "from the beginning . . . God 'made them male and female'"
(Mark 10:6). These changes in perspective are not merely abstract, as we know,
but have been accompanied by breathtaking alterations in our social fabric—a
metamorphosis that some even within the Orthodox fold seem prepared to
consider, or even to embrace.

It is, therefore, timely that the 2019 symposium for which this chapter was
originally written has focused upon "Chastity, Purity, Integrity: Orthodox
Anthropology and Secular Culture in the 21st Century." There are many aspects
to these conjoined themes, both practical and conceptual. In this offering, I
aim to focus particularly on humanity as male and female, gleaning wisdom
from pertinent scriptural passages, Church fathers, and contemporary Orthodox thinkers. We will begin by questioning why humanity has been considered
as a holy mystery in the Church, go on to troubleshoot questions that emerge
regarding the Incarnation and our anticipated eschatological state, suggest
some boundaries intended to mark off danger points in our necessary discussion of such ineffable matters, and finally close with an appeal to the Christian
imagination to grasp the mystery of "masculine and feminine" as something
even larger than male and female.

## Why Humanity Is Mystery

Why should we think in terms of humanity, male and female, as a mystery?
After all, our sexuality is something that we share with the animals, linking us
with this present age, rather than (in any obvious way) with God, in Whom,
the fathers insist, there are no passions, or parts. It was the pagans, not the
Christians, who believed in erotic relationships between gods and goddesses,

as mysteries of fertility. What is it, then, about our sexuality that could possibly be understood as anything but carnal, so far as the Christian is concerned?

For the answer we go back to origins. In both of the first two chapters of Genesis, we are presented with the creation of humanity as a great mystery. In Genesis 1, God "deliberates," so to speak, with Himself, before creating the crown of His creation. Of course, we know that God's willing is nothing like the "gnomic" necessities of human decision-making, as differentiated by St Maximus. Yet the Holy Scriptures use this anthropomorphic picture of God not simply to entertain, but, it would seem, to differentiate *this* creation qualitatively from the other forms of life that have preceded it: humankind warrants God's special attention. Moreover, the story goes on to proclaim a paradox: "So God created [Adam] in his own image; in the image of God He created him; male and female He created them" (Gen 1:27). Here we are given a glimpse of our complexity: our unity, as Adam, which can be translated "human being" or "humanity;" and our duality as male and female. In this we see our complexity as, to use the phrase of C. S. Lewis, "amphibious" beings—reflecting the image and likeness of God, but sharing sexuality with the animals.[137]And the mystery is deepened in Genesis 2, where we hear, for the first time, about something that is *not* good: "It is not good for the Adam to be alone." So this chapter backtracks, to fill in the story of *how* the female was formed. This taking of Eve from Adam, and his recognition of her as "bone of my bone and flesh of my flesh," adds to what we have learned about God's unitive and dual creation of Adam: it is not just that Adam is comprised of man and woman, but that woman has been taken from man, and therefore is his glory, as St Paul will explain in 1 Corinthians 11.

Christians may think of this as a faint reflection of the eternal begetting of the Son from the Father, or the procession of the Spirit from the Father. Together, the man and the woman are *Adam*; yet they are distinct, and the one comes from the other. Together they reflect the image of God, and are given dominion over the rest of creation (see Genesis 1:28)—a nurturing monarchy, showing forth the righteousness of God. And together, they partake of that world, too, for they are embodied, sexual beings like the animals. So they stand as a bridge, in a "priestly" position, says Fr Alexander Schmemann, between the rest of the world and the loving God Whom they represent.[138]

The narratives in Genesis, then, describe a great mystery. From these primordial stories have arisen many speculations, as theologians try to push against the boundaries of what we do not understand. Was the original Adam a hermaphrodite, and only became male after God made the differentiation?[139] Is our sexuality, therefore, not a basic, or foundational thing, but a second stage, which will eventually be dissolved? Should we see a human being, whether male or female, as only *half* of what it is to be human—something "not good" in itself, but only good when completed by the other half? The first idea of a double-sexed Adam was posited by ancient rabbis. The second, that a single person is incomplete, is implied in certain contemporary Christian circles—often evangelical—where the married state is considered the norm, and the single state as a default position. It would seem that these two perspectives push Genesis to say more than it really does. For we know that the *perfect* Adam, the Lord Jesus, was no hermaphrodite—He was circumcised on the eighth day! Furthermore, He was by no means incomplete without a female partner, though He yearns and cares for the Church as His mysterious Bride.

Alongside Genesis, we also have more distinct clues concerning the human mystery in Ephesians 5:21–32, 2 Corinthians 11:2, and the book of Revelation, all of which picture God's people as the Bride of Christ, and anticipate the time when we shall be presented, completely pure, to Him. Together, then, we bear a *feminine* iconic nature, responding to the One Who is pictured in divine and masculine terms as our Bridegroom. This is not a sideline in the Scriptures, but so important that it is enshrined in our worship, particularly in the Bridegroom Services of Holy Week. We recognize, then, a symbolism that is accentuated in the Bible and continued in the life of the Church: redeemed humanity is feminine to Christ's masculine grandeur.

Besides this persistent imagery in the Scripture, however, we also must take seriously the corrective words of Jesus to the Sadducees, who were mocking the doctrine of the resurrection. In all three synoptic gospels, we hear of how that ancient sect of Jews, the ruling priestly class, sets a riddle for Christ, a story in which a woman is married to several men sequentially throughout her life. The question, intended to stump Jesus, like the question about taxes to Caesar, is "Therefore, in the resurrection, whose wife does she become? (Luke 20:23)" (see Mark 12:18–25; Matthew 22:23–30; and Luke 20:27–36). Jesus, true to style, does not answer an insincere question. Instead, He says that they know neither the power of God nor the Scriptures, for in the resurrection, there is no giving or taking in marriage, but they are *"like* the angels." Furthermore, in Luke's version, he adds "and cannot die." Many have failed to notice the little word "like," and so some popular versions of Christianity have pictured those who have fallen asleep in the Lord as actually being angels. Others seem not to have noticed the explicit purpose of Jesus's remarks—to correct the scornful on their dismissive picture of the resurrection—and have, it seems, pushed His comments about "giving" and "taking" in marriage to speak more systematically about the marriage bond having an ephemeral nature.

But what happens if we read Jesus's remarks to the Sadducees not so much in terms of theological anthropology, and the dismissal of marriage in the Kingdom, but as a sharp response to the way that they have sarcastically framed the question? The Sadducees have asked, "*Whose* wife will she be?" Perhaps the Lord's emphasis on "giving" and "taking" amounts to this sort of response: "You don't know the power of God or the resurrection. It isn't like that . . . she doesn't *belong* to anyone, since there is no giving or taking, but they all, male and female alike, have glory like the angels. There is no more curse: and they won't die." On this reading, Jesus is explaining that the effects of the fall—undue power of a man over his wife, and death—don't pertain in the resurrection. The Sadducees have been ridiculing the resurrection because they are picturing it in the wrong way. Jesus's rebuke to them has to do with their assumption that the doctrine of the resurrection would be like a resuscitation—something like the Jehovah Witness pictures in our day. Certainly, Jesus is qualifying the importance of sexual intercourse and reproduction: as the fathers would put it, it is in our "garments of skin" that these things pertain. But to push Jesus's words beyond this rebuke is to miss the point of the narrative. It is a similar mis-step as those make who take the parable of Lazarus (see Luke 16:19–31) as proof that there can be no communication between the righteous who are asleep in the Lord, and those of us who pray for and to them: the parable is not intended to work out the geography of the afterlife, complete with the "gulf" that Protestants see to be unbridgeable. Similarly, this dominical word to the Sadducees does not contradict Orthodox teaching concerning God's eternal crowning of husband and wife.

Thus, while on the one hand many speak in the Church of human marriage as having eternal implications,[140] and celebrate its exalted status as an icon of Christ's communion with the Church, on the other hand we know that the resurrected life is not exactly like the current one, and our genders will be expressed differently. All these things point to the mystery of humanity as male and female. But how do we come to terms with this mystery?

First, it is wise to consider how the Virgin and Theotokos Mary, in relation to Christ, helps us to understand. Fr Alexander Schmemann, in his exhilarating book, *The Virgin Mary*, says that "being the icon of the church, Mary is the image and personification of the world—that is to say, of the new world that God is making."[141] Most particularly he means that she is the personification of God's redeemed people, the Church: "Mary is not the representative of the woman or women before God, she is the icon of the entire creation, the whole mankind as response to Christ and to God."[142] As we say in the hymn, "we bring a virgin mother" to the Lord as our offering. All of creation rejoices in her, and as it does so, it fulfills St Paul's words that the creation is "on tiptoe" waiting "the moment when God's children will be revealed" (Romans 8:19 (NTE)). Mary is the present sign of that great day to come, when the effects of the curse will be fully reversed, and there will be no more decay or death. Because of holy Mary's consistent "yes," she has become, as Fr Schmemann explains, "the locus of Christ's transformation, not just of woman, but of all humankind, and even of the entire creation."[143]

## Wherefores: Mapping Out Questions, Partial Solutions, and Dead Ends

Mary's role in all this helps us with the "wherefores" that come up when we think of our salvation, and of our gendered condition. Some have agonized: if Christ is male, and if salvation depends upon Christ assuming our human nature, how can the female have been "assumed" in the incarnation, and how can women be saved? Next, to put it a bit too plainly, does the risen/ascended Christ have male properties? What does this mean for eschatology, for the risen saints and for us? Finally, does it help to distinguish between male/female and the masculine/feminine?

There is not enough space in an essay of this nature to be thorough with such questions, since the focus here is upon theological anthropology rather than Christology proper. To begin with, however, it seems advisable for us to drop the Western distinction of "essential" versus "accidental" when thinking about sexuality. The maleness or femaleness of a particular human being is *neither* essential to his or her humanity, *nor* merely an outward accident (or appearance) of who that one is. The woman Eve is not a second creation, separate from humanity—but she is distinct from Adam. As St John Chrysostom explains, she is distinct in her relationship, especially since the fall, but not in her nature: "For had Paul meant to speak of rule and subjection . . . he would not have brought forward the instance of a wife, but rather of a slave and a master. For what if the wife be under subjection to us? It is as a wife, as free, as equal in honor. And the Son also, though He did become obedient to the Father, it was as the Son of God, it was as God."[144]

Father and Son are both divine in nature; Adam and Eve are both *Adam*—human, created from the same material by God for His purpose. Moreover, as the second Adam, Christ recapitulates *both* Adam and Eve, despite their distinctness in gender. Jesus is fully male, for He is a particular human being, but His humanity is drawn exclusively from the woman. (We might reflect on how that is even more amazing for us than for Christians of an earlier day, given what we know about genetics: any rudimentary parthenogenesis that we have seen issues in a female, or quasi-male. But from Holy Mary, without a human husband, the second Person of the Trinity became Incarnate. As we chant in the Theotokion for Pentecost, "Every mind is overawed with your childbearing!") As a first step in understanding our nature and how Christ took it upon Himself, the unique role of the Theotokos helps us to see how woman is fully involved in the Incarnation, and so fully recapitulated in Christ. And so we are led to be amazed at a mystery.

Second, in our worship, we consider the risen and ascended Christ to be masculine, the Theotokos feminine, and the saints intact in their gendered natures. The fathers *have* differed regarding the glorified body, whether it retains sexual characteristics or not.[145] In our own day, there are theologians such as Paul Evdokimov who have taken a page from the rabbis, and speculate that our eschatological state is hermaphroditic, in conformity with how they misinterpret the protological state of undifferentiated Adam in Genesis.[146] But in our icons, in our worship, and in our reverence we continue to relate to those who are glorified as masculine and feminine. Though we may not be able to discover from Scriptures or Tradition whether *physical* maleness and femaleness is eternal, it would seem that the distinction between masculine and feminine is something that we must preserve. Woven into the theological grammar of the Scriptures, and our worship, is the idea that gendered language points to a mystery even bigger than that of a male and female in a single marriage.

In our day, both Paul Evdokimov (despite his views on the final resurrected body) and C. S. Lewis have held on steadfastly to this idea that the physical male and female states are intimations of something greater. Evdokimov has speculated concerning mysterious "enstatic" and "ecstatic" realities to which female and male point, whereas Lewis has painted pictures and created characters that gesture toward an ineffable duality. I frankly find the approach of Lewis more helpful, and less apt to lead us into theological quagmire.[147] Pictures can feed our imaginations where discursive reason is more difficult.

**Boundaries to Help the Explorer "Watch Out!"**

Our minds, however, matter. Indeed, part of rationality is for us to recognize where reason cannot take us. Orthodox theology has formally recognized this in its distinction between kataphatic and apophatic theology, especially as we deal with mystery. In appreciation for the limitations of human reason, I would like to suggest nine boundaries, marking off the danger points connected with potential discussion regarding gender, anthropology, and theology, and giving practical guidelines within which I believe that our ongoing exploration can safely take place.[148] So, then, these boundaries adopt the patristic method of approaching a mystery apophatically—what we *cannot* say—in order not to stray beyond what we know:

1. We cannot say that all symbols are merely human expressions, and that language and action are detachable from the reality to which they point.
2. We cannot say that gendered language is expendable in talking about God or humanity.
3. We cannot say that the relations of Father, Son, and Spirit are symmetrical, nor can we say that they are not mutual and equal.
4. We cannot say that the relations of husband and wife are totally symmetrical, nor ought we to say that there is no mutuality or equality.
5. We cannot say that woman and man are two different creations, but we also cannot say that man and woman are indistinct from each other.
6. We cannot say that there is an absolutely confined role for each gender—reversals are part of our story.
7. We cannot say that there are no "higher" gifts and no "lesser" gifts—but all are necessary, and the higher need the lower, so that sometimes it is impossible to discern which is more important.
8. In God-talk, we cannot forbid the use of feminine imagery, for the Bible uses it.
9. In God-talk, we cannot ignore the usual or normative use of masculine language, even if it is uncomfortable to us.

These, I think, give us some parameters, both guarding us from danger and honoring the mysteries of theological anthropology and trinitarian theology. The first two hedges recognize our need to speak in metaphor, and the particular value and deep significance for our faith of gendered language and realities, as revealed to us in the Scriptures. Indeed, the pervasive use of masculine and feminine language in the Scriptures and ongoing Christian Tradition marks out this territory as sacramental—that is, we are offered in the male and female signs that points to an ineffable mystery, and even partake of it.

The second two are predicated on St Paul's statements in 1 Corinthians 11:3–16, where he acknowledges both *taxis* and mutual honor, both in the Godhead, and between male and female. These two boundaries could be the subject of an entire book, let alone an article. Some theologians, particularly within the evangelical community, have engaged for the past few decades in a heated debate on how 1 Corinthians 11:3–16, and other passages in the New Testament, ought to be understood—both in terms of male–female roles, and in terms of trinitarian theology. A major problem here seems to be that the real impetus of the debate is concern for women's roles in the Church, rather than the quest for an understanding of the Trinitarian mystery: God's nature thus becomes a mascot for ecclesial polity, rather than a mystery in itself that gives insight into the nature of humanity, created after His image.[149]

The next three boundaries are meant to safeguard the complexity of our human relations. It may be that in this triad we will find the means to respond sensibly to the evangelical complementarians, who are certainly not semi-Arian, as charged by their egalitarian counterparts, but who do sometimes demonstrate a rigidity concerning the charisms of woman that might be deepened by a sacramental view of the universe such as the Orthodox account provides.

The final paired boundaries move from talk about male and female per se into our Christian naming of God. We must not reject, even in reaction against our confused age, the Biblical and traditional use of feminine similes and imagery for God; on the other hand, masculine language is normative, enshrined in the prayer that Jesus made us bold to say, and essential, rather than mere window-dressing, for our faith.[150] It is, after all, from the heavenly Father, that every form of "fatherhood" (*patria*) in heaven and earth is named (see Eph 3:15)!

These intertwined mysteries of theological anthropology, with all its unusual contours, and the ineffable Trinity, we must guard, but also probe, in order to give reasons to our sexually confused age. We want to remain in Christ, to learn more and more of Him *and* of our world, and to commend what is real and true to others. It is my prayer that this symposium is only the beginning of a movement to address the skepticism, incoherence, and fragmentation of our day. May it be that in meeting these challenges we become a stronger and wiser Church concerning the human mystery, just as the challenges of Arius, the Spirit-fighters, Nestorianism, and Monophysitism issued in our deeper appreciation of the One Who is holy.

We have suggested some chastening boundaries for the future exercise of Christian minds. It may now be helpful for us to dwell upon an image to enliven our imaginations—*for "the refreshment of the spirit,"* as Lewis puts it.[151] We may not be able to *define* the final resurrected state (for it is even more mysterious than our present human situation), but luminous pictures will certainly help us to anticipate it. We need such glimpses of glory in our wounded and soiled state!

Here is one such picture from Lewis's novel *Perelandra*, the second of his cosmic trilogy. At the climax of the story, the reader meets the King and Queen of Perelandra, victorious over temptation, newly come into their inheritance of the green world, and commanding even the homage of the huge angelic beings (with masculine and feminine aspects) whom the reader has already met. Consider the wonder of these two-in-one, the way in which they are both "very good" in themselves, but point sacramentally beyond themselves to the One from whom all good things come. Mark also the main character of the book, Ransom, and his awareness of his own deficit—a lonely longing for a true mother and father, in our fallen world. May his yearning give voice to our present need to truly see and appreciate male and female, as God created us, pointing toward mysteries that we can hardly fathom.

All was in a pure daylight that seemed to come from nowhere in particular. He knew ever afterward what is meant by a light "resting on" or "overshadowing" a holy thing, but not emanating from it. For as the light reached its perfection and settled itself, as it were, like a lord upon his throne or like wine in a bowl, and filled the whole flowery cup of the mountain top, every cranny with its purity, the holy thing, Paradise itself in its two Persons, Paradise walking hand in hand, its two bodies shining in the light like emeralds yet not themselves too bright to look at, came in sight in the cleft between two peaks, and stood a moment with its male right hand lifted in regal and pontifical benediction, and then walked down and stood on the far side of the water. And the gods kneeled and bowed their huge bodies before the small forms of that young King and Queen.

There was a great silence on the mountain top, and Ransom [the main character of the book] also had fallen down before the human pair. When at last he raised his eyes from the four blessed feet, he found himself involuntarily speaking though his voice was broken and his eyes dimmed. "Do not move away, do not raise me up," he said, "I have never before seen a man or a woman. I have lived all my life among shadows and broken images. Oh, my Father and my Mother, my Lord and my Lady, do not move, do not answer me yet. My own father and mother I have never seen. Take me for your son. We have been alone in my world for a great time."[152]

# PART TWO

## Remedies: Moral, Pastoral, and Social

# Acquiring an Orthodox Ethos

## Archpriest Peter Heers

Today we are increasingly faced with challenges to the age-old, universally accepted, and canonically codified moral order *from elements within* the Orthodox Church. How should we understand this new wave of innovation wherein certain professors or hierarchs subtly modify or change the teaching of the Church with regard to, for example, homosexuality?

Every teaching, every word, given by the Lord, whether directly as the Incarnate *Theanthropos*, or indirectly, through "το στόμα τοῦ Χριστοῦ," the chief of the Apostles, Paul, will remain until the Second Coming, according to the words of the Lord: "For assuredly, I say to you, till heaven and earth pass away, one jot or one tittle will by no means pass from the law till all is fulfilled (Matthew 5:18)." Therefore, anyone, no matter the rank, who sets aside the sacred deposit of the faith, far from improving on or updating the Lord's teaching, simply makes himself irrelevant.

In rejecting His words, His commandments, His teachings, the innovator rejects Him and His Grace and His Way to Himself. Either we accept every word of the Word and submit to Christ, or we hold back and reject, or desire to "improve" on, aspects of His teaching, and hence lose everything, first of all communion with Him.

This may seem harsh, but it arises from a clear understanding of the Orthodox outlook or *phronema* which maintains that DOGMA and ETHOS are inseparable, as the source or spring is inseparable from the water flowing from it. Likewise, the Ethos or the Way of Christ flows from the Dogma or the Truth of Christ.

In the West, morality became an autonomous science, a matter pertaining to this life and world, separated from the Source of Good and Eternity. In the theology of the Middle Ages, Christian "ethics" as a distinct branch of theology was born, as "ethics" came to be understood within the twofold framework of jurisdiction or authority, and practice. In this context, a legalistic ethical system was contrived with its conceptual roots Blessed Augustine's theology.

Scholastic theology saw the faith of the Church as a system, a set of established reasonable certainties, which can be established rationally. Faith became an ideology, which was confirmed when put into practice in the ethical domain.

This system of ethics, which bases moral value on the likelihood that good actions will produce "happiness," combined with Anselm's theory of satisfaction of divine justice (the sacrificial theory of atonement), opened the way for the "religionization" of Christianity. Seeing the Body of the Theanthropos as a religion replaced faith (trust) in the Person of Christ with a moral code of conduct which, when observed, imparts salvation.

It was, thus, inevitable that such an ethical teaching, based on so-called "metaphysics," would eventually collapse.

In the Orthodox Church, such an idea of "Christian ethics," as we encounter in Western theology, does not exist. We simply have the Cross—which is to say *asceticism*, which is to say *purification* and *illumination*.

In the Church, "being good" is not the aim, per se, but rather, participating in the One Who is the Only Good One. Being good is seen within the context of salvation, never outside of it. In the Church, it is not what we are doing as much as who we are becoming.

We have the example of the prodigal son. How is sin understood here? As departure, exile, loss of identity, alienation from sonship, and a break in communion. In short, the loss of a relationship with the Person of Christ.

Sin is a missing of the mark, and that mark is *communion with God*. Sin is not simply or mainly "doing something bad," but rather falling away from communion—falling from life into death, from well-being into existing.

For a glimpse of what this communion and life is, we read from the *Gerontikon*, or the Sayings of the Desert Fathers:

> Abba Lot went to see Abba Joseph and said to him, "Abba, as far as I can, I say my little office, I fast a little, I pray and meditate, I live in peace; and as far as I can, I purify my thoughts. What else can I do?" Then the old man stood up and stretched his hands towards heaven. His fingers became like ten lamps of fire, and he said to him, "If you will, you can become all flame." (Sayings of the Desert Fathers, Bk. 12, part 8)

This is our "ethics:" become aflame with the Grace of the Holy Spirit.

The central mystery of Orthodoxy is CHRIST, the *Theanthropos*, fully God—united with the Holy Trinity—and fully man, united with all men who constitute His Body, the Church. This truth is at the center and constitutes the entire dogma of our Faith. Christ the *Theanthropos* is our way of believing, living, thinking, and doing. This truth must be stressed from the outset when we are speaking of the Orthodox Ethos.

The Orthodox Ethos presupposes and begins and ends with our communion with the Father in Christ through the Holy Spirit and the purification and illumination of our entire being on the path of divinization or *Theosis*. This state, the acquisition and realization of the Christian Ethos, presupposes the Orthodox Faith.

Every departure, no matter how slight, from the Orthodox Faith, brings with it a falling away from the Orthodox Ethos and Spiritual Life. There are, unfortunately, many examples of this in ecclesiastical history, the most notable being the introduction of the *filioque* and the subsequent loss of the Orthodox Ethos in the West.

However, the opposite is also true: departures from the Orthodox Ethos bring in their wake departures from Orthodox Faith. In our own day, this interdependence of Dogma and Ethos is most apparent in the loss of the ascetic life, which has ensured the spread of secularism, the very spirit of antichrist, which has given birth to the ecclesiological heresies of ecumenism and phyletism.

Right Faith, *Orthodoxy*, is the foundation and the content of our new life in Christ and of the ethos of the Church and of every believer, who is regenerated as a "new creation."

For someone to be a "new creation" in Christ, to be filled, in other words, with the Orthodox ethos, means that the "old things have passed away; behold, all things have become new" (2 Corinthians 5:17). In other words, the ancient and modern delusions and heresies and idol worshipping have been put away, and the true Knowledge of God and Orthodox worship in the Holy Spirit and Truth have arrived. Or, according to St Cyril of Alexandria, «τα της εν αληθεία θεοσέβειας δόγματα» (the Godly dogmas in truth; PG 74.537).

The Apostle Paul writes that only in Christ Jesus is there a "new creation." Then he immediately adds: "as many as walk according to this rule, peace and mercy be upon them" (Galations 6:15–16). This rule which all Christians must walk is, according to St Irenaeus, "the rule of faith," "the immovable rule of truth," which we received at our Baptism with our confession of the Symbol of Faith.

Catechism is not learning *about* God, but purification from delusions about God, man, and creation, and purification of our *way* of life, which is to say the supplanting of this old way with *the ethos of Christ*.

Thus, properly understood, dogma is an expression of experience and a guide to the same. Orthodox Dogma leads those who accept it through purification to illumination and, if God wills, to glorification. "This means that Orthodox theology forms a circle: it starts from the revelation granted to the God-seers; and then this experience of the God-seers is put into words, as far as this is humanly possible, in order to guide those who accept it into an experience of revelation. It is in this sense that we say that dogmas are closely linked with man's cure."[153]

Correct diagnosis + Correct treatment = health and salvation.

In contrast, separating dogma from experience and cure can easily lead one into heresy, which can differ little from the theology of demons "who believe and tremble." The most tragic of all heresies (and one very popular today) is that which supposes that theology is done in an armchair, when reflecting deeply and thinking great thoughts about the things of God. Yet this is the Frankish delusion, coming about as a result of the dissolution of the unity of Dogma and Ethos, of Faith and Life, of Revelation and Experience. Whereas the Orthodox Way—the Orthodox Ethos—means that we experience dogma, we learn it empirically. Saint Paul writes:

> For this reason I bow my knees to the Father of our Lord Jesus Christ, from whom the whole family in heaven and earth is named, that He would grant you, according to the riches of His glory, to be strengthened with **might through His Spirit in the inner man**, that **Christ may dwell in your hearts through faith**; that you, being rooted and grounded in love, may be able to comprehend with all saints what is **the width and length and depth and height**—to know the love of Christ which passes knowledge; that you may be filled **with all the fullness of God**. Now to Him who is able to do exceedingly abundantly above all that we ask or think, according to the power that works in us, to Him be glory in the church by Christ Jesus to all generations, forever and ever. Amen. (Ephesians 3:14–21) (emphasis added)

This is all experienced in the Church. Many believe in Christ, but many do not trust in Him, *in* His Body and *with* His Body. In other words, we often do not believe in Him as the Church. Consciously or unconsciously, we separate Him from His Church, His Body, which is His *flesh*. This is tragic, for it is a missing of the mark, a falling away. For Christ is confessed and experienced only within His Church, which is His Theanthropic Body.

Christ, with His "enfleshment," took upon Himself a Body and became Himself Body, and this very Body is the Church. As St John Chrysostom says, Christ assumed the body of the Church, and the Church He made His own Body (PG 52.429).

Thus, Christ is inseparable from the Church, which is His Body; and the Church is inseparable from Christ, Who is the Head, Life, and Ethos.

In Holy Baptism we are united to the Holy Trinity in Christ, which means that we are planted into the Body of Christ, the Church. This is exactly how it is put in the prayer of Baptism: "Implant him as a plant of Truth in Thy Holy Catholic and Apostolic Church."

Therefore, when we separate Christ from the Church or the Church from Christ, we commit the greatest of errors and fall into the greatest of heresies: we de-incarnate Christ and cast Him away from His Body, and likewise from man and the world. If we do this, we are no longer Christians, and we certainly can no longer approach the acquisition and realization of the Orthodox Christian Ethos.

That which characterizes the Orthodox ethos is its Christological and Christ-centered character. Faith itself IS Christ, according to St Ignatius of Antioch: "Perfect Faith is Jesus Christ" (Epistle to Smyrna, 10:2). Or, according to St Maximus the Confessor, "Christ is the enhypostatic faith" (PG 90.332).

The Christ-centered ethos of the Orthodox Church is life IN Christ, nothing less. One cannot acquire the Way of Christ by imitating Christ externally. As the Lord has said, "I am the vine, you are the branches: he **who abides in Me**, and I in him, bears much fruit; for without Me you can do nothing" (John 15:5) (emphasis added). We are made His Body *in the Eucharist*—not mechanically or magically, but having fulfilled the presuppositions, the first and most important being that we have "put on Christ" in *Baptism* and *Chrismation* and through the evangelical virtues.

There are presuppositions of the Mysteries, and presuppositions of acquiring the Orthodox Ethos. Both presuppose asceticism, coupled with mysteriological initiation. Nothing can be taken in isolation; the entire Tradition must be taken as a whole. All the elements are at once dogmatic and ethical.

We can and must become, with the Holy Apostles themselves, "eyewitnesses and ministers of the word" (Luke 1:2) and of His Majesty (see 2 Peter 1:16). As the beloved Apostle John wrote:

That which was from the beginning, which we have **heard**, which we have **seen** with our eyes, which we have looked upon, and our **hands** have handled, concerning the Word of life—the life was **manifested**, and we have seen, and **bear witness**, and declare to you that eternal life which was with the Father and was manifested to us—**that which we have seen and heard we declare to you**, that you also may have [communion] with us; and truly our [communion] is with the Father and with His Son Jesus Christ. (1 John 1:1–3) (emphasis added)

This is dogma by experience: experience expressed as dogma. In this way, in every generation, *the Incarnation continues*, and the Truth, Way or Ethos, and Life—Christ Himself—is imparted. The imparting in every generation happens in the same way it took place in the beginning: as being eyewitnesses of the Incarnation in time and space, from those who have become Christ-by-grace, *Theanthropoi*-by-grace.

Many converts to the Church embrace the Truth, but without the Way, and thus remain without Life abundant. The hardest part of "becoming Orthodox" today is not having examples, not seeing the incarnation of the virtues, not seeing holiness incarnate.

Who is the "holy man"? He is nothing less than that one in which the entire man—his thoughts, words, deeds, impulses, glances, decisions, and desires—are embedded with the Grace of the Holy Spirit. We cannot obtain holiness—which is the Orthodox Ethos—in any other way other than through encountering it incarnate, and seeing, and hearing Christ in our own time and space.

St John Chrysostom provides us with a rule of life when he says *that a good thing cannot happen in a bad way.* The embracing of Truth, therefore, must be accompanied by the acquisition of the Way.

The West lost the Way—the ascetic way—and then lost the Truth. This departure has led to our days, to this present apostasy, to the embrace of corruption. To our great detriment, there are an increasing number of Orthodox today, including prominent hierarchs, who are on this same path—a path which will lead them into becoming "the world," to the embrace of corruption. This is a sure sign of the times.

According to St Jerome, when the cup of corruption overflows and formerly Christian people embrace the sins of the flesh, which is a turning away from life, this will usher in the end of history: *When homosexuality multiplies among Christian people, then the end of history is at hand.* (Όταν θα πολλύνει η ομοφυλοφιλία στους χριστιανικούς λαούς, τότε πλησιάζει το τέλος της Ιστορίας»)

What are we to do, then, when we face those "mockers of the last time who would walk according to their own ungodly lusts" (Jude 18)? What is our response to the innovators in our midst, those "clouds without water, carried about by the winds; late autumn trees without fruit, twice dead, pulled up by the roots; raging waves of the sea, foaming up their own shame" (Jude 12–13)?

We must do the same as Christians have done since the Day of Pentecost and the giving of the Revelation of Saint John, in which it is said:

> And he said to me, "Do not seal the words of the prophecy of this book, for the time is at hand. He who is unjust, let him be unjust still; he who is filthy, let him be filthy still; he who is righteous, let him be righteous still; he who is holy, let him be holy still. And behold, I am coming quickly, and My reward is with Me, to give to every one according to his work. . . . Blessed are those who do His commandments, that they may have the right to the tree of life, and may enter through the gates into the city. But outside are dogs and sorcerers and sexually immoral and murderers and idolaters, and whoever loves and practices a lie. . . . And the Spirit and the bride say, "Come!" And let him who hears say, "Come!" And let him who thirsts come. Whoever desires, let him take the water of life freely. (Revelation 22:10–12, 14–15, 17)

Amen.

# ICXC NIKA: The Liberty of *Theosis*[154]

## Prof. Alfred Kentigern Siewers

> True love for one's neighbor is established on faith in God. It is in God
> Himself. "That they all may be one," said the Saviour of the world to His
> Father, "as You, Father, are in Me, and I in You; that they may also be one
> in Us" (John 17:21). Humility and loyalty to God destroy carnal love.
> That means that it lives through lack of faith and arrogance.
> —St Ignatius Brianchaninov, *The Field*[155]

Recently, I was talking with a young Orthodox Christian, most of whose social contacts are online, at coffee hour at our college-town mission. He told me that he found it impossible to have respectful conversations as a traditional Christian with non-Orthodox friends about issues of sexual politics, which are shaped by the conformity of the online "hive mind." They would end the discussion by labeling him a hater, he explained, and cut him out of their networks.

I also heard that week from an Orthodox friend who said that a longtime secular professional mentor had just cut off their friendship without any conversation because my friend had publicly signed an online document opposing ordination of deaconesses in the Orthodox Church. The ex-mentor in another part of the country saw the statement in cyberspace and deemed it hateful, although he is neither Orthodox nor religious.

Locally, our small college town of about 5,000 people was simultaneously debating an "Human Relations Ordinance" that echoed the proposed U.S. Equality Act in redefining sex to include "sexual orientation" and "gender expression." Revised provisions would make it illegal to aid and abet illegal discrimination in those areas, making it unclear whether Bible Studies or Church homilies could be rendered illegal if following Orthodox teachings. Christians opposing the proposal were accused of being haters and blocking civil rights for LGBTQ+ people. Meanwhile, on campus, advocates of a "trans-affirming" statement by the university community referenced neo-Nazi and anti-Semitic violence in the United States in recent years to imply that, if you were not on board publicly with the statement at the workplace, you were with the haters.

This essay identifies such micro-incidents with a macro picture of growing sexual totalitarian culture in the global West, related to an ethos of individualism with deep historic roots, accelerated by new technological networks. It offers recent developments in Russia as an alternative, to suggest how Orthodox culture provides a remedy to today's self-destructive Western sexual politics, based in distinctive Orthodox ideas of uncreated grace as natural law, of *sobornost*, and of *theosis*. In such teachings and practice, Orthodoxy highlights a Christian "otherworldly queerness" that does not essentialize passions, objectify identities, or fragment humanhood, but which integrates us in personal relationships with God and one another. This Orthodox remedy surprisingly meshes well on a deep level with foundational aspects of the American republic, as this essay also seeks to explain.[156]

On the national level in the United States, the current proposed Equality Act would redefine the term "sex" in the sense of transgender, to erase the traditional sense of "engender" linking sex to trans-generational and organic begetting or birth. This proposed new official anthropology would be inimical to traditional Christian views of family and sex that shaped American culture and its constitutional republic. It would ban traditional views of sex from the public square, with no religious exemption. It labels alleged discrimination or prejudice contradicting its redefinition as illegal "sexual stereotyping," and also could limit scientific and medical critiques of LGBTQ+ ideology.[157] In 2019, the U.S. House voted in favor of the bill 236 to 173. In the Senate the bill had forty-six sponsors, including one Republican. It was supported by all major Democratic presidential contenders in the leadup to the 2020 election. A Democrat majority in the Senate after the next national election could make it law in January 2021. The country as a whole is at another major inflection point.

The landmark 2015 U.S. Supreme Court decision *Obergefell* v. *Hodges*, seeking to redefine the Christian definition of marriage by rendering same-sex marriage a constitutional right, was but a link in a long trend in secular American culture, culminating in today's secular transhumanism, a combination of transgenderism and technocracy. Orthodox Christianity, as a resistant minority faith in the United States, will increasingly find itself in the crosshairs of the movement to establish transhuman secular anthropology as the official ideology of the global West. In secular transhumanism, old distinctions of men and women are deemed oppressive. Forced devotion to a virtual reality of a technologically driven secular state, not voluntarily to another person in marriage and family, and ultimately to the personhood of Jesus Christ, shapes this new "cultural" or "soft" totalitarianism. Yet Orthodox Christianity presents an anthropology capable of radically transfiguring this debate over sex and technology, with its own Christ-centric theistic experience of transhumanism, an otherworldly queerness. Focusing on the purpose of human beings as *theosis*, or life-transfiguring oneness with God, Orthodoxy offers humanity a relational and communal—yet solitary and ascetically fearless—beautiful and natural life in Jesus Christ, apart from the modern commodification of human beings. But before examining the capacity of Orthodoxy to bring healing to the suffering rendered by technocratic transhuman oppression, it is necessary to examine the link between today's secular anthropology in the global West and rising "soft totalitarianism."

### Sexual Totalitarianism

Secular transhumanism today seeks to override physical and traditional forms of the human body with technology, to establish a new type of all-controlling regime. For example, dominant online search engines generate algorithms that provide a matrix for secular sexual ideology. Searches for the keyword phrase "men can" produce hits such as "men can have babies," "men can get pregnant," "men can have periods."[158] Such cyber-pedagogy reflects a new technological social consensus that would seek to erase the traditional Church culturally, as much as Soviet Communism attempted to block Orthodoxy's inter-generational transmission physically.

Such Internet messaging offers a glimpse into the growing effort by public–private "surveillance capitalism" or "woke capitalism" to shape social mores, in a virtual culture heavily engaging men, in particular, with cyberporn and its latest innovation, "sexbots."[159] Such high-tech society paradoxically celebrates a "liquid modernity" that denies God and the reality of created nature, while asserting near-absolute rights for customized sexual personas. This cultural climate fosters a culture of isolation and anxiety easily tending toward terror and terrorism, and the type of demonizing and nihilistic ideas that Hannah Arendt discerned in her post–World War II study of totalitarianism.[160]

Totalitarianism has been defined as "the monopoly of an ideology governing all ideas in all fields . . . and all means of dissemination," creating an administrative state and manipulating people through forms of mass terror and economic control.[161] It produces an all-encompassing "discourse" of society, which is "the discourse of the party, the ideal body of the revolutionary, which traverses each of its members," causing a break with external Creation, and with God.[162]

Orthodox anthropology, by contrast, bases human identity on the freedom of *theosis*, becoming more and more like Jesus Christ, through a synergy of divine grace and human asceticism. Its definition of sex is based on experience of otherworldly reality expressed iconographically in the physical bodies of males and females. This is not the fluid consumer-materialism that today emphasizes autoeroticism and sexual activity, in a disembodied, atomistic false biology, divorced from reproduction and face-to-face complementarity of the sexes. Orthodoxy's view of sex is based on the cosmology, anthropology, soteriology, eschatology, and ascetic-liturgical practice of *theosis*, which illumines freedom as both self-restraint and service to universal Truth, Who is the God-man Jesus Christ. But secular transhumanism essentializes the passions to lay the groundwork for an anarchistic society vulnerable to totalitarian control through manipulation of sexuality by technology.

The political scientist Eric Voegelin decades ago warned of the emergence of this technocratic culture, embodied by the administrative state and enforcing a modern form of "gnosticism"—a culture of disembodied individual will, dominated by elite experts, wielding technological control, in a revolt against created reality to eliminate traditional ideas of freedom.[163] Contraceptive technology and the technologically shaped affluence of postwar American culture both nurtured this tendency in the West. Social data outline the change. The U.S. birthrate in 2019 reportedly hit a thirty-two-year low, and the percentage of Americans over twenty-five who have never married has nearly doubled since 1960. The percentage of adults who have never married in the United States (20 percent), percentage of unmarried parents (25 percent), and number of unmarried adults cohabiting (eighteen million) are at all-time highs in America according to recent studies, with a sharp increase in "involuntarily celibate" young men. Only 65 percent of U.S. children now grow up in homes with a married mother and father, down to 36 percent in African American households.[164]

The weakening of traditional family structure in the United States parallels a decline in the kind of organic nongovernmental social networks, including religious communities, that writers such as Edmund Burke and Alexis de Tocqueville described as essential to the project of free societies in the West. A survey in 2019, four years after the *Obergefell* decision, shows that "nones," those Americans who do not belong to any particular religious body, are at a modern high, now equaling the percentage of the population who identify as either Evangelical Protestant or Roman Catholic, the two largest faith groups in the country.[165] Efforts to undermine traditional family and organic social networks, originally identified with agrarian life, were priorities of Marxist revolutionary and intellectual agendas from the nineteenth century into what is called the "cultural Marxism" of twentieth-century Western academia. But such efforts today positively engage corporate interests seeking profit from an atomized consumer society with a rising proportion of singles or two-income households, who have high disposable incomes but no or few children and are ideal consumers for "woke capitalism." Medical trends supporting this trend include refined forms of artificial conception and surrogate mothering, aborting births to increase the odds of desired characteristics in children, and techniques for changing male or female bodies from one to the other "gender." Legally and culturally, acceptance of "no fault" divorce, abortion "rights," online pornography and autoeroticism, a growing global sex industry, and greater acceptance of sexual transgressions by married adults, all paved the way for the advances of the LGBTQ+ agenda in recent years.

Constitutionally, the legal trend pivots on the paradox that each individual's ability to pursue his or her identity, unencumbered by traditional anthropologies of sex, marriage, and family, should be coercively enforced.[166] This culminates the longer dismantling since the late 1940s of whatever was left of America's "soft establishment" of Christian values, by judicial overturning of prayer and Bible readings in public schools, bans on pornography and abortion, and once-ubiquitous state and local anti-sodomy laws. Today Christian bakers, florists, photographers, corporate executives, and professionals face prosecution or persecution for exercising rights of faith-based conscience.[167] Most prominently seen in *Obergefell*, the trend was echoed even in the newly realigned Supreme Court's decision in 2019 to remove legal prohibitions on immoral or scandalous trademark names, on the grounds that laws cannot enforce traditional morality in speech and expression.[168] Instead, an establishment of secular transhumanism has emerged. Gay Pride celebrations in some cities now eclipse the Fourth of July, marking a new civil religion of "social justice."[169] Judicial overturning of laws passed by vote, such as California's 2008 constitutional amendment against the civil redefining of marriage (Proposition 8), underlines the elite nature of the secular transhumanist movement.

## Russia's Christian Cultural Dissent

Post-communist Russia, on the other hand, with a reviving predominantly Orthodox Christian culture, has resisted secular transhumanism. Russian President Vladimir Putin asked:

[H]ave we forgotten that all of us live in a world based on Biblical values? Even atheists and everyone else live in this world. We do not have to think about this every day, attend church and pray, thereby showing that we are devout Christians or Muslims or Jews. However, deep inside, there must be some fundamental human rules and moral values. In this sense, traditional values are more stable and more important for millions of people than this liberal idea, which, in my opinion, is really ceasing to exist.[170]

The internal conflict in Western secular sexual ideology, between sex as socially constructed and sexual passion as essential identity, remains unresolved and unexamined.[171] To prevent such self-examination arguably is the goal of today's sexual totalitarians. They would remove identity from larger cosmic connections, and ostensibly make it serve the authority personified in the individual. But the reality becomes what Alexander Solzhenitsyn suggests is an "egotocracy," as people dissipated by self-indulgence become ruled by systems of control enabled by technology under a strong-willed head.[172] The hidden but all-pervasive control of the transhuman Western technological state goes unexamined even as its advocates target Putin, for perhaps deserved criticism of violations of human dignity, but without acknowledging how his public support of Orthodoxy follows decades of massive anti-Church persecution under Communism.

To secular transhuman anthropology, the Orthodox Christian view of the purpose of the human being as *theosis* stands as not only a reproach, but an antidote. It opposes the progressive gnostic disembodiment of the Incarnation of Christ in transhumanism, and thus of man as made in His image. It is no coincidence that much of the hostility directed by the secular West today against Russia involves its status as the world's largest Orthodox Christian nation, rejecting sexual identity politics. Between the fall of communism in 1991 and 2019, the number of Orthodox churches in Russia has grown from 6,000 to an estimated 36,000. In 2019, an estimated 1,593 candidates for the priesthood were expected to begin training, up 19 percent from the previous year.[173] The civic culture has become majoritarian Orthodox in support of traditional family life and sexual anthropology.[174] At the same time Orthodox Christian tradition takes a constructively critical view of Western ideas of natural law. The latter's secularized legalism often morphed into enabling secular sexual transhumanism under the banner of individual rights. For example, John Locke's influential view of the self, originally based in Protestantism, emphasized individualism with a never-ending dialectic between self-fulfillment and moral law, in a way that over time defined natural rights in terms of self-will. Orthodoxy, basing its anthropology on *theosis*, or realization of self in relationship with God, offers a remedy for the inadequacy of any Enlightenment-style moralism to oppose today's secular emphasis on sexual self-fulfillment in the global West.[175]

In his 2019 *Financial Times* interview, Putin said liberal governments in the formerly Christian West had failed their peoples by pursuing "sexual diversity" among efforts to undermine their traditional cultures. "I am not trying to insult anyone because we have been condemned for our alleged homophobia. But we have no problem with LGBT persons. God forbid, let them live as they wish," he said. "But some things do appear excessive to us. They claim now that children can play five or six gender roles. . . . Let everyone be happy, we have no problem with that. But this must not be allowed to overshadow the culture, traditions and traditional family values of millions of people making up the core population."[176]

Russian cultural resistance, on the basis of Christian tradition, to codifying LGBTQ+ agendas into law has encouraged American Christian leaders such as Franklin Graham, son of the leading Protestant preacher Billy Graham, to flock to visit or engage post-Communist Russia, as if on pilgrimage.[177] The Russian Orthodox Church's Synod and leaders in the past two decades have promulgated crucial documents on *The Basis of the Church's Social Concept* or "Jubilee Document" in 2000 and the *Basic Teaching on Human Dignity, Freedom and Rights* in 2006, strongly supporting a traditional Christian anthropology of sex and family, reflected in recent state policies. Russia in 2013 passed a law prohibiting promotion of homosexuality to minors, which has resulted in restrictions on media, businesses, and public events.[178] Although often labeled an "anti-gay law" in the West, Russian officials term it an "anti-gay-propaganda law" designed to resist secular Western influence on young people, noting that it reflects social mores that existed in Western countries until recently. Russian leaders also support efforts globally to shore up traditional families (in the sense of C.S. Lewis's "Tao," incorporating aspects of traditional family found in major world religions including Confucianism, Islam, and others[179]), such as the World Congress of Families organization. This has drawn fire from Western groups such as the cyber-influential U.S. Southern Poverty Law Center, which has all but labeled the Russian Orthodox Church a hate group, despite SPLC's own recent struggles with alleged bias and corruption.[180]

Reflecting decades of history under communism, followed by the recent disruptive transition to an era of Western-dominated capitalism in the 1990s, abortion and divorce rates continue to be high in Russia, and its population remains in decline, amid an economy now hobbled by Western sanctions. But longer-term cultural trends are moving in a more traditionally Christian direction, as seen in government promotion of large families. Similar efforts to shore up traditional ideas of sex and family in other non-Western countries portray political and economic lobbying for sexual transhumanism globally as Euro-American neocolonialism. Thus, African and Asian United Methodists in 2019 engineered a surprise rejection of their worldwide but American-based denomination's expected endorsement of homosexuality and transgenderism. Many Asian and African Christians argue that secular Western sexual mores follow American state and financial interests today. Even Communist China to some extent shores up traditional ideas of family and sex for nationalistic reasons, although in a context of state control that dominates family life, targets faith, and has forced abortions. None of these efforts in any way justifies from a Christian standpoint violence against people in various societies for sexual issues, including especially as done in traditional Muslim countries. Such acts have been condemned as sinful and beyond the pale of Orthodox Christian mores in a Russian Church-related website.[181] But the cultural efforts mentioned above do suggest the Euro-American-centrism of secular transhumanism. In that context, Russia is the one major power whose public culture evidences a traditional Christian approach to issues of sexual anthropology, while culturally outside mainstream Western religious and intellectual history.

Distinctive emphases of Orthodox Christian tradition on sex go deep into history, drawing on a shared heritage with the West. But Orthodox tradition is based more solely in pre-Scholastic first-millennial patristic foundations, developed in ascetic-centered monastic and liturgical practices across subsequent centuries. The Russian Orthodox philosopher-exile S.L. Frank in his book *The Unknowable* (1939) described the deep apophatic definition of freedom in this tradition in layers:

> [P]otentiality, the potency to become what it is not, lies in the deepest core of being. This is what we call "freedom." Since all concretely existent

things are rooted in the total unity of being and are permeated by the "juices" of the total unity, the element of primordial freedom is present, to varying degrees, in all concretely existent things . . . .[182] This primordial freedom in which we are driven by forces of our own inner being and which enslaves us is opposed by another, higher freedom which emanates from our selfhood . . . . This freedom is realized through self-overcoming . . . This is not yet the ultimate and highest freedom, genuinely 'true' freedom which can never emanate from man's inner being along . . . for it is freedom only in the form of struggle . . . But it is nonetheless true freedom insofar as it is self-overcoming.[183]

"True freedom," for Frank, draws on the above-mentioned primordial freedom of potentiality and self-restraint, but freedom in his Russian Orthodox definition must also involve what he calls "the ground of reality as antinomian monodualism." That means man's independent yet connected relation to God, fulfilled in *theosis*. He called this, "The coincidence of being *for another and in another* with what is, in essence, *being in itself and for itself* . . . revealed in the phenomenon of love."[184] Such love, Frank concluded, must be rooted in God through *theosis*. Thus, Frank argued, the Orthodox definition of freedom is voluntary service to universal truth, in the Person of Jesus Christ. That is the basis of Russian Orthodox anthropology and its resilience in the face of twentieth-century totalitarian persecution. It differs in emphasis, though overlaps in part, with modern Western definitions of freedom as simply individual right and choice. But the latter, when emphasizing self-will without God, forms secular transhumanism from its secularization of natural law and natural rights.

## Western "Egotocracy"

The Orthodox retention of the original form of the Nicene-Constantinopolitan Creed, the primary source of the Schism of Western from Eastern Christendom in the eleventh century, helps to explain why Orthodoxy rejects Western ideas of individualism, secularized natural law (see the next section below), and the corporate-administrative technocratic state, as seen in the aforementioned *Social Concept* document.[185] All the latter merge into secular trans-human cultural trends today. But they have deep roots. The Roman papacy's unilateral Western addition of the *filioque* ("and from the son") to the Creed in Latin—stating that the Holy Spirit proceeded from the Father and the Son together, rather than from the Father alone, as in the original Greek text of the Creed—led, from the Orthodox standpoint, to subordination of the Holy Spirit to an imagined melding of the Father and the Son. In other words, it shaped the Trinity into more of a binary or linear model. The Western-Latin tendency to find reflections of an individualistic human psychology in the Trinity came to emphasize the melded Self of the Father-Son, acting upon the Other, the Holy Spirit, instead of the Orthodox sense of the Most Holy Trinity as mystery, with aspects of both monarchy and conciliarity, experienced through uncreated energies rather than in unknowable Essence.[186] The Western Trinity thus became a type of the human self in a way that the Orthodox viewed as idolatrous. Personalism in the West came to center around the personhood of the individual self, rather than on the Person of Christ, as it remained in Orthodoxy. In first-millennial Christian tradition, the historian Peter Brown argued, sex "was embedded in a cosmic matrix in ways that made its perception of itself profoundly unlike our own. Ultimately, sex was not the expression of inner needs, lodged in the isolated body. Instead, it was seen as the pulsing, through the body, of the same energies as kept the stars alive. Whether this pulse of energy came from benevolent gods or from malevolent demons (as many radical Christians believed) sex could never be seen as a thing for the isolated human body alone."[187]

During its Scholastic era in the High Middle Ages, Western culture moved to a more individualized sense of both the body and the self, "from seeing the body as microcosm reflecting in itself a cosmic story, to seeing the body as interpreter of human inwardness," according to the Orthodox patristic scholar Fr Andrew Louth.[188] That trajectory, according to the psychoanalytic theorist Julia Kristeva and others, fulfilled the individualistic logic of the *filioque, contra* Orthodoxy.

Development of individualized identity in the West was integrally linked from post-Roman times to the emergence of an idea of the corporate state identified with the body of the individual ruler, whether king or pope. The idea of the "king's two bodies," in the feudal "absolute right of kings," distinguished the monarch's human body from his abstract body, the latter morphing into the corporate state in Western medieval Christianity. But in Byzantium, the ruler was seen more as an icon of the human nature of Christ, rather than the embodiment of the state as a virtual corporation as in the papacy of Roman Catholicism. The *symphonia* between Church and State in Orthodox political culture, which came to be symbolized by the two-headed eagle, was based in a principle of *sobornost* or conciliarity, a spiritual unity. *Sobornost* (by the fourteenth century the Slavonic gloss for "catholic" in the Nicene Creed) "means togetherness, wholeness, communality; it emphasizes a oneness, but without uniformity or loss of individuality," wrote the Russian émigré scholar Nicolas Zernov. It "means a symphonic Church which forms a harmonious unity out of the diverse gifts of its different members; like a well-conducted orchestra it produces one harmony, although each musician plays his own part on his own particular instrument."[189] It has also been defined, through Dostoevsky's literary expression, as organic collectivity, "a free, inner, organic 'unity in multiplicity,'" or the freedom of human personhood realized in the Person of Christ.[190]

The West developed a trajectory toward totalitarianism from the Augustinian emphasis on Original Sin, by separating the human sphere from the divine, as in Scholastic ideas of "created grace" combining with the emphasis on individual will related to the *filique*. This ultimately extended a type of individualism to the super-individual state and private corporations. These became "immortal" but abstract legal persons, operating in a secular sphere apart from God's rule, under secularized "natural law" and "natural rights." An apotheosis of this was Marx's "dictatorship of the proletariat," introduced into Russia by military coup and Lenin's brutal "vanguard" strategy.[191] This involved a "logic of identification, secretly governed by the image of the body," a "condensation that takes place between the principle of power, the principle of law and the principle of knowledge," according to the French political theorist Claude Lefort.[192] Therein lies the origins of contemporary Western identity politics. In Orthodox tradition, by contrast, law, associated with *logos* meaning "principle," ultimately becomes identified with the dynamic *uncreated* grace or energies, the "harmonies" (another translation of *logoi*), of God. These divine energies transfigure materialistic ideas of sexual identity, too.

## Orthodox "Natural Law," Based in Grace

Unlike the binary focus of the Western-Latin Trinity on Self vs. Other, Orthodox Triadology does not encourage individualized corporate bodies that assume evermore totalizing forms in the virtual "mega-individuals" of governments and corporations melding together in globalization today. Caesaro-Papism in Protestant Northern Europe, and the Papo-Caesarism of the Papal States, both emerged from the West, as did ideologies of communism, fascism, and global capitalism emerging from them. In Byzantine tradition, by contrast, the historian Anthony Kaldellis concludes there was a melding of

Classical Roman republicanism with Christian culture. The removal of emperors by the military, and protests by monks and lay crowds, were integral parts of established checks and balances on power, involving the sense that the ruler must adhere to higher law. Kaldellis writes:

> Byzantium was a republic in the broader sense. The Roman people remained the true sovereign of the political sphere, and they both authorized and de-authorized the holding of power by their rulers. The latter, "the emperors of the Romans," must be understood in relation to the political sphere constituted by the totality of the Roman people. The *politeia* was the Byzantine Greek translation and continuation of the ancient *res publica*.[193]

Frank argued from a Russian Orthodox standpoint that the "spiritual foundations of society" must involve the interpenetration of *sobornost* (the Slavonic translation of "catholic" in the Nicene Creed) with mechanical and individualistic aspects of society, *obshchestvennost*, to be healthy.[194] Otherwise the latter would be susceptible to dehumanizing technocracy. Frank, as noted, articulated an Orthodox Christian definition of *freedom* as unforced service to universal truth, grounded in the divine Personhood of Christ guaranteeing human dignity. *Justice* thus becomes the opportunity for all to engage in such service. That is very different from secularized Western ideas of social justice that came to justify Western sexual transhumanism. To Frank, *sobornost* expresses the Christian typology of marriage as between Christ and His Church, and thus becomes a symbol for Orthodox anthropology and society as well. Natural law is founded in the Cross, the intersection of grace with ascetic suffering, or "joyful sorrow," and freedom as self-restraint rather than assertion of individual right.

The late Orthodox bioethicist H. Tristram Engelhardt articulated this different Orthodox sense of natural law:

> Natural law is, after all, the spark of God's love in our nature, not the biological state of affairs we find in broken nature. Natural law is not an objective external constraint, but the will of the living God experienced in our conscience. It is this natural law, the law of God in our nature, which calls for carnal sexuality to be accomplished only within marriage. Anything else is unnatural in violating the law God established in Eden and renewed through Christ. . . . These are not judgments about the

unnaturalness, perversity, or deviance of acts in a secularly biological or medical sense of those behaviors constituting unsuccessful adaptations by reference to either inclusive fitness or personal fulfillment. The Christian moral-theological reference point for the appropriateness of sexual behavior is the creation of humans as male and female and the restoration of the union of Adam and Eve in the Mystery of matrimony. . . . [F]ollowing St. Paul, certain sexual activities such as homosexual relations are profoundly unnatural. . . . The law of God found in our nature and announced in Genesis and the Gospels is to be found in the union of husband and wife. In these terms, fornication and adultery are unnatural.[195]

Engelhardt based his description on a statement by St Basil of Caesarea on how "the spark of divine love latent within you" is enkindled by ascetic effort in synergy with grace, or *theosis* as the transfiguring and dynamic basis for natural identity.[196] The influential Orthodox Christian theological writer Vladimir Lossky further observed, "The Eastern tradition knows nothing of 'pure nature' to which grace is added as a supernatural gift. For it, there is no natural or 'normal' state, since grace is implied in the act of creation itself."[197] Real nature is not the fallenness of man and Creation. In the seventh-century AD, St Maximus the Confessor wrote:

The mystery of the Incarnation of the Logos is the key to all the enigmas and typology in the Scriptures, and in addition gives us knowledge of created things, both visible and intelligible. He who apprehends the mystery of the Cross and the burial apprehends the inner essences of created things; while he who is initiated into the inexpressible power of the Resurrection apprehends the purpose for which God first established everything.[198]

That is why St John of Damascus wrote in the eighth century that "it is of the nature of all things that they may be apprehended through industry and toil, and before all and after all by the grace of God, the Giver of grace." To "apprehend" with the mind's eye, St John argued, one must "knock hard, so that the door of the bridal chamber may be opened to us and we may behold the beauties within."[199] Marriage thus becomes the master figure for understanding identities as relational in Orthodox Christianity. What St Maximus the Confessor termed the *logoi* of the Logos as the source of identity, he also associated with divine energies: the *logoi* are the ways in which the energies are manifest or experienced by mortals in Creation. *Logoi* have a multiple meaning of "words," "stories," and "harmonies" in Greek (the latter relating directly to energies), but also "principles" or law, reasons.[200] A "marriage" of human beings in the Church with Christ involves unity through the divine energies with God, and exemplifies the source of identity, which is not found in self-will or passion, or assertion of rights to the same. The mystery of marriage in Orthodoxy exemplifies a covenant with God, not a contract between persons.

### Marriage and *Sobornost*

The controversial Russian nationalistic philosopher Alexander Dugin implicitly highlights this connection between marriage and anthropology in Orthodoxy by describing a "fourth way" of thinking about sex, apart from Western fascist, Communist, and liberal models. He draws on traditional Russian Orthodox models, while using language of postmodern theory to call for subverting current Western sexual ideology. (Dugin is an Old Believer in communion with the Russian Orthodox Church, whom Western journalists have characterized, pejoratively, as "Putin's brain.") His writing suggests how Orthodox views of sex may be profoundly anti-modern or trans-modern, a kind of Christian transhumanism that surpasses the radicalness of secular transhumanism through *theosis*, but in a way compatible with Orthodox tradition.

In his discussion of gender, Dugin draws on a Russian philosophical interpretation of the Heideggerean term *Dasein* ["being there"]. He defines *Dasein* as "the 'between' in the space between the subject and the object," undermining the opposition of Self and Other in Western individualism by emphasizing a relational sense of identity. That relational identity is a mystery in Christ transfiguring male or female in any individualized secular sense.[201] Sex in Dugin's "fourth way" is based in identity that is relational to God, not essentialized passion. He employs the term sex not to describe an essential binary humanity, but rather a "radical androgyne," representing "the primordial, untouched unity" of humanity in Genesis 1:26—the wholeness found in *theosis* via *sobornost*. This is like St Maximus' view discussed below. Dugin's foundation in revealed Christian teaching on marriage subverts Western notions of secular "postmodern gender," with the latter's relativistic view of gender and sex as socially constructed.

Dugin argues that such secular transhumanism claims to be universal, but is only a projection of the culturally particular identity of modern Western liberal man onto the world at large. Thus, secular feminism and transgenderism reflect a Eurocentric type of gnostic self-will, the "gender of globalization," claiming to supersede traditional models. For Dugin, secular feminism and transgenderism reflect norms coming from the model of elite Western males: for example, professional women who wish to emulate the personas of successful men. Today's coercive secular transhumanism, Dugin argues, involves the idea that "women are not yet fully liberated men," and "this all-consuming archetype [of the sexually liberated Western self] becomes meaningless."[202] To Dugin, secular transhumanist sex follows a Western sense of Being that falsely claims universality. He argues that Heidegger's attempted alternative, offering a more apophatic view of Being as mystery, can be deepened from the standpoint of Russian Orthodox philosophical ideas.[203] The latter include the idea of *sobornost*, or spiritual unity, leading in the Church to *theosis*.

So what Dugin calls his "fourth way" of sex, "not in the sense of half of something else" but rather a "radical androgyne," representing "the primordial, untouched unity" of humanity, actually draws on ancient Orthodox Christian tradition. He calls this an angelic practice of sex. Dugin calls for a move "beyond the limits of gender which we know," as defined by the West today as socially constructed, to "sex as practiced by the angels." "The [angelic] gender of Dasein [present-being]," he writes, "represents a root reality, that . . . belongs to *l'imaginaire*."[204] *L'imaginaire*, or the Imaginary, is a term evoking the deep structure of human ecology, which shapes the self beyond sex, but in Orthodoxy ultimately in a resurrected body still expressing the cosmic complementarity and symbolism of Christ and His Church, and a life of freedom as service.

In the Gospels, Jesus Christ observes, "[I]n the resurrection they neither marry, nor are given in marriage, but are as the angels of God in heaven" (Matt. 22:30).[205] Advocating an "angelic" practice of sex, Dugin argues for a parallel between the ascetic nature of marriage and the "angelic" life of ascetic monasticism. The monastic's goal is the angelic life, epitomized in the prototypical monastic figure of St John the Baptist portrayed often in iconography with angel wings in the desert. A shared ascetic spirit in monogamous lifelong marriage and monasticism, captured in Church canons and other teachings and confessional practices,[206] stems from a common emphasis on *theosis*, reflected in what might be called "Dugin's Christian transhumanism."

Russian Orthodox Bishop (then-Hieromonk) Luke (Murianka), Abbot of Holy Trinity Monastery and Rector of Holy Trinity Seminary in Jordanville, New York, wrote in 1997 that the mystery of marriage in the Church should not be denigrated. He added, however, that it is important not to fall into the opposite extreme of considering sex to be an avenue for *theosis*, or believing that the categories of male and female are fundamental to deification:

The assumption that God created man and woman with the intention of them

> engaging in carnal, sexual relations is faulty and can lead to dangerous conclusions. God created mankind in an unfallen, sinless, pure, angelic state. Carnal relations, as we can see from the Fathers cited above [St Gregory the Dialogist, St Athanasius the Great, St Mark the Ascetic, the Byzantine exegete Euthymius Zigabenos, Bishop Ignatius Brianchaninov], came about as a result of the fall. Finally, there came a time in the life of the Old Testament Church, when it was time for it to be replaced by the New Testament, revealed by the incarnate Word of God, in Whom man's nature was finally made whole. Man's wholeness was not accomplished through the carnal union that occurred in blessed marriages throughout the Old Testament, but rather man's wholeness was accomplished in Christ, Whose incarnation occurred without carnal relations.[207]

Even within marriage, Orthodox tradition (through canons, saints' lives, and instruction by elders) suggests regulation of days when sex cannot occur (possibly more than half the year for those who commune regularly and observe fasts traditionally), as well as ways in which husband and wife should engage in sex, the rejection of abortion and a disdain for contraception, and the avoiding of medical/technological means for prolonging sexual activity into old age, instead of encouraging consensual celibacy for older married couples. Sex is not a path to spiritual enlightenment.

The angelic orders, like the orders of the Church, are cosmically hierarchical. Orthodox marriage also entails a created hierarchy, as a living embodied symbol of the unity between Jesus Christ as the Bridegroom and the human community of the Church, as both His Bride and His Body. But the hierarchy in human marriage is apophatic as a mystery, and the division between male and female likewise not absolute. Man's identity in Christ is not reducible to essentialized sex and passions. Hierarchy in this ancient sense, which ultimates in the unknowable essence of God, involves networks of divine energy in love, not oppressive control by human power. It includes direct access by all to divinity. Saint Paul's writings tell of the reciprocal love of man and woman in marriage involving the husband as the head of the wife, but imitating Christ in laying down his life for her. The woman is to serve the husband, but exercising her own form of service as leadership in Christian terms, as the Apostle Peter described (I Peter 3:1–6), winning husbands to the word of God by chaste conversation with fear and adornment of the "hidden man of the heart."

In Orthodoxy, human beings are embodied, but like angels in eschatological purpose, as Christ's statement about marriage indicates. Man is made, God says in Genesis, "in our image, after our likeness," and is given dominion over the earth (Gen. 1:26), without reference to sex. But Genesis then states: "So God created man in His own image, in the image of God created He him; male and female created he them" (Gen. 1:27). Orthodox teachings on this basis both deepen and clarify human notions of sex. They strip away any identity with sexual passion, while establishing marriage as between two created sexes, as Jesus Christ said in the Gospels. The human body even in its fallen state potentially is a living and embodied typology of holy iconography, expressed in the beauty of saints who continue as intercessors for us in the afterlife in their respective male and female forms. But in Orthodoxy this should be understood not as idolatrous deification of the male and female sexes (for it is the human being who is deified, not his or her sex per se), but as a reminder, in humility, of how man as such is not God, except in the unique case of Jesus Christ.

Saint Maximus the Confessor in the seventh century articulated the mystery of male and female by concluding that the division will be transcended in the Second Coming of Christ. What he called the "extremes" and "means" of humanity entail "the productive and containing power of the divine energy" in relation to sex. One "extreme," or ultimate, state is that of the origin of man in Genesis 1:26—man created according to Christ the Logos, Who Himself is the image of God the Father. The Confessor describes "the mean," or instrumentality, expressed in Genesis 1:27, "male and female He made them," as the present condition of humanity. The other "extreme" he describes as the Apostle Paul's observation that, in Christ Jesus "there is neither male nor female" (Galations 3:28).[208] In the dynamism of the divine energies we may experience both "extremes" and "mean" at the same time. Hieromonk Damascene Christiansen suggested that, at the time of bodily resurrection, "human beings will bear some kind of 'imprint' of maleness or femaleness," citing the Church's regard for the resurrected and ascended Christ and the Theotokos beyond death as "still in some sense man and woman." However, "one should be careful not to try to define this point too precisely."[209]

Orthodox anthropology could be categorized at once as "single sex" (St Maximus' "extreme"), "two sex" (the Maximian "mean"), or "three sex"—as in the "third gender" or "third sex" sometimes assigned in Byzantine writing to ascetic celibates and eunuchs. Monastic virginity is the angelic standard of transfigurative chastity in Orthodoxy. But that norm is not exclusive of marriage. The goal of Orthodox Christocentric anthropology is not to essentialize any passions, but to progress on the journey to *theosis* through ascetic struggle and cultivation of the virtues with the vital assistance of divine grace in the Church. Natural law governing man is, from an Orthodox standpoint (following Engelhardt and St Basil), ultimately what is natural according to Paradise and the final Resurrection to come, sparkling as transfigurative grace in a fallen world and fallen human nature.

### True Freedom

Claude Lefort in his essay "The Image of the Body and Totalitarianism," and the Soviet dissident Orthodox writer I.R. Shafarevich in his study of socialism, warned of a psychological "death wish" embedded in the utopian ideals of both fascist and liberal-socialist systems. Lefort concluded that the "organicist" nature of totalitarianism, with the state assuming the role of social body that supplants the individual body, leads to self-murder as well as mass murder.[210] Shafarevich saw this "death wish" in events such as the killing fields of the Pol Pot regime in Cambodia, Soviet food-genocides and labor camps, and the Chinese Cultural Revolution.[211] Extinguishing humanity has become a type of social euthanasia, perversely envisioned as pleasurable.

Such ideas, in turn, contribute to the promotion of erasing human sex. Dostoevsky unforgettably wrote of suicide as the end-trajectory of nihilistic radicalism in his novel *Demons*, which explored the revolutionary eschatology of self-extinction. Within this context, tragically and ironically, high suicide rates among people identifying as LGBTQ+ become the pre-eminent justification for the coercive enforcement of secular transhumanist ideology, at the expense of traditional family norms that are accused of promoting suicides and mental illness.[212] However, a lack of definitive studies not sponsored or carried out by LGBTA+ advocates and controlled for other social and psychological factors makes the blame placed on Christianity especially hateful (given that strictures against homosexual and trans-sexual behavior are found in numerous other traditional faiths, including traditional Islam, Judaism, and Buddhism). This is deeply true in regions of the West now dominated by secular transhumanist public culture, in which communities of traditional faithful often have become marginalized minorities, including some regions of the United States.

Orthodoxy considers suicide a sin and its prevention a social priority, because each human being (regardless of behavior or identification) is
infinitely valuable as an icon of Christ. Any persecution or hatred of people
is un-Christian and abhorrent and needs to be opposed. But individual cases
are often complex, as in the tragic death of Matthew Shepard, whose remains
are now enshrined in the Episcopal Church's so-called National Cathedral.[213]
His demise is the subject of competing narratives of bigotry and drug-dealing.
In terms of "trans" youth, studies indicate that the vast majority will desire to
revert to their biological sex by their twenties, and that, at older ages, those who
have attempted to change their sex medically still have a high suicide rate.[214]
Trans youth have higher suicide rates, but trans populations appear to increase
proportionately with establishment of official secular transhumanism, in a
social-conformity phenomenon.[215] The psychoanalytic theorist Slavic Žižek
suggested that a naïve belief in transgender ideology, the faith that releasing
one's self from sexual norms will solve psychological issues, may hide other
problems.[216] For example, other critics suggest that parents who "come out"
as trans, and who leave children and families for new partners of the same
original sex, indulge in or may be overcome by a paradoxically self-destructive
narcissism.[217] Such concerns fit Shafarevich's characterization of a "death wish"
in totalitarian movements, redirected to hatred of the Other, now evidenced in
what the sociologist George Yancey calls "Christianophobia."[218] LGBT+ advocates routinely invoke "transphobia" and "homophobia" to pathologize traditional Christian anthropology as a disease.

The Orthodox answer to secular transhumanism and its totalitarian tendencies, epitomized in the term *theosis*, grows from the living symbolism of
marriage known in many cultures. It is also reflected in the roots of the American republic in the Hellenic-Christian synthesis, a shared heritage with Orthodox culture. Christian marriage as a typology for *sobornost* formed the basis of
the American republic, according to John Quincy Adams, sixth president of
the United States:

> [T]he social compact, or body politic, founded upon the laws of Nature
> and of God, physical, moral, and intellectual, necessarily pre-supposes a
> *permanent* family compact formed by the *will* of the man, and the *con-
> sent* of the woman, and that by the same laws of Nature, and of God, in
> the formation of the Social Compact, the will or vote of every family
> must be given by its head, the husband and father.[219]

That echoes the words of his father, President John Adams: "Our Constitution was made only for a moral and religious people. It is wholly inadequate to the government of any other."[220] The elder Adams argued for the combination of monarchy, aristocracy, and democracy in the new republic, paralleling in spirit Kaldellis's analysis of the Byzantine republic-empire. By the time of Abraham Lincoln's Presidency in 1861, that vision had become *de facto* reality: a strong presidency, an aristocratic Senate, and a democratic House of Representatives. Lincoln most famously in his Gettysburg Address linked the Declaration of Independence to the Constitution as establishing a nation "under God." The Declaration's key invocations of the biblical God ("God," "Creator," "Providence," "Supreme Judge") echoed in Lincoln's capstone to the founding documents, referring to "our fathers" and "under God," reflected, arguably, the spirit of *sobornost* and *symphonia*. Traditional Christian marriage remains the prime nexus of the tradition of civic morality and faith invoked by both the two Adams and Lincoln as essential to the American republic.

The contrast between totalitarian tendencies of secular transhumanism and traditional ideas of marriage and family undergirding a Christian republic is highlighted in the *The Russian Orthodox Church's Basic Teaching on Human Dignity, Freedom, and Rights* from 2006. It discusses the significant difference between two Greek words for freedom in Scripture and the Church Fathers. When the Apostle Paul writes, "Where the Spirit of the Lord is, there is liberty" (2 Corinthinas 3:17), he speaks of liberty as an unveiling of the purpose of the hidden glory of God in Creation. There he uses the Greek term *eleutheria* for "liberty" or "freedom." However, that term for the Apostle has the double-meaning of libertinism unless informed by the Spirit in service—as in "do not use liberty as an opportunity for the flesh, but through love serve one another" (Galatians 5:13). When Jesus Christ says in the Gospels, "If the Son makes you free, you shall be free [*eleutheroi*] indeed" (John 8:36), that freedom means living in the goodness that man had in his primordial natural state in Christ in the eschatological role to come. The natural again stems from prelapsarian Paradise and in the general Resurrection at Christ's Second Coming. God created man originally with *autexousion*, or "freedom of choice," according to St Gregory of Nyssa. But that gift, though regarded as primary freedom in modern secularism, remains in Orthodoxy an accompaniment or means to a deeper sense of freedom from passion in service to truth—that is, *eleutheria* in Christ. Today in the secular West, however, the secondary term often subsumes the primary meaning, enabling secular transhumanism, whose emphasis on self-will becomes destructive of human nature in God.[221] Patriarch Kirill of Moscow has commented on this paradox of gnostic technocracy being based in materialistic passion:

> The problem is that transhumanism reduces a human being to his/her biological, or, in the patristic terms, bodily, constituent, and believes that with the view of perfecting it, it is permissible to give up moral norms and go beyond the limits of what is morally admissible. Transhumanism promises humanity "digital immortality," the overcoming of physical limitations and, practically, the creation of a new man. Through movies and literature an idea is penetrating the minds of our contemporaries that people need "alteration," "renewal" or, using computer terms, "upgrade." This is a new form of anti-Christianity that declares sincere concern for man's good, but in reality completely destroys the true notions of humaneness and of human being as an image of God.[222]

Secular cosmology today adapts outmoded Darwinist philosophy to try to replace Christian anthropology with a view of all things as having a common materialistic source, yet one physically fluid in categories of identity, and evolving through atheistic "natural selection."[223] In stark contrast, Orthodox Christian transfiguration in *theosis* provides a model for a resilient traditional anthropology for the twenty-first century, based on a sense of freedom as serving truth that is at once universal and personal. Its role in mooring a virtuous and trans-generational constitutional republic deserves legal and political privilege, to hold back the self-will of reckless elites in a rising global technocracy.

Saint John the Evangelist's revelation that the spirit of anti-Christ includes the denial of Jesus Christ's Incarnation (see 1 John 4:1–3) is pertinent here. Denial of the human incarnation of God as a man also involves denial of traditional biblical anthropology of sex, family, and marriage as practiced in Christian cultures. With such denial comes erasure of traditional marriage as a model of *sobornost* and ultimately *theosis*, and the replacement of its cosmological ethos of reciprocal service under God by the individual drive for sheer power and self-satisfaction. As a Russian proverb declares, "What anarchism starts, communism ends."

# Twenty-Six Foundations for Centering the Lives of Our Youth in Purity, Chastity, and Integrity

Prof. David C. Ford

> Train up a child in the way he should go; and when he is old,
> he will not depart from it.
> —Proverbs 22:6 (NKJV)

Our Holy Orthodox Church deeply affirms the tremendous importance of children, beginning with the service for the Sacrament of Marriage, during which there are numerous prayers offered for "fair children" for the newlyweds. Then, when a child is born, the priest is there on the eighth day for the service of the Naming of the Child. Next, of course, come the Baptism and Chrismation of the child after forty days, and these sacraments are immediately followed by the baby—the newly enrolled "warrior for Christ"— receiving the Holy Eucharist.

It's profoundly significant that of all the Christian groups, only the Orthodox include the babies at the Holy Chalice, completely recognizing and demonstrating their full incorporation into the Church, the Body of Christ. This alone, it seems to me, shows forth the truthfulness of our Church's claim to be the One, Holy, Catholic, and Apostolic Church, alone preserving the fullness of the Christian Faith.

The writings of the saints also proclaim the crucial importance of children in our Church. To cite three examples, I turn to two modern Church Fathers and one from the fourth century. Saint Theophan the Recluse wrote in late nineteenth-century Russia, "One must at all times keep the education of the child under the most abundant influence of the Holy Church, which by the whole order of its life acts in a saving way upon the formation of the child's spirit. . . . Of all holy works, the education of children is the most holy."[224]

Bishop Irenaius of Ekaterinburg and Sibirsk in Russia wrote to parents in the early twentieth century:

> Do you want your children to be obedient? Show them your love. Not a love that weakens them, that gives way to all their demands; but a wise and heartfelt love that looks to their true benefit. When a child sees such love, he will obey not from fear but from reverence. . . . Finally, never forget to invoke the blessing of God on your work in bringing up your children. Only then will your labor, struggles, and concern be crowned with success. With God's help, your children will learn obedience.[225]

And our Father among the Saints, St John Chrysostom, wrote in the late fourth century:

> To each of you fathers and mothers I say, just as we see artists fashioning their paintings and statues with great precision, so we must care for *these wondrous statues of ours.* Painters, when they have set the canvas on the easel, paint on it day by day to accomplish their purpose. Sculptors, too, working in marble, proceed in a similar manner; they remove what is superfluous and add what is lacking. Even so you must proceed. Like *the creators of statues, give all your leisure to fashioning these* **wondrous statues for God.**[226]

May the following twenty-six spiritual foundations be very helpful in raising our youth in purity, chastity, and integrity—indeed, in every virtue in the Christian life.

1. Sexual purity—in all its glory, wonder, beauty, dignity, sanctity, and safety—is an integral part of *an entire way of life,* centered in Christ in His Holy Church. This glorious way of life in godliness, which helps us immensely to experience the comforting presence of the Living God, and to be filled with His love, joy, and peace, is what every human being is created and designed for by the Holy Trinity in His infinite goodness, love, and beneficence! Through actively communing with Him as we follow this God-ordained, grace-filled path in humble obedience to our Creator and Saviour, we experience the most joy-filled, meaningful, and personally satisfying way of living that is possible in our life on earth. For we have the inner peace and joy that comes from knowing that we're pleasing our Creator and Saviour by living in the way He wishes for us to live. And most importantly, this is the only path that leads to eternal life with Christ in His Heavenly Kingdom.

2. Parents need to consider honestly their priorities for themselves and their children. *Are you parents dedicated* to making daily prayer, at least weekly Church attendance, and virtuous, godly living the foundations of your marriage and your family life? *Are you fathers determined* to be the servant-head of your home, taking the ultimate responsibility for the spiritual and material well-being of your family? Studies have shown that when the father goes to church with his children, the children are much more likely to remain in the Church after they leave home.[227]

3. Youth growing up in *Christ-centered homes,* in which purity, chastity, integrity, and all the virtues are emphasized and lived, will most likely naturally imbibe this grace-filled way of life. For a wonderful visionary and practical description of a Christ-centered marriage, I highly recommend a talk by Elder Aimilianos, an Athonite elder speaking to married Orthodox Christians. The talk is called "Marriage: The Great Sacrament."[228]

4. From the early moments parents are aware of a pregnancy, they should *pray for their child* to live in the Way of Christ, and for a godly future spouse—or an appropriate monastery—for their child.

5. *Godparents have a special God-given role and responsibility* in reinforcing the family's nurturing of the child in the Christ-centered life. As the parents prepare for the child's Baptism and Chrismation, do they choose godparents primarily for their dedication to the Orthodox Christian way of life, and for their willingness to help ensure that their godchild will grow up as an active Orthodox Christian? Are the new godparents willing to be instructed by the priest on the duties and responsibilities of godparenting?

6. Beginning with the Baptism and Churching of the child, *the entire parish* should be directly or indirectly involved in the Christ-centered nurturing of the child in purity, chastity, integrity, and all the virtues.

7. The priest of the parish should preach and teach periodically about *the glory, wonder, beauty, sanctity, dignity, and safety of sexual purity both in marriage and in the single life*—along with warning about the manifold spiritual, emotional, and physical dangers that come with any form of sexual impurity—such as spiritual estrangement from the Lord, requiring deep repentance; intense emotional turmoil and even psychological trauma; and sexually transmitted diseases. A great resource for such teaching is *Glory and Honor: Orthodox Christian Resources for Marriage,* a collection of essays and other writings on various aspects of marriage and sexuality, including the awesome and wonderful complementarity of husband and wife, as well as the full goodness of marital relations.[229]

8. All the parents in the parish should be steadily encouraged by the priest, and by one another, to **"make their home a little church,"** as St John Chrysostom urges. This entails daily prayer, Scripture reading, and reading the Lives of the Saints with the children, and regular church attendance by the whole family.[230]

9. Another aspect of making the home a little church is to *have icons in every room of the home*, with an icon corner in the room of each child, including an icon of the patron saint of the child.

10. A critically important aspect of providing an atmosphere in the home conducive to joy-filled Christian living is *to limit sharply and supervise carefully the use of TV, cellphones, and the Internet* by our children and youth, and as much as possible, by the adults also. An excellent new book by an Orthodox psychologist, Dr Claude Larchet, called *The New Media Epidemic: The Undermining of Society, Family, and Our Own Soul*, vividly describes the dangers of too much screen time in general, let alone the temptations to pornography, game-playing, and other addictive behaviors fostered by excessive TV, video, and Internet usage.[231]

11. Year by year the parishioners and the priest should cultivate *a relationship of trust and joy with the child*. This means the entire parish is devoted to making sure, as much as possible, that the youth will stay in the Church in their adulthood.

12. Year by year the parishioners and the priest should encourage the youth to be as involved as possible in *the liturgical life of the parish*—as altar boys, choir members, Readers, coffee hour helpers, workday helpers, special events helpers, and so on.

13. Every parish could have *an informal chess club* (or a club for other board games) during the regular coffee hour, when adults can bond with the youth, as well as the youth bonding among themselves.

14. Year by year the youth should be involved with the other youth in the parish, as well as those in nearby parishes, in regular, mutual activities of fellowship, led by a responsible, qualified youth leader and other adults. The *youth meetings* should include prayer, worship, Bible study, reading lives of the saints, and learning about Church History, the Sacraments, and the divine services; activities like Bible Bowls, skits, oratorial contests, games, musical performances, and sports events; and open discussion on topics including sexual purity, chastity, integrity, and the glory and awesomeness of Christian marriage. Additional youth activities could be held

in different settings, such as ice skating, bowling, hiking, camping, historically oriented field trips, and pool parties.

15. Ideally every parish should have *a dedicated youth group* that meets weekly. If a parish is too small for this, two or more parishes in a particular area could collaborate for a joint youth group.

16. Orthodox *summer camp programs* and other retreat settings for our youth are vital for reinforcing our youth in their pursuit of Christ-centered living. Such broader Orthodox experiences for the youth in our parishes will increase the chances that they will meet and marry fellow Orthodox Christians.

17. Orthodox *short-term missions trips*, such as to Project Mexico,[232] can be life-changing for our youth.

18. Strong *camaraderie* should be encouraged and fostered among the youth. Their friendships should last a lifetime!

19. A sense of identity as *warriors for Christ* and His Holy Orthodox Church (see the prayers in the Orthodox Baptismal service) should be fostered among the youth. This will help them understand themselves as *living for Christ and His Truth*—which entails following His life-giving, safe way of purity, chastity, integrity, and all the virtues. Together with regular participation in the Holy Eucharist and the Sacrament of Confession, cultivation of the virtues helps us tremendously to experience the strengthening and comforting Presence of Christ, Who is Himself the Way, the Truth, and the Life (John 14:6).

20. Our youth must stand not only *for Christ and His Truth* but also *against the various false opinions that are prevalent in the surrounding culture*. Many of those erroneous beliefs undergird our society's promotion of sexual promiscuity, abortion, experimentation with drugs, other addictive behaviors, experimentation with one's sexuality, suicide, and so on. Among the most prominent and damaging false claims are (a) that an unborn child is only a disposable clump of tissue; (b) that abortion is not physically, emotionally, or spiritually harmful for the mother; (c) that sexual promiscuity, in any of its manifold forms, is not physically, emotionally, or spiritually harmful; (d) that there's no reason why two persons of the same sex who deeply love each other shouldn't be allowed to get married; (e) that one's gender can be different from one's biological sex; (f) that men and women are basically the same, so they should be virtually interchangeable; (g) that a biological male really can be a female trapped in a male body, and so

he should try to become a female anatomically, and vice versa—and further, that this phenomenon can become evident at a very young age; (h) that the universe has come about solely as the result of random chance, so life is ultimately purposeless and meaningless. Guided discussion of those egregious errors, and how they are foreign to and incompatible with Orthodox Tradition, should be an important part of parish life for the youth—especially for those who attend public and even private schools, where our youth are often confronted with such false opinions from their teachers and/or schoolmates.[233]

21. Various *guest speakers/discussion leaders* could be invited to be part of the youth group program each year—including married couples relating their experience in marriage, monastics describing their lives as monks or nuns, and single persons talking about their efforts, with the help of Christ and the Theotokos and the saints, to live without indulging in sexual relations before marriage. Married couples who were able to preserve their virginity before getting married would most likely have the most credibility when speaking about the glory of waiting for the totally new adventure of the wedding night—when the bride and groom will become one flesh with no guilt feelings, with no fear of contracting a sexually transmitted disease, with no fear of getting pregnant, with no memories of previous sexual experiences that might diminish the awe-filled wonder, and with the life-long mutual commitment that such sexual intimacy requires in order for it to be God-pleasing and truly blissful. When the bride and groom have saved themselves sexually for each other until their wedding night, the crowns they receive during the marriage service will be most meaningful—as symbols of the couple's victory in having maintained self-control over their sexual impulses, as honoring each one's self-sacrifice on behalf of his/her future spouse, and as an acknowledgment of the faithfulness and steadfastness that they demonstrated, which bodes well for the future stability and flourishing of their marriage. And the bride will be able to wear the pure white of her wedding gown without a trace of hesitation, guilt, or hypocrisy.

22. An excellent program for Orthodox youth, called "Sex and God Education," is popular in Bp. Basil's Midwestern Diocese of the Antiochian Orthodox Church in North America. As part of this program, *Orthodox medical doctors* answer any questions regarding sexuality (probably in boys-only and girls-only sessions, in which questions may be asked anonymously).[234]

23. *Parenting toward the Kingdom: Orthodox Christian Principles of Child-Rearing*, written by Dr Philip Mamalakis, is *a stellar resource* for promoting Christ-centered Orthodox family life, including an emphasis on purity, chastity, integrity, and all the virtues.[235]

24. A youth group *visit to a monastery* can be life-changing for our youth.

25. As high school graduation approaches, and the youth decide whether to go to college, trade school, or directly into the workplace or military, their parents, godparents, and priest should make every gentle yet firm effort to encourage them to remain active in a local Orthodox church, and to attend a school where there is *an active Orthodox Christian Fellowship (OCF) chapter.*

26. *Trade school* should be a viable option for youth who are adept with their hands and prefer not to go to college. Skilled trades often may provide a steady field of employment much more quickly, at a fraction of the cost of college, and without the sexually permissive indoctrination that is now widespread in higher education. Attendance at a trade school might well afford Orthodox youth a greater chance to retain their traditional Orthodox worldview, while they learn a trade that will enable them at an earlier age to support a family.

To summarize and conclude, I turn again to St John Chrysostom, who taught his flock well: "Do you think it is something of small importance to their marriage that *both the young man and the young woman be virgins*? It is not a small thing, neither for the chastity of the young woman, nor for that of the young man. Will not the charm of their love be especially pure? And greater than all things, will not God then be more gracious, and fill their marriage with a myriad of blessings, when they are united according to His commandments?"[236]

Saint John Chrysostom also declared powerfully to the parents in his flock that *not* teaching their children virtue, *not* calling them to account for their actions, is *"to trample upon the noble nature of their soul."*[237] But if children *are* given diligent care and attention in the family and in the Church, St John was very confident that they would turn out well. In the spirit of Proverbs 22:6, the verse I quoted at the beginning of this article, St John asserts, "For it is not possible, indeed it is not, that one should turn out badly who is brought up with so much care, and has received such great attention. Sins are not so prevalent, so deeply rooted, by nature *as to overcome so much previous care*."[238]

# Restoring Young Men to Manhood

Fr Johannes L. Jacobse

By almost any measure, the breakdown of sexual morality in the Post-Christian West is nothing short of catastrophic. Although it began with the so-called Sexual Revolution in the 1960s, its intellectual antecedents were evident long before that. At its core lies a new anthropology, a new vision and understanding of who and what man is, that distorts and subverts the received wisdom that has shaped generations past. That ideology seduces the uninformed and innocent through the false promise that sexual licentious offers personal emancipation. Young men, in particular, are in the line of fire.[239]

Many young men today are suffering from a hidden affliction that the Sexual Revolution has foisted upon them, most through addictions to pornography and sexual self-abuse.[240] People old enough to remember the advent of this cultural shift have firsthand knowledge of the cultural rot that has ensued from it. The young are not so lucky. Their coming of age occurs amidst the decline, and in the innocence and inexperience of youth they believe that the way things are is the way they have always been.

Those addictions—all entailing a slavery to human passions and vice—are ruthless taskmasters that foster a great deal of suffering in a young man's life. They are primary causes of the "failure to launch" into integral adulthood in society that afflicts many young men today. They block healthy maturation by closing off the natural pathways that are necessary for masculine self-confidence and creativity. A young man almost always has the native—God-created and God-given—desire to flourish. But he faces a great deal of frustration and anguish when he discovers that the road to flourishing seems closed off to him by his vices. Moreover, he has no real idea how to wrestle himself free of them or, even worse, believes that freedom is not even possible.

The lie that holds men back is the promise that sexual license is the pathway to personal emancipation. That lie has power because the new anthropology posits that sexual feelings are a primary constituent through which a man defines who he is. As a result, that necessary journey into self-knowledge and healthy manhood that should begin in adolescence and needs to be guided throughout the teenage years gets off to a very shaky start. Many men end up stuck there.

Any Orthodox priest who hears the confessions of young men will tell you that almost all boys are deeply affected by our moral collapse. Adolescence is an awakening to the world in stages, but, instead of facing and conquering the challenges a boy normally faces in the course of his teenage years, the frustrations mount and are relieved through self-abuse. The easy availability of pornography makes this dysfunctional self-therapy more frequent, because it makes arousal easier.

So what happens to the young men afflicted with these vices? How does it affect their maturation and development? What counsel should be given to a young man, and what must he do to flourish?

### The Approach to Healing

The key anthropological insight by which healing can begin is this: All desire, even inordinate desire, is ultimately grounded in the soul's desire for communion with God. "Inordinate desire" is, of course, initially defined by the biblical Commandments. It is the first signpost, a preliminary indicator, which reveals that something is amiss, that some behaviors are sinful.

The Commandments are necessarily juridical, a conscription of behavior. These behavioral prohibitions, however, must be properly understood. Fundamentally, they have an ontological character, because they also bring into focus the desire that drives the sinful behavior and reveals it as being disordered. Healing, then, is not properly understood solely as obedience to a divine Commandment (a reduction that sees healing as little more than behavior modification), but rather as an *inner* reorientation.

One of things that compels young men to seek healing is the deep feelings of dissipation, of a soul-crushing weakness, which they experience through the sin of self-abuse. When they hear that the struggle against the vice may also entail increasing self-knowledge and self-confidence as well as growth into stable, mature, and creative manhood, they are willing to take up the challenge. Indeed, many even seek it out, willing to strive for the higher things often expressed in terms of aspirations that define what a man ought to achieve and the road on which he ought to walk.

It works like this. Sexual energy is primarily a creative energy. The sexual drive is given by God and it is good, and its primary end is the creation of new life. The energy is also a unitive force that, when exercised, brings the body, mind, and soul into a singular focus.

Properly understood then, sexual energy is a creative energy that courses through a person in ways that imply order and purpose. Proper order here is defined by the Commandments through moral proscriptions, although the proscriptions, while a useful metric in some situations, cannot reach into ontology, into the places where desire is grounded. The violations of the proscriptions, in other words, reveal the disordered desires, but offer no means for the re-ordering—the redemption and restoration—of the inordinate desire that fosters deeper self-integration and health. For the young men struggling with pornography and self-abuse then, the goal is to shift the sexual energy into the proper ordering.

It begins with understanding who and what a man is.

Men find themselves in work. Work is how a man expresses himself, where his creative prowess is actualized and made concrete. Men build skyscrapers and bridges and businesses. They fight wars. They yearn for strength and accomplishment. They coach baseball teams, write books, fix cars, and fly helicopters. Men differ from women in that it is in their nature to create things outside of themselves, using their bodies to make and do things. (Women may indeed do this as well, but their primary concern lies within, particularly the conceiving, gestating, and giving birth to children. Men, however, must work beyond the home, if they are fully to realize their manhood.)

But work requires ascetic discipline, and when discipline is applied in overcoming sexual vice, one of the first things a man experiences is a flush of creative energy. That energy, which used to be dissipated through self-abuse, needs to be directed, to be channeled. Otherwise the young man will fall into frustration and the cycle continues. It is not enough to say he needs to work. The mentor may need to teach him how to work, how to apply himself, how to overcome things that led to the frustrations that led to the dissipation.

This is especially true of young men. Almost all young men who struggle with pornography consumption and self-abuse started at a very young age, some as young as eleven years old. For many the cycle of consumption and dissipation has become habituated, a way of dealing with stress and frustration that has unfortunately blocked maturation in different areas of their lives. Most often it has to do with self-knowledge and self-confidence. They don't know what they were put on this world to do, and they don't know how to figure it out. They don't see the relation between the habituated dissipation and their inability to find out what it means to flourish. It leads to a self-perpetuating cycle of frustration and release that undermines the courage and confidence the young man needs to develop into the strong man he yearns to become.

These broken young men are the detritus of the Sexual Revolution whose proponents promised freedom but instead brought enslavement. There are ancillary behaviors that perpetuate interior dysfunction of broken young men, video games perhaps one of the worst. Boys who have lost their way into manhood escape into a virtual world. That world can feel as real as the concrete world but it is still a substitute world and cannot make up for what is lost. One of the first things most young men do who authentically embrace the struggle is get rid of their video games. The same with drugs. If the young man is to succeed, the marijuana has got to go as well.

### A Praxis of Healing

The depth and power of the potential transformation in a young man's life once he embarks on the path of healing should not be underestimated, although it sometimes occurs in fits and starts. When a man commits to the ascetic discipline necessary to break the grip of the vice, several things happen.

First his thinking gets sharper. Purifying the heart makes for a sharper mind (we call it "gaining clarity"), which makes focusing his intellectual powers easier. A mind that was often scattered by simple anxieties and other distractions becomes easier to direct.

Second, the moral logic of the Commandments becomes internalized and their rationale becomes self-evident. The ascetic discipline, coupled with the proper channeling of the energy it releases, is actually an awakening of the *nous*, the internal faculty of illumined seeing through which the true nature of things is revealed. When this happens (and it is a concrete event, an internal reordering and thus healing), a young man can choose whether to walk in this newness of life or return to the more familiar patterns of sin. Once a young man sees this, his interior orientation can change. Most choose the new life. If they fall, repentance is always available and often quick.

Third, it becomes abundantly clear to any mentor or spiritual father helping young men on this road of healing that they have no greater advocate than the Lord Jesus Christ Himself. No one desires their healing more than Christ. The prayers for them are answered quickly and the opportunities for flourishing are abundant. The blessings are manifold. They reveal the Lord's great love for them. To the mentor the blessings make clear that the forces that contributed to the brokenness of the young men and would keep them enslaved come from the depths of hell.

The healing begins with the deliberate effort to curb the pornography consumption and self-abuse it fosters. This is difficult at first but what the young man has to see is that the connection between temptation and sin is often reflexive. Usually many years of habituation need to be undone. While the young man has learned through bitter experience that he cannot defeat the vice by will power alone, his will (volition) has to be directed somewhere simply because healing is not automatic. Resisting the sin is self-evident, of course, but what remains unknown is how to deal with both the chronological and interior spaces that open up when the resistance begins. For this he needs a mentor or spiritual father because those spaces are where the healing takes place.

The chronological space needs to be filled with a more ordered life. The energy previously dissipated in self-abuse will come rushing back and it has to be directed somewhere. Young men in particular need to set goals and to define tasks. They need to clean their rooms or apartments, create a to-do list, strive to perform better in school or at work—all the things necessary for increased personal success. This will give the energy a new outlet, consonant with their native skills and aspirations, which fosters progress in their respective vocations, whatever they may be.

The interior space that opens also requires discipline. That includes establishing a prayer rule, regular Holy Confession and reception of the Holy Mysteries of the Body and Blood of Jesus Christ, and all the other basic spiritual practices necessary for sound growth. Obstacles may arise once the young men start down the path of healing, because the things that have impeded their maturation, the things that directed their sexual energy into the inordinate behavior, begin to surface again. They soon realize that their habituated behaviors began as ways to ameliorate pain, trauma, boredom, insecurities, whatever the case may be (it is usually a mixture of things). Until they deal with those issues, the habit will not be broken and they will remain stagnant. The guidance a qualified mentor or spiritual father can provide is invaluable in that struggle.

It is important to note that what drives the desire to be healed is to be free of the emasculation and all the variants that the sexual dissipation incites—insecurity, aimlessness, irritability, diminished energy, lack of focus and drive, among others. Self-abuse robs young men of manly self-confidence (they may sense this without always perceiving the direct connection), because self-abuse is the dissipation of masculine creative energy. That is why the healing of this vice requires that both the exterior and interior components work hand in hand.

Shame enters in, of course, but the best way to deal with that is to assure young men that a lot of other men have struggled with this powerful sin and overcome it. But again, the victory and the self-assurance that success fosters rest not so much in a celebration in overcoming the vice, but in experiencing the increase of masculine self-identity and self-confidence, in building the bridge or skyscraper, in creating something good and enduring, all in ways that complement each young man's native gifts and abilities. The confidence comes through accomplishment, by learning what they were put into this world to do, and by doing it. Shame dissolves when the struggle is approached in this way.

Moreover, the therapy that takes place in each young man's interior spaces need not be long or involved. Most of the time it is not necessary to go into any deep analysis of the past. Rather, simple awareness of how past experiences shaped the habitual thinking is enough. Psychological analysis may have informational value, but it has no real transformative power. The transformation comes in the doing of something, of saying "no" to what has been a habitual "yes." Again, that's why the interior therapy must be linked with exterior accomplishment. Once that success occurs and the flush of masculine self-confidence is experienced, the old patterns of thinking are more easily abandoned, because strength vanquishes the numbing weakness of dissipation.

Accountability is necessary. Accountability, however, is more than a confession of temptation or fall (although it can be that). Accountability requires a trust between men that teaches the younger how to become a man. For that reason the mentor to the young man has to be male. A woman cannot meet those masculine needs. Accountability structures can vary from a simple text message to internet filters such as "Covenant Eyes." Approaches will differ depending on the person.

### Fatherhood, Manhood, and God

For many young men the absence of a father who could model healthy manhood contributed to their confusion in the first place. Young men assimilate unhealthy and immoral attitudes largely through cultural osmosis. A significant part of their healing requires that the flawed anthropology of such ideologies as radical feminism and homosexuality be addressed as well.

Restoration and redemption occur in the relation between the mentor or spiritual father and the young man. In a very real sense that kind of proper male bonding, which was missing in childhood and otherwise could have directed a young man away from the pitfalls that snared him in adolescence, is finally realized, enabling the young man finally to stand on his own two feet. It is grounded, of course, in the Fatherhood of God Who desires that all men come to the knowledge of the truth. Much of that knowledge is gained and expressed experientially, so that as a young man comes to know himself, he will also come to know God. As a man comes to know God, he will also come to know himself.

For the mentor or spiritual father, to watch a young man grow into self-knowledge, to guide him on the path he was created to walk, to see him develop into the man that God created him to be may be one of the most rewarding tasks a mentor can accept. It is more blessed to give than to receive, St Paul teaches, and the mentor often receives much more than he gives as he guides a young man into manhood. One learns how deep and boundless the love of God truly is.

# The Eucharist as Antidote to Secularism: Insights from a Twentieth-Century American Orthodox Perspective

## Archpriest Chad Hatfield

Although many scholars, both Orthodox and others, continue to address the work and memory of Protopresbyter Alexander Schmemann, I am deeply concerned that they do not properly reflect Fr Alexander's profound insights, but are, instead, remaking him in their own image. Indeed, too many are trying to hijack him, to turn him into something which he simply was not.

We must hear Fr Alexander himself, because he was, in so many ways, as contemporary today as he was when he was alive. Born in Tallinn, Estonia, in 1921, he taught Russian literature and poetry and wrote extensively on Orthodox liturgical theology as a professor at St Vladimir's Orthodox Seminary in New York from 1951 (and as dean from 1962) until his death on December 13, 1983.

A significant portion of his personal and scholarly efforts addressed the rise of secularism and where it might lead us culturally. As far back as April 1, 1975, Fr Alexander was the sole Orthodox participant in a remarkable ecumenical effort among eighteen mostly traditional Roman Catholics and Protestants that produced the landmark document known as "The Hartford Appeal." That document, which received widespread publicity in the American media owing, in part, to the prestige of its co-signatories, lamented in thirteen specific propositions, "an apparent loss of a sense of the transcendent," a reduction of salvation and the meaning of moral "good" to "human fulfillment," relativism among the world's religions, and a worldly agenda for the world instead of a Christian agenda for the world.[241] In short, Fr Alexander et al. warned the American people about the dangers of creeping radical individualism and secularism.

Even before "The Hartford Appeal," Fr Alexander connected the question of secularism to worship in a secular age:

> To put together, in order to relate to them to one another, the terms "worship" and "secular age," seems to presuppose that we have a clear

understanding of both of them, that we know the realities they denote, and that we thus operate on solid and thoroughly explored grounds. But is this really the case?[242]

He was convinced that, despite modernity's widespread preoccupation with semantics, it was important for us to maintain our vocabulary as Orthodox Christians and to define the terms and words that we use:

[T]here is a great deal of confusion about the exact meaning of the very terms we use in this discussion. Not only among Christians in general, but even among the Orthodox themselves, there exists in fact no consensus, no commonly accepted frame of reference concerning either *worship* or *secularism*, and thus the problem of their interrelation. Therefore my paper is an attempt not so much to solve the problem as to clarify it, and to do this if possible within a consistent Orthodox perspective.[243]

Fr Alexander pointed to the adverse results of that confusion:

In my opinion, the Orthodox, when discussing the problems stemming from our present "situations," accept them much too easily in their Western formulations. They do not seem to realize that the Orthodox Tradition provides above all a possibility, and thus a necessity, of reformulating these very problems, of placing them in a context whose absence or deformation in the Western religious mind may have been the root of so many of our modern "impasses" And as I see it, nowhere is this task more urgently needed than in the range of problems related to *secularism* and proper to our so-called *secular age*.[244]

That "secular age" is the same one in which we are living almost four decades later. Surveys in North America reveal some shocking statistics. Our people are not well formed in their own theological mind. Abortion, same-sex "marriage," euthanasia, and many other vexing issues of our day are gaining increasing acceptance among Orthodox believers. So we cannot, as Orthodox Christians, simply sit in judgment on anybody. Our own house is in crisis, and we have to put it in order.

Secularism has been analyzed and defined in recent years in a great variety of ways. Fr Alexander argued that, to the best of his knowledge, none of those descriptions stressed the essential point that reveals the true nature of secularism, which thus shapes the discussion of secularism properly.

Fr Alexander defined secularism as "above all, a *negation of worship*."[245] It was a remarkable definition, perhaps unique for his time. When we consider today how to respond to the political and cultural tsunami about to hit us so very hard, we would do well to heed Fr Alexander's summons to return to the Eucharist, to return to our worship, and to be true and authentic to who we are as baptized Orthodox Christians.

Fr Alexander insisted that secularism is not an appeal to "some kind of transcendence and therefore some kind of new religion. If secularism in theological terms is a heresy, it is primarily a heresy about *man*,"[246] not God. Again, that was a remarkable twist on the usual arguments against secularism. Furthermore, he wrote that secularism

> is the negation of man as a worshiping being, as *homo adorans*: the one for whom worship is the essential act which both "posits" his humanity and fulfills it. It is the rejection, as ontologically and epistemologically "decisive," of the words which "always, everywhere, and for all" were the true "epiphany" of man's relation to God, to the world, and to himself. "'It is meet and right to sing of thee, to bless thee, to praise thee, to give thanks to thee, and to worship thee in every place of thy dominion.'"[247]

One of the things that we glean from Fr Alexander's scholarship is that we live in a secularized world that trumpets its embrace of atheism. But I think we have learned a lesson that differs from Fr Alexander's insights—namely, that secularism has, indeed, become, in our time, a competing *religion*.

Another of Fr Alexander's primary concerns during the second half of the twentieth century was the steady loss of the younger generations from our Orthodox religious household. We thought that Caesar, and our genetic makeup, would transmit our holy Orthodox Tradition. In fact, that is a fallacy. In the United States, the Orthodox constitute less than 1 percent of the population![248]

What kind of global culture will surround our children in the generations to come? It will not be an Orthodox one; and if, unlikely as it seems now, it is Christian, it will be Protestant, the primary religious force in American history from the initial colonization in the seventeenth century. We Orthodox have to fight all the more to transmit our Orthodox Tradition. That is why I believe Rod Dreher's book, *The Benedict Option*, has become so popular with traditional Christians in America. We all need to be looking at ways to survive the coming two-front tsunami of secularism and Islamism.

We have to admit that we have lost the younger generations, and we have lost them because we have failed to catechize and to teach, not only our young people, but also our adults. I have said for years, as I look at Orthodox parishes in America, that we teach theology to our kids and let the adults play games. This needs to be flipped around; we need to get the attention of our mature faithful, or we will simply lose the fight. We have to formulate compelling answers to the questions, doubts, or disinterest of adult Orthodox, if we are to preserve the next generations in Holy Orthodoxy, recover those who were lost, and come out on the other side like Noah after the flood.

The preface of Fr Alexander's last book, published posthumously in 1988, *The Eucharist*, helps me to make an important point. Matushka Juliana, his wife, said that, of all of his writings, that book was the most difficult for him, because he knew the importance of worship and Eucharist, and he had to get it just right. As someone who stands at the holy table in worship, I often return to that preface to regain a proper direction.

Fr Alexander oriented us back to the Eucharist:

Perhaps many people will be astonished that, in response to this crisis, I propose that we turn our attention not to its various aspects but rather to the sacrament of the eucharist and to the Church, whose very life flows from that sacrament. Yes, I do believe that precisely here, in this holy of holies of the Church, in this ascent to the table of the Lord in his kingdom, is the source of that renewal for which we hope. And I do believe, as the Church has always believed, that this upward journey begins with the "laying aside of all earthly cares," with leaving this adulterous and sinful world. No ideological fuss and bother, but a gift from heaven—such is the vocation of the Church in the world, the source of her service.[249]

In the West, we recognize that a prophetic voice is struggling to be heard in the so-called Free World of Western Europe and North America. In our time we have clearly moved from being a "Post-Christian" society to an aggressively "Anti-Christian" society. Basic social values and moral teaching are suffering erosion at a rapid pace. Social media plays an active role where there is little accountability and much influence on a younger generation filled with "Nones" and "Dones."

The latest Pew Research Center report on religion in America, released on October 17, 2019, found a deeply troubling decline in the numbers of Christians in America since in 2009: Protestants now constitute only 41 percent of the adult population, down from 51 percent in 2000; Roman Catholics are 20 percent, down from 23 percent in 2009; and Orthodox Christians remain well below the radar at less than 1 percent. Meanwhile, the ranks of those who do not identify with any religion ("Nones") and those who are simply former Protestants, Roman Catholics, or Orthodox ("Dones") have risen from 12 percent in 2009 to 17 percent in 2019. But here is the most shocking statistic: "only half of Millennials (49%) describe themselves as Christians; four-in-ten are religious 'nones,' and one-in-ten Millennials identify with non-Christian faiths."[250] The so-called millennials, born between 1981 and 1996, are, of course, the young adults of our current generation and those most likely to become parents of the next generation of Americans—that is to say, the children who, if we extrapolate from the Pew findings, may emerge even less religious than their parents!

The Orthodox Churches (and others who identify as Christians) have failed to teach and preach to the faithful, who now seem to have their worldview formed from the entertainment industry rather than from the teachings of Christ and His Church. Toward the end of the fourth century AD, St John Chrysostom lamented that the people were not in church but in the Hippodrome.[251] Are we not living with a modern variation of the same scenario?

Robert P. George, a traditional Roman Catholic and McCormick Professor of Jurisprudence at Princeton University, has described forcefully the attacks on religion and pro-family values that have accelerated in recent years:

> [A]ttacks on the family, and particularly on the institution of marriage on which the family is built, are common in the academy. The line here is that the family, at least as traditionally constituted and understood, is a patriarchal and exploitative institution that oppresses women and imposes on people forms of sexual restraint that are psychologically damaging and that inhibit the free expression of their personality. As has become clear in recent decades, there is a profound threat to the family, one against which we must fight with all our energy and will. It is difficult to think of any item on the domestic agenda that is more critical today than the defense of marriage as the union of husband and wife and the effort to renew and rebuild the marriage culture.
>
> What has also become clear is that the threats to the family (and to the sanctity of human life) are necessarily threats to religious freedom and to religion itself—at least where the religions in question stand up and speak out for conjugal marriage and the rights of the child in the

womb. From the point of view of those seeking to redefine marriage and to protect and advance what they regard as the right to abortion, the taming of religion (and the stigmatization and marginalization of religions that refuse to be tamed) is a moral imperative.[252]

This "taming" of religion has now become an attack from the *inside*. The drift and decline of mainline Protestant denominations is, of course, well documented. The dance with the *Zeitgeist* has left those once influential denominations in steep numerical decline.[253] Rodney Stark, a self-described "independent Christian" and Distinguished Professor of the Social Sciences at Baylor University, reflected wistfully on that phenomenon:

> The wreckage of the former Mainline denominations is strewn upon the shoal of a modernist theology that began to dominate the Mainline seminaries early in the nineteenth century. This theology presumed that advances in human knowledge had made faith outmoded. If religion were to survive, it must become "modern and progressive and . . . the meaning of Christianity should be interpreted from the standpoint of modern knowledge and experience" (as the theologian Gary Dorrien puts it). From this starting point, science soon took precedence over revelation, and the spiritual realm faded into psychology. Eventually, Mainline theologians discarded nearly every doctrinal aspect of traditional Christianity.[254]

In the landmark U.S. Supreme Court decision *Obergefell v. Hodges* in 2015, which legalized same-sex "marriage" throughout the United States, Justice Samuel Alito wrote a dissenting opinion that is already, four years later, proving prescient. He denounced that infamous 5 to 4 ruling as a way eventually to silence those, including traditional Christians obviously, who persist in affirming universal verities in Western civilization such as marriage between one man and one woman alone. They, Alito predicted, "will be able to whisper their thoughts in the recesses of their home, but if they repeat those views in public, they will risk being labeled as bigots and treated as such by governments, employers, and schools."[255] I would add that many of "their churches" and "their pastors" will also label their more faithful, traditional counterparts the same way. That, too, has already come to pass.

# "Radechesis": A Radical Return to the Roots of Catechesis

### Archpriest John E. Parker

In 1951, H. Richard Niebuhr, a very prominent liberal American Protestant theologian, wrote a widely read, very influential book titled, *Christ and Culture*. Here are some crucial excerpts:

> A many-sided debate about the relations of Christianity and civilization is being carried out in our time. Historians and theologians, statesman, churchman, Catholics, and Protestants [he didn't mention Orthodox], Christians and anti-Christians participate in it. It is carried on publicly by opposing parties, and privately in the conflicts of conscience. Sometimes it is concentrated on special issues such as those of the place of Christian faith in general education, or of Christian ethics in economic life. Sometimes it deals with broad questions of the church's responsibilities for social order or the need for a new separation of Christ's followers with the world.
>
> The debate is as confused as it is many-sided. When it seems that the issue is clearly defined as lying between exponents of Christian civilization and non-Christian defenders of a wholly secularized society, new perplexities arise as devoted believers make common cause with secularists, calling, for instance, for the elimination of religion from public education. Or, for the Christian support of apparently anti-Christian political movements. So many voices are heard; so many confident, but diverse assertions about the Christian answer to the social problems are being made, so many issues are raised that bewilderment and uncertainty beset many Christians.

Does that sound familiar?

Niebuhr continued:

> In this situation it is helpful to remember that the question of Christianity and Civilization is by no means a new one; for Christian perplexity

in this area has been perennial, and the problem has been an enduring one through all the Christian centuries. It is helpful also to recall that the repeated struggles of Christians with this problem have yielded no single Christian answer, but only a series of typical answers which together, for faith, represent phases of the strategies of the Militant Church in the world. That strategy, however, being the mind of the Captain, rather than the lieutenants, it is not under the control of the latter. Christ's answer to the problem of human culture is one thing; Christian answers are another. Yet His followers are assured that He uses their various works in accomplishing His own.[256]

Thanks be to God that He indeed accomplishes His own works through our efforts to do His will in the world.

I would encourage Orthodox Christians to read Niebuhr's book and to consider how we, in light of the Jordanville Conference in March 2019, might assess how Niebuhr contrasted Christ and "culture"—that is, how he enumerated six distinct ways that Christians, in ancient times and modern, have tried to deal with the question of the interaction of our Lord and where and how *we* live. Those six ways Niebuhr neatly captured as Christ in Culture; Christ above Culture; Christ next to Culture; Christ beneath Culture; Christ informing Culture; and Christ transforming Culture.

All I know with confidence is how to be the pastor of a church. For my entire adult life, that's what I've had the opportunity to do. I've been to school many times, and I know how to read a book, and I know how to write a paper, but I do not consider myself an academic. Instead, what informs my perspective is observing and interacting with parishioners for the last fifteen years as an Orthodox priest, and a few years before that as an Episcopal priest.

A personal story might serve as a concrete example. It was the year 2008. I know that because it was about the first month that we were in our brand new and very beautiful church building, when a young man from the University of South Carolina came to me during coffee hour. He was visiting Charleston from Columbia, the state capital—about two hours away. He shook my hand and said, "Hi, Fr. John, I have a question for you." I thought, "Great! Is he going to ask us why we built this beautiful, Byzantine Church?" Or maybe he wants to know, "Where did we get our iconographer?" or "How did you make the iconostasis out of reclaimed barn wood from North Carolina?"

Instead, the young man asked, "Fr John, what is the canonical penalty for fornication." First question! I would have guessed he was about twenty-two years old. And I thought to myself, "Good Lord! Couldn't we have started with something simple and southern, like, 'Love your hair! How's your mother?'"

But his question did address, implicitly, a valid concern of the significance of purity, chastity, and integrity, and the Orthodox approach to those virtues. Some people who come to our Orthodox Church from the outside, as well as some of our own faithful, treat those questions strictly from a moralistic perspective. Speaking as one who stresses at every opportunity the evangelism of folks outside, specifically to bring them into our Churches, I am concerned that those who are coming in be treated according to what my bumper-sticker biblical verse for my Christian pastoral life says in one of those beautiful Hymns of the Servant: "Behold, my servant, whom I uphold; my chosen, in whom my soul delighteth: I have put my Spirit upon him; he will bring forth justice to the Gentiles. He will not cry, nor lift up his voice, nor cause it to be heard in the street." The next verse is the pastoral keynote for me, and I propose that it serve at your pastoral keynote, too: "A bruised reed he will not break, and a dimly burning wick he will not quench" (Isaiah 42:1–3 (ASV)).

It is extremely important for us, as we fight the battles that face us, not to extinguish dimly burning wicks—which is the easier of the two images to consider. A bruised reed? Perhaps many Americans have never seen a reed (much less a bruised one). However, if you visit Charleston, South Carolina, you can see some beautiful sea grass, and you'll see how that works. But every serious Orthodox Christian is familiar with the vigil lamps hanging all around the church, and what happens when the wick is not trimmed well, and the oil is barely getting up into it, and the flame is so slight that all you have to do is wave your hand past the lamp, and the flame goes out. That is a most appropriate image of the world right now!

The world appears inhospitable to Orthodoxy now because it is like a gigantic teenager. It asserts itself boldly, but underneath it is simply a completely bent, broken reed. We keep that in mind as Orthodox Christians who wish to welcome and nurture spiritually those who are coming from the outside. The affront to us from opposing voices in the mass media, in the intense ideological arguments, is true and real, and at some level we have to deal with it as it comes to us. But we have to remember constantly to say, "I hear you," since we understand more deeply what is going on—that underneath it all there is a grave spiritual problem. (Maybe we have to keep silently in the back of our minds a beautiful southern saying: "Bless your little heart!")

So here is a proposal for attempting to instill respect for and practice of the virtues of purity and chastity among those who come to us from the outside. It is vitally important for us to remember the words above of the Prophet Isaiah. I hope they will ring in your ears all the more when you hear them in your own Orthodox church in Great Lent: "*A bruised reed he will not break, and a dimly burning wick he will not quench*" (Isaiah 42:3 (ASV) italics added).

In his chapter in the present book, Professor David Bradshaw discusses the beautiful Greek word, *agnos*, which means both purity and chastity. However, we usually interpret "purity" as the opposite of carnality. That is a very *bodily* definition. Chaste. Modest. Immaculate. Clean. No stain.

Yet *agnos* has another, perhaps more inspiring definition: "exciting reverence," or "venerable" or "sacred." I think that is the aspect of beauty that Professor Bradshaw addresses. It is also what we saw even in the building of our beautiful Church in Charleston, South Carolina. At the blessing of the cornerstone, Archbishop Dmitri (Royster), of blessed memory, said these beautiful words: "This little piece of acreage—0.6 acres in Charleston, South Carolina —is removed from the thorns and thistles of the fallen world, and restored to paradise." And then, by the providence of God, we constructed a church building on that site in which all but one visitor from 2008 until 2019, when I left to become Dean of St Tikhon's Seminary, said, *twice* upon entering it, "Wow!" They would look toward the altar and say, "Wow!" Then they would look upward at the frescoed dome and again say, "Wow!" Everyone but one! That fellow offered a non-committal, "Interesting!" (He must have been an iconoclast!) The conversion of that place into something so beautiful was so critical and so captivating! I would suggest that it was a place reclaimed for paradise.

Even before we designed the church building, we informed the architect that we would prefer a building, to quote those beautiful words from the Gospel, that "if [we] were silent, the very stones would cry out!" So when visitors would come into the church, we did our best to be quiet, because the stones did cry out—and spoke better than we did: many visitor embraced the Orthodox Church and our teachings, including one who heard about our architect as he was rebuilding a house in her neighborhood. She saw his name on a sign, visited his website, and discovered that he had also built our church. She came to see the architecture, walked in, was drawn immediately to the icon of the Holy Ascension, wept before the icons, and never left. She came to look at a piece of architecture and became an Orthodox Christian. That is beautiful, amazing, good, important!

However, as much as I encourage us to build beautiful architecture for the glory of God (our first and most important reason), we also should do so for what that does for those coming in from the outside. To revisit Archbishop Dmitri's eloquent blessing of our church, "This little acreage is reclaimed from the thorns and thistles of this world, and restored to paradise," I suggest that we think of that sentence preeminently *for people*, not just for stones. The stones are only a reflection of you and me. It's not the other way around. That is, we are coming from that brokenness in the world and being restored to paradise in each Orthodox church.

In the 1980s an amazing Episcopal priest—and his wife—were amazing influences in my life and my wife's. They had a bumper stick on their Volvo, which read, "Know Jesus, Know Peace. No Jesus, No Peace." (That Episcopal couple were Fr Gregory and Frederica Mathewes-Green—Fr Gregory was my parish priest when I was a boy.) For that reason I have titled this chapter a call for *radical* catechesis (Greek for "instruction") or, to coin a term, "radechesis." Alas, our own Orthodox parishioners are largely ignorant of the Orthodox Tradition. (I regret my bluntness, but we have to acknowledge that reality.)

The world is a stream flowing a thousand miles an hour. Even if we suppose, generously, that our faithful spend ten hours a week in church (are there many?), that is less than 10 percent of waking hours in a week, while allowing eight hours of sleep per night. Given such a generous sleep schedule, our parishioners still spend 102 of 112 hours a week "in the world."

That is all the more true for our children. It already had begun when I was a school teacher in 1994, in Bryn Mawr, Pennsylvania. There were already little pink triangle stickers in classroom windows, which meant a "safe space" for homosexuals. Now—remember my motto: "A bruised reed he will not break, and a dimly burning wick he will not [snuff out]"—what I am describing is not "snuffing" or "breaking." My point is that "our time" has already been going on for a long time—it is not new today. But what is new today is little children coming home from school and asking about Susie having two moms. How do we deal with that?

That question is exponentially more complex with respect to teenagers, because the tide is strongly against us. At the School of the Arts in Charleston, a public magnet school, the "LGBTQ+" lifestyles are the norm. To be a teenage boy interested in a teenage girl is not the norm!

High school "prom" night used to be mean that you went to the prom—you got a date, you went to the dance, you went home. Sometimes you asked to stay out extra-late if you went to the prom. Or some would stay out all night and watch the sun rise. Then there was the "prom house": rent a house and stay there after prom, with all of your friends (let the reader understand!). Then it evolved to this: go to the prom house *instead* of the prom itself at the local high school. So what to do when yours is an Orthodox Christian family and your son or daughter comes to you and asks, "Can we have a prom house?"

Good catechesis furnishes a simple one-word: "No!" But we have to offer "No" with an alternative. You probably recall the Gospel verse that cautions if you exorcise a demon from a certain place and do not fill that void, seven more demons will come in. (Once, to my son's surprise, when he asked if he and his friends could have a prom house, I said, "Yes." Astonished, he asked the drawback. "I'm the chaperone—and I'll be up all night" was my reply. He opted out!)

How do we deal with those situations in the world? We have to recall my earlier point: the world is a teenager. How do teenagers live? According to their feelings. You can hear that in their words—it is pervasive in our language: "I feel like I saw that guy at that movies yesterday!" "I feel like I forgot to do such-and-such last night." "I feel like I ate this before."

No, you don't "feel" like that. You *believe* that you did this or that earlier. You *recall* that you saw that guy yesterday. It is not just a silly language issue; it is a serious one, in my opinion, because everything now is all about feelings. That is why marketing works so well on our children. It also explains why we encounter such difficulties when we try to teach ourselves and one another about *apatheia*—that is, the spiritual discipline of leaving behind the emotions in order to focus on Jesus Christ—when the whole world is a teenager and everything is about feelings.

Turning finally to catechesis, I would note at the outset that I recently studied at St. Vladimir's Seminary and earned a Doctor of Ministry (D. Min.) degree. My project focused on catechesis for adult converts to Orthodoxy. Please be advised that none of the adult Orthodox laity, none of the adults coming into the Church, and none of our children needs to know the dates of the Seven Ecumenical Councils. Nor do we need to know about the Uncreated Light or how to plumb the depths of Christian mystery *in order to become a Christian*. These are indeed important facets of Orthodoxy, and critical to our history. But our faithful, including our children, need to know the Creed, the Code, the Services, and the Scriptures. The Creed—that is, the original the Nicene Creed—proclaims the basics of the Faith. The Code is a succinct way to say, the "moral teachings of the Church." The Services entail how we worship and why. And the Scriptures are, of course, the Old and New Testaments of the Bible, on which all the above founded and sustained.

In the ancient Church catechesis for a person who came to the Orthodox Church to become a Christian entailed, first, instruction in the moral teachings of the Church. That also meant that an inquirer could not be enrolled as a catechumen (i.e., a "learner") unless, on the first day of Great Lent, the inquirer's sponsor testified to the bishop that the prospective catechumen *already* had changed his or morally bad behavior. After that testimony, the newly enrolled catechumen went to church to listen, three hours a day for forty days, to sermons by the bishop, who explained the Scriptures. The catechumen would learn what the services meant only after her or she had been received into the Church, having heard the Scriptures so intensely for the whole Lenten period.

I would propose that we turn that sequence slightly around, specifically that we teach through the Creed and the Scriptures (in whichever order one prefer): "Who is Jesus?" "Why did He die?" "How did He live?" "To what life does He call us?" Then we can teach our people, "And here is how to live as a result." In today's culture, I think, if we begin by saying, "We don't do this. We don't do that. It's bad. It's immoral. It's not right," visitors and inquirers are going to hear just another form of moralism. And while it is true that "it is bad," "it is not right," "it is immoral," we have to teach them first *why* those things are true, and how those teachings could inspire them toward right living.

What I have proposed here is equally true for our children, for our parishioners, and for those coming to us from the outside to become Orthodox Christians. Therefore, I urge a radical return to the ancient form of catechesis, where we lay aside the deeper levels of discipleship, and the Master of Divinity (M.Div.) graduate-level instruction that we are now giving to adults exploring conversion to Holy Orthodoxy, and get back to the basics: the Creed, the Scriptures, the Services, and only then, "How are we to live?"

# "The Benedict Option" and Orthodox Anthropology

## Rod Dreher

Since my book *The Benedict Option* was published in 2017, I've given count-less talks about it. The book has now been translated into nine languages, and I've delivered a number of addresses about it to Christians in Europe. Believe it or not, it's easier to talk about the decline and fall of Christianity in the West when you are among European Christians, as opposed to Amer-ican Christians. European believers have lived through several generations of de-Christianization. They are not deceived about the depth and breadth of the current crisis of our civilization. American Christians often have to be convinced of it.

But this is the first time I have had the chance to talk about the Benedict Option and Orthodoxy. Though I am an Orthodox Christian, I wrote the book for a general audience of what I call "small-o orthodox Christians"—the term I use to describe morally and theologically conservative Christians. The truth is, I believe that for reasons I will explain in this chapter, Orthodox Christianity is by far the best suited of all Christian confessions to endure this crisis—and not simply because Orthodoxy is theologically true. Orthodoxy is *anthropologically* true in particular ways. I don't say that as an apologist for Orthodoxy. I say that as someone who has read about how men hold on to their faith in a time of dissolution and disintegration. We Orthodox have been given an incredible gift, passed down through the centuries. As Bishop Irenei said during his key-note address at the Jordanville Conference, we Orthodox have the antidote to the sickness of this age, and of any age. We offer deliverance for the besieged Christians of the West.

I'm going to explain this, but first, let me provide my diagnosis of the crisis of our civilization, and why I believe that monasticism offers a way through it.

These are not normal times. We in the West are in the worst crisis since the collapse of the Roman Empire. We don't see this collapse clearly because it's hidden by our wealth. But make no mistake: the fundamental pillars of West-ern civilization are crumbling—none more severely than the Church.

Our crisis is actually a combination of crises.

It is a crisis of MEANING. In the West, we have arrived at a place where many people no longer believe that meaning exists at all, and that we can know it.

The modern historian Yuval Noah Harari says that the world today can be explained by a simple transaction: people have exchanged MEANING for POWER. That is, to gain the right to do whatever we desire with our bodies and with nature, we surrender the idea that objective meaning exists. We are free to do as we like, but the cost of that freedom is nihilism.

It is also a crisis of TRUTH. We have lost the ability to determine what is true or false. We can no longer agree on a narrative that allows us to reason together. This is one reason why we cannot resolve our conflicts.

It is also a crisis of FRAGMENTATION. In our time, people have lost a sense of unity and purpose. We no longer feel that we are part of a wider community. Radical individualism is the new normal. The old bonds of family and community have mostly dissolved.

It is, finally, a crisis of IDENTITY. We have cut ourselves off from God, from our past, from family, from our places, and from any traditional sources of the Self. We don't know who we are. Today, in the name of freedom, we even deny our biology as males and females.

All of these crises are manifestations of what one critic has called "liquid modernity." This critic, the late sociologist Zygmunt Bauman, says that the modern condition is one in which everything changes so quickly that it becomes impossible to find stability. The one who thrives in liquid modernity is the one who has no relationships and no commitments. Modern man is not a pilgrim—that is, a man who goes on a meaningful journey with others toward a certain destination; rather, he is a tourist, who travels wherever his whims take him.

This is nothing new. In his famous sixth-century Rule, St Benedict of Nursia identified this kind of person as a "gyrovague," and called him "the worst kind of monk."[257] He goes from monastery to monastery, without stability, taking what he can and then moving on. A gyrovague is lost.

The Rule of St Benedict is a way of life that offers everything that the *gyrovague* refuses. It trains communities that live by the Rule to discover meaning, truth, community, wholeness, and identity. The Rule is a source of life and hope for a dark, confused world, precisely because Benedict wrote it out of his own experience of the collapse of Roman civilization. As a young Christian, he fled from the city of Rome, went to live and pray in a cave in Subiaco, and eventually emerged to found monasteries, and to write his Rule.

When he died in the year 547, there were only a few Benedictine monasteries. But over the next centuries, the movement grew. Historians credit the Benedictines with laying the groundwork for the rebirth of civilization in the West.

How did they do it? Benedict was a Christian who sought a way to serve God in community, amid a world where all certainties and all moral structures were in collapse. The early Benedictine monks did NOT seek to save civilization. They only wanted to put the search for God first, and to order everything else from that.

To find God, they established a way of life that consecrated everything to His service. Prayer, work, study, worship, eating, living together—all of it was ordered by the Rule, to keep the members of the community always on an inner, orderly pilgrimage to unity with God. Theirs was a life of constant conversion.

The fruits of that conversion were shared throughout Western Europe over the next centuries. The monks did not stay only inside their monasteries, but rather they became a blessing to all the people around them. They taught them how to pray, most of all, but they also taught them how to cultivate gardens, how to build things, and how to do all kinds of things that people forgot after Rome's collapse. And within the monastery libraries, the monks preserved the cultural memory of Greco-Roman civilization.

I believe that today we Christians who live in the world have a lot to learn from the Rule of St Benedict, and the historical example of the Benedictine monks and nuns. What I call the "Benedict Option" is the choice all Christians must make if we want to hold on to our faith in this Age of Darkness. Christians today must understand ourselves as exiles, and develop ways of living that keep the Faith alive through this long trial the Church is now enduring.

The most common misconception of the Benedict Option is that it is a call to head for the hills and build fortresses. This is not true. There is no real escape from modernity any more than there was high ground to escape to during the Great Flood. Besides, unless we have been called to the actual monastery, we must live in the world. I think we should understand ourselves as like the Hebrews in their Babylonian exile. Through the prophet Jeremiah, the Lord told His people that He allowed them to be carried into exile for His own purposes. It will not last forever, He said. He told them to settle in Babylon and pray for the peace of the city.

But if we look to the Book of Daniel, we see the story of Sedrach, Misach, and Abednago, three Hebrews who were the king's servants. You can hardly be more assimilated into Babylonian society than that. But when the king demanded that the men bow down before a graven idol, they chose the prospect of death before sacrilege. Today, we have to ask ourselves: how did those three holy young men live there in Babylon such that when they were put to the test, they chose death before abandoning God? Whatever they did, we must do also in our own Babylonian exile.

The term "Benedict Option" comes from a famous passage from philosopher Alasdair MacIntyre's book *After Virtue*. In that book, MacIntyre says that the disintegration of the West has reached a breaking point. He compares it to the collapse of the ancient Roman imperial order in the West. Today, he says, there are those who have ceased to identify the moral life with maintenance of the contemporary social order. Instead, not always recognizing what they are doing, they will choose to devote themselves to creating new forms of community within which the moral life can be continued in this new Dark Age. He writes that we await another, and doubtless very different, St Benedict.[258]

What's his point, for us Christians? That we face a decision. We can continue to labor to build up this failing post-Christian order, or we can opt to focus primarily on building communities within which the Faith can survive this cultural revolution.

Let me be clear: we lay Christians are not monks. We are called to live IN the world. But if we are going to live *faithfully* in the world, then we must spend far more time and effort away from the world—in prayer, study, fasting, and other things to root the Faith deep in our hearts. Our spirituality must become more disciplined, and yes, more monastic.

Because our calling is to live in the world, we must always offer the Gospel, in word and in deed, to the world. But today, we Christians are weak in faith, and we cannot give to the world what we do not have.

I mentioned that it's hard to convince many American Christians about how perilous our situation is. Nobody who has examined the literature on Christian belief and practice can possibly be optimistic. The Faith has been declining during recent generations, but with the Millennials, it has walked right off a cliff. Among those who still profess belief in Christianity, what they actually believe is a pale imitation of the historic Faith. The sociologist of religion Christian Smith calls this pseudo-Christianity "Moralistic Therapeutic

Deism."[259] It's what happens when the bourgeois spirit casts out the Holy Spirit and parasitically inhabits the language and traditions of Christianity. Moralistic Therapeutic Deism—or MTD—teaches that God exists, but all He wants of us is that we be happy and fulfilled, and nice to others. That's pretty much it.

MTD is the de facto religion not simply of American teenagers but also of American adults. To a remarkable degree, teenagers have adopted the religious attitudes of their parents. We have been an MTD nation for some time now, though this may have been disguised.

Christian Smith told me in an interview: "America has lived a long time off its thin Christian veneer, partly necessitated by the Cold War. That is all finally being stripped away by the combination of mass consumer capitalism and liberal individualism."[260]

We Orthodox Christians can't look down on Roman Catholics and Protestants. We are also failing to impress upon our people, and our children, what it means to be faithful Orthodox Christians. This is a particular tragedy, because, unique among all Christian traditions in the world today, Orthodoxy has retained the premodern vision that was once universal to all Christians before the advent, in the Late Middle Ages, of modernity in the West.

This is not the place to get into the philosophical details, but I can say that only in Orthodoxy does one find in the ordinary life of the Church the incarnation of that vision.

In premodern Western Christianity, according to philosopher Charles Taylor, there were three basic bulwarks upholding their vision of the world.

First, the world and everything in it is part of a harmonious whole ordered by God and filled with meaning. All things that exist are signs pointing to God.

Second, social relations are grounded in that higher reality.

And third, the world is charged with spiritual force.

It would not be accurate to say this doesn't exist at all in contemporary Roman Catholicism, but as someone who spent half his Christian life as a Roman Catholic, I can say that Catholicism in the United States has in most places lost this vision, and has entirely absorbed the flattened, disenchanted modern vision. Roman Catholic life, liturgically and otherwise, has become bland, moralistic, and mechanical. I should say that it does not have to be that way. Whatever its theological errors, Roman Catholicism still retains immense resources with which to resist the disintegration and de-sacralization of our age. But since the 1960s, at least, ordinary Roman Catholics have to work very hard to find them.

In this chapter, though, I don't want to compare and contrast theological teaching between East and West. Instead, I prefer to focus on how the practical, ordinary life of Orthodoxy fits what anthropologists say is necessary for traditions to thrive. When I first encountered Orthodoxy fourteen years ago, my first thought was, "This is what I thought Catholicism would be when I converted back in the 1990s." This was BEFORE I knew much of anything about Orthodox theology. This was from what I learned by worshiping liturgically with the Orthodox, and discovering the role of asceticism and related practices in Orthodox life. Years later, as I was writing *The Benedict Option*, I discovered in anthropological texts why some version of monastic practices is necessary for lay Christian life today, and also why Orthodox Christianity is UNIQUELY SUITED for the Benedict Option.

Paul Connerton, a social anthropologist at Cambridge University, wrote a brilliant little book called *How Societies Remember*, in which he examined small traditionalist societies to discover how they managed to hold onto their traditions in liquid modernity, which dissolves everything it touches.[261]

In modernity, the individual conceives of himself as self-determined. By contrast, traditional societies believe that the individual is determined in part by things external to himself: religion, society, the past, and so forth.

Our experience of the present, says Connerton, largely depends upon our knowledge of the past. The struggle of traditional societies in the modern world is the struggle of memory against forgetting. The more radical a social order's aspirations, the more it will try to control the memories of the people within it. A people that has been cut off from its past—whether they have been denied access to those memories, or whether they have chosen to be indifferent to them—is a people that can be dominated.

In the case of the Church, those who make the Christian life about mere good works, or only about the individual's personal experience of God, surrender to outside domination and disintegration. The anthropologist Mary Douglas has said that when a religion turns away from its mystical, cosmological teachings, and begins to focus mostly on the individual's spiritual experience, it is on the way to decline. Then, when it turns to what we call the social gospel, the religion is in terminal decline. It all begins, though, with losing a palpable sense of the sacred, rooted in historic community.[262]

For his part, Paul Connerton finds that no culture can exist without shared memories—that is, traditions.[263] So how do small traditional cultures that manage to hold onto their shared memories in the face of modern disintegration do it? He found that they had several things in common.

First, these communities have a sacred story that tells them who they are.

Second, these communities commemorate their sacred stories more or less by ritual performances. These performances must do specific things. They must tell the sacred story in the same way. It must be understood by the community that the sacred rite in some sense takes its participants out of ordinary time and connects them to past generations of the community.

And third, this ritual telling of the sacred story must involve the body. The sacred story, in Connerton's lovely phrase, must be "sedimented into the bones." In this way, the sacred story and all it implies must become a matter of what Connerton calls "habit-memory."[264]

All of that should sound familiar to Orthodox Christians. Reading Connerton for the first time, I understood from an anthropological point of view why Orthodoxy is so powerful. The beauty and power of the Divine Liturgy, with its chants, candles, prostrations, icons, and its conscious evocation of eternity, is an incomparable bulwark against the disintegrating forces of liquid modernity.

But the Divine Liturgy is not magic. As anthropologist Mary Douglas has written, a culture's rituals express its cosmology, and in so doing constructs its sense of reality. But that cosmology must also be lived outside the ritual. If we live as if there is a separation of religion from life, we rob it of all its power. Attending the Divine Liturgy is necessary, but not sufficient. The liturgy must be part of submitting to what Douglas calls "a total pattern of symbols."[265]

Let me speak concretely. If we are to "sediment" the Orthodox Christian Faith into our bones, then we must constantly submit the body to the purification of spiritual life and practice. We have to pray, and pray with our bodies. Crossing ourselves, making prostrations, kissing icons—these things are not empty gestures at all. These seemingly minor gestures are among the most meaningful things we can do.

And Christian asceticism, which is only practiced in any serious way today by Orthodox Christianity, is absolutely necessary. Again, I don't want to get into the theological reasons here, but from an anthropological point of view, ritual asceticism—fasting, in particular—"sediments" into our bones the reality of the religion's cosmology. We Orthodox know that fasting disciplines the body and brings it into greater harmony with God. It is necessary to *theosis*. Before I became Orthodox, I thought of fasting as a kind of punishment. I did not realize that fasting is necessary for our ultimate healing.

To underscore that point, I need to speak very personally about how sexual asceticism worked for my own healing. I came to Christ as an adult through

Roman Catholicism. As a single man, aged twenty-five, living in a big city, I found that giving up my sexual freedom was the only serious sacrifice I had to make. But it was a big one. There was nothing in the culture to support my struggle, and very little in the culture of contemporary Catholicism.

Nevertheless, I knew the Egypt from which I had come in search of Christ, and I was not going to go back there. I lived in the desert, so to speak, for three years, not knowing if God had in mind for me to marry. I knew only that I had to obey the Lord. Eventually I met the woman that I would marry—and the meaning of my three years of ascetic chastity became clear. Through my ascetic obedience, the Holy Spirit healed brokenness within me, and prepared me for marriage. Had I not allowed the Lord to reorder my erotic desires through obedience and asceticism, I would not have been able to marry—or to sustain the marriage through difficult times.

We all know that sexuality is the most divisive issue in contemporary Christianity. Mainline Protestantism has abandoned the prohibition against homosexuality. Many younger Evangelicals are rejecting that prohibition, and within Roman Catholicism, under Pope Francis, homosexuality is fast becoming normalized. Even in Orthodoxy, there are academics and clerics who are trying to change the Church's teachings to conform to the spirit of the age. This is not a minor thing. From a Christian anthropological point of view, this is an existential crisis for Christianity.

Is sex the linchpin of Christian cultural order? Is it really the case that to cast off Christian teaching on sex and sexuality is to remove the primary factor that gives—or gave—Christianity its power as a social force?

Though he might not have put it quite that way, the eminent sociologist Philip Rieff would probably have said yes. Rieff's landmark 1966 book *The Triumph of the Therapeutic* analyzes what he calls the "deconversion" of the West from Christianity.[266] Nearly everyone recognizes that this process has been under way since the Enlightenment, but Rieff showed that it had reached a more advanced stage than most people—least of all, Christians—recognized.

Rieff, writing in the 1960s, identified the Sexual Revolution as a leading indicator of Christianity's demise. In classical Christian culture, he wrote, "the rejection of sexual individualism" was "very near the center of the symbolic that has not held."[267] He meant that renouncing the sexual autonomy and sensuality of pagan culture and redirecting the erotic instinct was intrinsic to Christian culture. Without Christianity, the West was reverting to its former state.

The point is not that Christianity was only, or primarily, about redefining and revaluing sexuality, but that within a Christian anthropology sex takes on a new and different meaning, one that mandated a radical change of behavior and cultural norms. In Christianity, what a person does with his or her sexuality cannot be separated from what man is. In a sense, moderns believe the same thing, but from a perspective entirely different from the early Church's.

Describing how men and women in the early Christian era saw their bodies, historian Peter Brown says the body

> was embedded in a cosmic matrix in ways that made its perception of itself profoundly unlike our own. Ultimately, sex was not the expression of inner needs, lodged in the isolated body. Instead, it was seen as the pulsing, through the body, of the same energies as kept the stars alive. Whether this pulse of energy came from benevolent gods or from malevolent demons (as many radical Christians believed), sex could never be seen as a thing for the isolated human body alone.[268]

Early Christianity's sexual teaching does not come only from the words of Christ and the Apostle Paul; more broadly, it emerges from the Bible's anthropology. The human being bears the image of God, however tarnished by sin, and is the pinnacle of an order created and imbued with meaning by God.

In that order, man has a purpose. He is meant for something, to achieve certain ends. When Paul warned the Christians of Corinth that having sex with a prostitute meant that they were joining Jesus Christ to that prostitute (cf. I Cor. 6:15–17), he was not speaking metaphorically. Because we belong to Christ as a unity of body, mind, and soul, how we use the body and the mind sexually is a very big deal.

Evangelical Christianity and the Roman Catholic magisterium both say the same thing, but only within Orthodox Christianity is the reality of the unity of body and soul made manifest in everyday devotional practice. I'm not saying that Orthodox Christians are necessarily holier than the non-Orthodox. What I am saying, though, is that within Orthodoxy we can more fully appreciate the meaning of the Incarnation, and only Orthodoxy gives believers today the means to "sediment" the meaning of Christianity within our bones.

Orthodox Christianity is the most radically countercultural form of Christianity in the modern world. This is not a bug; this is a feature. It's not easy to be faithfully Orthodox in America today—thank God! In her well-known 1970 book *Natural Symbols*, anthropologist Mary Douglas, an English Roman

Catholic, lamented the English bishops' abandonment of the Friday fasting requirement in the wake of the Second Vatican Council. Instead, they encouraged the faithful to do works of charity on Fridays. In their statement, the bishops said that this would make it easier for Roman Catholics there to assimilate to modern English life. The Friday fasting rule, the bishops wrote, caused other English people to regard Roman Catholics as odd.

So, they ended the practice. Mary Douglas wrote, with sadness and a tinge of bitterness: "Now there is no cause for others to 'regard us as odd.' Friday no longer rings the great cosmic symbols of expiation and atonement. It is not symbolic at all, but a practical day for the organization of charity. Now the English Catholics are like everyone else."[269]

Let us American Orthodox NOT be like everyone else! Let us insist on our difference! To make the Faith acceptable to post-Christian America is to kill it. We have to keep it mystical. We have to keep it embodied. We have to keep it countercultural.

Wise Christians across centuries including the writer Fyodor Dostoevsky have said that the best arguments for the faith are not syllogisms and apologetics. Rather, the best arguments for the faith are the saints the Church produces, and its beauty. We Orthodox understand that very well. Encountering the beauty of the liturgy, and the iconography, and the chants, and entering into the lives of the saints all around us—these are doorways leading to the truth, Who is Jesus Christ. Beauty and goodness made incarnate lead people to a life-changing encounter with the Lord.

Bishop Irenei is right in what he said in his keynote address to the Jordanville conference: we Orthodox do have the answer for what man longs for. We return him to his body, and his body to His Lord. We immerse him in beauty and goodness. We help him know who he is, and who he will become. We teach him how to "sediment" the truth into his bones.

What else is there? Has anybody who lives an Orthodox life ever encountered a form of Christianity more powerful than Orthodoxy? If not, then we have a story to tell the world. Use words if necessary.

# "Benedict," "Constantine," and "Prophecy": *Three* Options in the Coming Storm

### Archpriest Alexander F. C. Webster

> If we lived in a State where virtue was profitable, common sense would
> make us good, and greed would make us saintly. And we'd live like animals
> or angels in the happy land that/needs/no heroes. But since in fact we see that
> avarice, anger, envy, pride, sloth, lust and stupidity commonly profit far beyond
> humility, chastity, fortitude, justice and thought, and have to choose, to be human at all
> . . . why then perhaps we/must/stand fast a little—even at the risk of being heroes.
> —Sir Thomas More in Robert Bolt's play, *A Man for All Seasons*

## The "Benedict Option"?

"A specter is haunting Europe . . . " Not Communism, as Karl Marx and
Friedrich Engels optimistically began their *Communist Manifesto* in 1848. The
"specter" that we traditional Orthodox and others face, particularly in North
America and Europe, is the demonic movement of militant radical secularism that seeks to grind every vestige of Christendom and Christians into the
ground.

Enter Rod Dreher's "Benedict Option." In response to the deluge of political, social, and cultural marginalization, harassment, suppression, and eventual
persecution that he foresees, Dreher begins in 2017 where Alasdair MacIntyre
concluded his prescient book *After Virtue* in 1986 with a plaintive hope: "What
matters at this stage is the construction of local forms of community within
which civility and the intellectual and moral life can be sustained through the
new dark ages which are already upon us. . . . We are waiting not for a Godot,
but for another—doubtless very different—St. Benedict."[270] Dreher advocates
a radical, "strategic withdrawal" of Christians from society. "[W]e have to
develop creative, communal solutions," he counsels, "to help us hold on to our
faith and our values in a world growing ever more hostile to them." That entails

"a decisive leap into a truly countercultural way of living Christianity . . . "—or, to put it concisely, "exile in place."[271]

*The Benedict Option* offers a cornucopia of communities that Dreher extols as such small Christian countercultural communities. Surprisingly for a devout layman of the Russian Orthodox Church Outside Russia, Dreher overlooks *this* community, the one hosting this academic conference! Here in Jordanville, New York, we *strive to* live the "Benedict Option" each day.

The monks here are, in classic military parlance, the FLOT—"Forward Line of Own Troops"[272]—through their constant prayer and "the whole armor of God" (Ephesians 6:1) in the spiritual warfare against "principalities" and "powers" (Ephesians 6:12), whether political or demonic. Meanwhile, Holy Trinity Seminary shapes the "mind" of this community. Finally, the wives and families of the faculty, administrators, and seminarians, together with more than a dozen local families and other individuals who regularly attend the liturgical services at our Cathedral—not to mention the hundreds of pilgrims who flock here each year—constitute the body of this community. We are prepared and determined to endure whatever our secular society throws our way. But even Jordanville may not be able, alone, to withstand the coming storm.

Dreher does, fortunately, summon traditional Christians "to speak prophetically" to our political leaders, even while praying for them, before, alas, taking the wind out of his own sail by timidly adding this cautionary note: "Christians should not seek conflict and instead should submit to their workplace and legal authorities as much as possible . . . . Silence can be a shield."[273]

Perhaps Dreher had in the back of his mind the remarkable example of Sir Thomas More in King Henry VIII's increasingly Protestantized England. As chancellor of the realm, More, a devout Roman Catholic loyal to the papacy, studiously refrained from any public or private discussion of the king's divorce and remarriage or the king's supplanting of the pope in Rome as head of the English church, trusting in the legal maxim that "silence betokens consent," not dissent. We know, however, how that prudent effort failed, when his former law clerk, Richard Rich, perjured himself at More's trial, the court found More guilty of treason, and More, with no hope of survival, finally discharged his private opinion in the hearing of all in Parliament. The quotation of More at the beginning of this presentation presages More's ultimate decision to "stand fast a little," speak truth to power, as the contemporary saying goes, and become a "hero" to Christians in all times and places.

Nonetheless, I must confess that I am disappointed that Dreher has proposed a rather passive public posture for traditional Christians in the present crisis. A fundamental problem with the key premise of the "Benedict Option" is the radical, dramatic difference between St. Benedict's early medieval era and our own precarious time.

St. Benedict of Nursia and the other monastic abbots in Italy and northwestern Europe from the sixth through eighth centuries had to survive waves of uncivilized pagan "barbarians."

*We* must endure relentless assaults from militant apostates from Christian civilization. Most of them (or their immediate ancestors) have *known* the Church (or its splinter entities), *belonged* to it, and *lived*—or tried to live—according to its theological, moral, and spiritual revelations and guidance.

The challenge to St. Benedict, et al., was, arguably less onerous and more promising than ours, however crude, fierce, rapacious, and destructive the Germanic and other migrant peoples were. The invaders and conquerors from whom the early medieval monks in the West hunkered down in their monastery fortress communities were not *personally* hostile to Christians *qua* Christians, or impelled by a radical secularist iconoclastic ideology, hellbent on eradicating every trace of the divine presence among men, women, and children—especially the divine virtues of faith, hope, and love, as well as chastity, purity, and integrity.

In short, St. Benedict, et al., tried to survive in a post-Roman, uncivilized, pre-Christian world. Through patient, exemplary evangelism and persuasion, they helped convert half a continent. We Orthodox Christians in Europe and North America in the second decade of the twenty-first century must persevere in a post-Christian, nihilistic, spiritually suicidal world. "Patient, exemplary evangelism and persuasion" will hardly suffice and will, most probably, fail in our time. Something other than the "Benedict Option" alone is required.

### The "Constantine Project"?

To address that deficiency, John Mark Reynolds, Ph.D., founder and headmaster of the Saint Constantine School in Houston, Texas, whom Rod Dreher lauds among many others in *The Benedict Option*, has proposed the "Constantine Project."

Reynolds is under no illusions that hunkering down and trying to ride out the coming storm would prove effective. Although he acknowledges Dreher's BenOp as an invaluable model of mutual support within a religious community for traditional Christians, Reynolds hastens to add that it is quixotic and unrealistic by itself. "I'm looking for allies both here and globally to protect me," he admits, "from the political pressure that will come if we're successful. Because I think we're too big to be left alone. I don't think that the current shadow of that hideous strength is going to let me just live in Nursia."[274]

Reynolds is right. If the new secular sexual political order will not tolerate individual bakers, florists, and photographers all over the United States who politely decline to offer their professional services for homosexual "weddings" as a matter of religious duty or moral conscience, then entire communities of like-minded Christians can hardly expect to escape notice and the vicious wrath of the militants. The many pockets of small-scale, non-public Christendoms that the BenOp envisages would, almost certainly, become high-value targets for elimination through one means or another.

Turning his attention from St. Benedict of Nursia eastward to another sixth century Christian whose contributions to Western Civilization were larger than life, Reynolds suggests the profound relevance of St. Justinian the Great, Emperor of New Rome in Byzantium and, for a generation, Old Rome as well, to our current crisis in the twenty-first century West. Justinian's numerous achievements in the realms of imperial governance, reconquest of western Mediterranean regions of the Roman Empire, an unprecedented codification of ancient Roman law together with his own additions (the *Novellae*), his architectural vision of the Great Church of Hagia Sophia in Constantinople, to name only a few, dwarfed the legacy of St. Constantine the Great, the Roman emperor whose Edict of Milan in AD 313 ceased the persecution of Christians by the state and its minions, legalized Christianity in the Roman Empire, and paved the way for the unique partnership of *imperium* and *sacerdotium* that we know as Christendom.

St. Benedict and his fellow monks were able to preserve and extend St. Constantine's legacy of Christian culture in the barbarian, former Roman Christian West, precisely because St. Constantine's legacy continued uninterrupted in the Byzantine Orthodox East. The flickering flames of Christian civilization that St. Benedict et al. kept alive in the West perdured as a continual display of fireworks in Byzantium, which also provided "political protection" to the Christians in the West, if only through its imperial shadow from East to West—much as "the Russian Orthodox Czar" was able, as an external, distant, but ever-present military threat, to provide such "protection" to the Greek Orthodox Christians in the Ottoman Empire.[275]

In the present fight for survival of Orthodox Christians and others in the West, Reynolds reminds us, we are *not* alone, just as St. Benedict et al. were never on their own. Reynolds warns that "without some equivalent of Constantinople or Moscow" the small BenOp communities that Dreher envisions will "have a hard time surviving."[276] But Reynolds sounds a hopeful note when he observes: "just as Christianity is decaying a bit [*sic*] in places like the United States and Western Europe, it's advancing in some form or another all over Eastern Europe, the former Soviet Union, China, and South Korea."[277] Consider the magnificent, providential irony if the global power of "the Russians" in the Russian Republic today (so disdained, scorned, and demonized by so many American elites across the political spectrum despite having cast off the shackles of Soviet tyranny, state atheism, and decades of persecution), with the Russian Orthodox Church headquartered in Moscow as the religious and moral force, were to furnish the ballast to keep afloat the fragile ship of faith in the post-Christian West!

How might our potential "protectors" in Orthodox Russia today (in league, perhaps, with Orthodox Serbia, Romania, Bulgaria, Greece, and Georgia) know who and where we are hanging on for dear life in the apostate West, as well as the depths of our spiritual distress? How might some of us in the West actively resist those in power here who seek to extirpate traditional Christian morality, spirituality, doctrinal teachings, liturgical practices, schools, and even families? One answer that I wish to propose is a call for the social virtue of justice and the personal virtue of righteousness.

### The "Prophecy Option"!

To Dreher's "Benedict Option" and Reynolds' "Constantine Project" I would add the "Prophecy Option."

The "three-fold" ministry of our Lord Jesus Christ on earth—priest, prophet, and king—is quite familiar to most Christians, particularly us Orthodox Christians. But the second of those roles is the least understood and appreciated of the three. In ancient Israel the Hebrew word that we translate as "prophet" was *nabi*, or, literally, "one sent to speak." Thus we can appreciate how that term applies perforce to Moses the Prophet and Lawgiver and the numerous prophets whom God raised up to speak on His behalf to the Israelites, often with the exclamation, "Thus saith the Lord!" The Greek term for *nabi* in the New Testament—"*prophetes*"—makes the divine connection clearer: "one who speaks *for another*." A biblical prophet was someone called by God, sent by God to His own people, and empowered to speak for God as their conscience—to "rattle their chains," as it were, or to "rock the boat," or, as the nineteenth-century humorist Finley Peter Dunne's fictional bartender Mr Dooley declared the mission of newspapers, "to comfort the afflicted and to afflict the comfortable"![278]

The ancient biblical prophet—and here I would include our Lord Jesus Christ in one of His Incarnate roles—was neither a magician nor a fortune-teller nor a hypnotic visionary. When he spoke, as the biblical texts capture so well, he did not offer mere predictions of the future. The biblical prophet was concerned with all three verbal tenses. He summoned God's people to abandon one or more of the three deadly "I's"—idolatry, injustice, and immorality—and to act morally and spiritually in the *present* in accordance with the Law of God, the Covenant given by God through Moses, in the *past*. Only when necessary did the prophet warn of dire consequences in the *future*, if the people continued to ignore God's will for them and for their own good. Whether a cliché or a truism, the biblical prophet did not so much *foretell* the future as boldly "forthtell" the will of God for the *present*!

Though overshadowed in the popular Christian perception of our Lord Jesus Christ as a gentle, accepting, non-judgmental Son of God, His public debut in Galilee as Messiah, as announced in Matthew 4:15–16, fulfilled the Old Testament Prophet Isaiah's vision: "the people who sat in darkness have seen a great light, and for those who sat in the region and shadow of death Light has dawned." His was a light of great heat: of warmth and love for those who hear His will and do it; but of searing, purging heat for those who persist in their godlessness, unselfishness, cruelty, and downright indecency! How many times did our Lord warn the scribes and Pharisees: "Woe to you . . . hypocrites," "blind guides," "serpents," "brood of vipers," "like whitewashed tombs which indeed appear beautiful outwardly, but inside are full of dead men's bones and all uncleanness" (Matthew 23:16. 33; 23:27)? That's not the namby-pamby Jesus in the American imagination. To be sure, nor was the Incarnate Son of God a fire-breathing, misanthropic street-corner prophet of doom and gloom.

The renowned American civil rights advocate and Baptist minister, Dr Martin Luther King Jr, often quoted this verse from the book of Amos in the Old Testament: "let justice run down like water, and righteousness like a mighty stream" (Amos 5:24, (NKJV)). But the Prophet Amos also loved his wayward fellow Israelites and interceded on behalf of them with the Lord, pleading, "O Lord, Lord, be merciful! Who will raise up Jacob? For He is small!" (Amos 7:2).

Much more than Amos, our Lord Jesus Christ spoke "truth to power" with abundant divine love to save His wayward creation in the divine hope that they would turn from—that is, "repent"—their evil ways.

What we need in the coming storm, in addition to Dreher's small BenOp communities and Reynold's contemporary "Constantine," is those intrepid Christian souls among us who can and will respond to God's question, "Whom shall I send, and who will go to this people?" by echoing Isaiah's reply, "Behold, here am I, send me" (Isaiah 6:8).

One way that any one of us, even the "least" of the Orthodox faithful, can exercise a minimal prophetic role in the coming storm is by saying "No!" to those in positions of power over us who would harass, oppress, or even persecute us for our Orthodox Christian fidelity. That simple kind of resistance ought not to be dismissed. In the magnificent film "Spartacus" (1960), the two remaining survivors of a massive slave revolt against Rome in 73 BC, a Thracian who named Spartacus who instigated and inspired the revolt and a Sicilian "singer of songs" named Antonius, discuss the failed revolt on the eve of their own crucifixion the following morning.

Antoninus asks, "Could we have won, Spartacus. Could we ever have won?"

Spartacus replies, "Just by fighting them we won something. When just one man says, "No, I won't," Rome begins to fear. And we were tens of thousands who said no. That was the wonder of it. To have seen slaves lift their heads from the dust, to see them rise from their knees, stand tall, to hear them storm through the mountains shouting, to hear them sing along the plains."

Although Antoninus rains on that eloquent evocation of joyous defiance of tyranny by remarking, "And now they're dead," it is the exemplary spirit of Spartacus that lingers from that moment in the film. Any one of us can say "No" instead of cowering in fear or desperately hoping not to be noticed by the terrestrial powers arrayed against us.

Recently a Baptist pastor in the environs of St Louis published a brief article in *Touchstone Magazine* appropriately titled, "Must Say No." Joshua Steely explains when and why Christians, in good conscience and fidelity to the Gospel of Jesus Christ, cannot compromise with "the sexual revolution." He focuses on the "Fairness for All" (FFA) compromise crafted by the National Association of Evangelicals (NAE) and the Council for Christian Colleges and Universities (CCCU). The FFA concedes the inclusion of "sexual orientation" and "gender identity" as "protected classes" in the public arena in America, particularly antidiscrimination laws, provided that such laws specifically "protect religious liberty." Pastor Steely steadfastly opposes such a fundamental compromise with the purveyors of perversion as self-defeating, self-contradictory, and even what I read as a selfish sectarian concern by Christians. Saying "No" to this sexual Zeitgeist may have adverse consequences, but Steely's resolve is steeled: "That foe may defeat us and take away our religious freedom. But at least we will not have given it away."[279]

But even that "everyman a prophet" approach will not suffice in the coming storm. We need Orthodox Christian prophets for today like those whom our Lord has sent into spiritual harm's way ever since the Incarnation of the Son of God—prophets who, like Isaiah, respond to the divine call with extraordinary moral and political courage such as these twelve:

- **St John the Forerunner,** Prophet, and Baptizer, who confronted King Herod Antipas for his unholy "marriage" to Herodias, his brother's wife;
- St. Ambrose, Bishop of Milan in Italy, who refused to allow the Byzantine Emperor Theodosios I to commune in the Milan cathedral after turning loose Goth mercenary soldiers to massacre thousands of civilians, including children, in the Greek city of Thessaloniki in AD 390;
- **St John Chrysostom,** Archbishop of Constantinople, who, a few years later, excoriated the Byzantine Empress Eudoxia for her excessive, self-indulgent love of luxury and pleasure, while many others in the Empire languished in poverty—even calling her another Jezebel and Herodias;
- **St Mark,** Bishop of Ephesos, who, alone among all the hundreds of Orthodox bishops at the misbegotten "reunion" Council of Florence in AD 1439, rejected the urgent appeals of Patriarch Joseph II of Constantinople and the Byzantine Emperor John VIII Palaiologos to submit to the papal claims and heresies;
- **St Philip,** Metropolitan of Moscow and All Russia, who, when Tsar Ivan IV ("the Terrible") attended the Lenten Liturgy for the Sunday of the Veneration of the Holy Cross in the Moscow cathedral in 1568, refused to bless the tsar and rebuked him publicly for the numerous murders by his political police, the Oprichniki—only to be strangled to death on December 23, 1569, by another minion of the tsar;
- **Archimandrite Melentije Pavlović** (later the first Metropolitan of Belgrade in Serbia, 1831–1833), who publicly defied the Sultan of the Ottoman Empire by blessing with a hand cross the Serb revolutionary Milosh Obrenovic at the Takavo Uprising on Palm Sunday, April 23, 1815;
- **St Tikhon (Belavin),** Patriarch of Moscow, who, having already appealed worldwide for financial support to alleviate widespread famine in the new Soviet Union, publicly denounced as sacrilege the Bolsheviks' confiscation of consecrated liturgical items in March 1922 for ostensibly the same end;

- **Metropolitan Stefan (Shokov) of Sofia,** Bulgaria, during World War II and the Nazi Holocaust, primate of the Bulgarian Orthodox Church and "undaunted in the face of... personal attacks and frequent threats of arrest," whose public "protests ranged from simple objections to the compulsory wearing of the Star of David by converted Jews to a prophetic letter to King Boris of Bulgaria in May 1943, 'warning him not to persecute the Jews, lest he himself be persecuted' through the judgement of God!"[280]
- **Mother Maria Skobtsova,** an unconventional Russian Orthodox nun from Latvia whose quiet but profound resistance to the Nazi Holocaust in Paris, France, included an answer to fervent prayer—namely persuading sanitation workers to hide Jewish children in "garbage bins, haul them out on the trucks from the stadium, and then under the cover of night, sneak the children to the house on rue de Lourmel where she then could orchestrate their continued passage to the south of France, an area outside of Nazi control, and to safety."[281] For which she was found out, sent to the gas chamber at the all-female Ravensbruck Concentration Camp in Germany, and martyred on Holy Saturday in 1945;
- **Archbishop Iakovos (Coucouzis)** of the Greek Orthodox Archdiocese in North America, who, on March 21, 1965, joined the third civil rights march in Selma, Alabama, in the front line with Dr. Martin Luther King, Jr., "way out in front of the rest of the Orthodox community on one of the most vital moral issues of the day," and who, for that "visible prophetic stance, . . . earned acclaim from most of the members of his church but bitter enmity from others, who were not yet ready to embrace the civil-rights movement or its demands for equality."[282]
- **Aleksandr Solzhenitsyn,** the author of the *Gulag Archipelago* and other celebrated novels, short stories, and expository writings, who exposed Soviet abuses of human dignity and human rights within the Communist state and who, after his forced exile, turned his prophetic voice also toward the non-Communist West for the first time in June 1978, when, during his outstanding, albeit controversial, Harvard Commencement Address at Harvard University, he chastised the United States for its failure of nerve in not pursuing victory in the Viet Nam War![283]
- **Metropolitan Onuphry of Kiev and All-Ukraine,** besieged primate of the loyal canonical Orthodox Church in the country, which is also an integral autonomous part of the Russian Orthodox Church (Moscow Patriarchate), who, in his public address at a meeting of the All-Ukrainian Council of

Churches as recently as March 21, 2019, with Petro Poroshenko, then President of Ukraine in attendance, protested "the seizure of churches, the interference of the authorities in Church affairs, and other offenses" perpetrated against the canonical Church by Poroshenko's government, concluding with this bold, prophetic challenge to Poroshenko: "All that I have mentioned above only harms the state. Make it stop. I am sure it is within your power!"[284]

That is, indeed, a veritable roll call of noble prophets through the ages who have lived the words that Robert Bolt puts in Sir Thomas More's mouth in the quotation at the beginning of this chapter. All of them took "the risk of being heroes" and have been enshrined in our collective Orthodox memory as Heroes of the Faith. Theirs was a prophecy with a price that perhaps few Orthodox Christians today, unlike the countless confessors and martyrs for our Lord from age to age, may be willing to pay. In every case mentioned above, the prophet lost his or her position and sometimes his or her life. Is it any wonder there is never a surfeit of genuine prophets anywhere or at any time? There are no unemployment lines here: the job of prophet is always begging for applicants—to paraphrase the current slogan of the U.S. Marine Corps: "The Few, the Humble, the Prophets!"

The life span of a prophet tends to be short and marked by stages: inspiration, trepidation, perspiration, exasperation, validation. Too often the last stage—validation—is after the prophet's life on this earth. Even our Lord Jesus Christ Himself lamented the way Israel mistreated those divine spokesmen, those special proclaimers of God's will: "O Jerusalem, Jerusalem, killing the prophets and stoning those who are sent to you!" (Matthew 23:27). But we Orthodox Christians have, from the beginning of the Church, cherished the memory of those confessors and martyrs and honored *them* via icons, *not* those Christians who simply tried to survive political, religious, or cultural trials at all costs.

Our Lord seems to raise up such prominent prophets in every era to oppose idolatry, injustice, or immorality on behalf of divine truth, justice, or purity—and to inspire the truly faithful to endure whatever the "principalities" and "powers" of this world might inflict upon us.

May He do so again in the coming era of spiritual and moral darkness. Our survival with integrity as the Church in the West may depend on it.

# List of Contributors

**Dr David Bradshaw**, B.S. in Physics from Auburn University and Ph.D. in Philosophy from the University of Texas, is Professor of Philosophy at the University of Kentucky and the author of *Aristotle East and West: Metaphysics and the Division of Christendom* (Cambridge University Press) together with numerous articles on ancient, patristic, and medieval philosophy. He has edited two volumes of joint consultations between Russian and Anglo-American philosophers, *Philosophical Theology and the Christian Tradition: Russian and Western Perspectives* and *Ethics and the Challenge of Secularism: Russian and Western Perspectives*, both published by the Council for Research in Values and Philosophy.

**Dr Mark J. Cherry** is the Dr Patricia A. Hayes Professor in Applied Ethics and Professor of Philosophy at St Edward's University in Austin, Texas. He earned his undergraduate degree in philosophy from the University of Houston and his doctorate degree in philosophy from Rice University. His research encompasses ethics and bioethics, together with social and political philosophy. He is the author of *Kidney for Sale by Owner: Human Organs, Transplantation and the Market* (Georgetown University Press, 2016) and *Sex, Family, and the Culture Wars* (Transaction Publishers, 2016), together with fifteen edited books and more than 100 peer-reviewed book chapters and journal articles. He is Editor of *The Journal of Medicine and Philosophy* (Oxford University Press), Senior Editor of *Christian Bioethics* (Oxford University Press), and Editor-in-Chief of *HealthCare Ethics Committee Forum* (Springer), as well as Co-editor of the book series *The Annals of Bioethics* (Routledge) and Editor of the book series *Philosophical Studies in Contemporary Culture* (Springer).

**Rod Dreher** is a senior editor at *The American Conservative*. He has written and edited for the *New York Post*, *The Dallas Morning News*, *National Review*, the *South Florida Sun-Sentinel*, the *Washington Times*, and the *Baton Rouge Advocate*. Rod's commentary has been published in *The Wall Street Journal*, *Commentary*, the *Weekly Standard*, *Beliefnet*, and *Real Simple*, among other publications, and he has appeared on NPR, ABC News, CNN, Fox News, MSNBC, and the BBC.

A former publications director for the Templeton Foundation, he has also authored four books, *The Little Way of Ruthie Leming* (Grand Central Publishing, 2014), *Crunchy Cons* (Crown Forum, 2006), *How Dante Can Save Your Life* (Regan Arts, 2017), and *The Benedict Option* (Sentinel, an imprint of Penguin Random House, 2018). The latter was described by David Brooks in the *New York Times* as "the most discussed and most important religious book of the decade."

**Dr Bruce Seraphim Foltz** is Professor of Philosophy *Emeritus* at Eckerd College in St Petersburg, Florida. He is the author of *Inhabiting the Earth: Heidegger, Environmental Ethics, and the Metaphysics of Nature* (Humanities Books, 1995) and *The Noetics of Nature: Environmental Philosophy and the Holy Beauty of the Visible* (Fordham University Press, 2014), as well as coeditor of *Rethinking Nature: Essays in Environmental Philosophy* (Indiana University Press, 2004), and *Toward an Ecology of Transfiguration: Orthodox Christian Perspectives on Environment, Nature, and Creation* (Fordham University Press, 2013). Most recently, he is the editor of *Medieval Philosophy: A Multicultural Reader* (Bloomsbury Academic, 2019) and author of *Byzantine Incursions on the Borders of Philosophy: Contesting the Boundaries of Nature, Art, and Religion* (Springer, 2019). He has founded or cofounded three professional societies, including the International Association for Environmental Philosophy and the Society for Nature, Philosophy, and Religion.

**Dr David C. Ford** is Professor of Church History at St Tikhon's Orthodox Seminary, in South Canaan, Pennsylvania. His publications include *Marriage as a Path to Holiness: Lives of Married Saints* (St Tikhon's Monastery Press, 2013); *Women and Men in the Early Church: The Vision of Saint John Chrysostom* (St Tikhon's Monastery Press, 1996); *Wisdom for Today from the Early Church*; *Saint Tikhon of Moscow: Instructions and Teachings for the American Orthodox Faithful (1898–1907)* (St Tikhon's Monastery Press, 2016); *Church History*, vol. 3 in the revised catechetical series entitled *The Orthodox Faith* (St Vladimir's Seminary Press, 2016); Saint John Chrysostom's *Letters to Saint Olympia* (St Vladimir's Seminary Press, 2016); and the booklet *Prayer and the Departed Saints* (Conciliar Press, 1991). He also contributed to and helped to edit, along with his wife Dr Mary Ford and Dr Alfred Kentigern Siewers, *Glory and Honor: Orthodox Christian Resources on Marriage* (St Vladimir's Seminary Press, 2016). Along with numerous other articles, he also, along with Dr Mary Ford and Fr Theodore Petrides, wrote and edited the twenty-one-page thematic articles in the Old Testament portion of the complete *Orthodox Study Bible* (Thomas Nelson, 2008).

**Dr Mary Ford** is Associate Professor of New Testament at St Tikhon's Orthodox Seminary. She has published, in addition to numerous articles, *The Soul's Longing:*

*An Orthodox Christian Perspective on Biblical Interpretation* (St Tikhon's Monastery Press, 2015). She coauthored, with her husband, Dr David C. Ford, *Marriage as a Path to Holiness: Lives of the Married Saints* (St Tikhon's Monastery Press, 2013); *Women and Men in the Early Church: The Vision of Saint John Chrysostom* (St Tikhon's Monastery Press, 1996); and she contributed to and coedited *Glory and Honor: Orthodox Christian Resources on Marriage. Marriage* (St Vladimir's Seminary Press, 2016).

**Reader Gaelan Gilbert, Ph.D.,** is Visiting Professor in Arts & Humanities at the University of Saint Katherine in San Diego, California, where he has served in faculty and academic administrative roles since 2013. He is also the Headmaster of Christ the Saviour Academy, an Orthodox Christian classical academy connected with St George Antiochian cathedral in Wichita, Kansas. His undergraduate degrees are in English education and philosophy/theology, and his graduate work focused on premodern European literature, culture (including gender), philosophy, and theology. His current research and writing includes a chapter on Eastern Orthodox Christianity for the *Bloomsbury Religion North America* series; a larger project on liturgy, philosophy, and culture; a book proposal on Orthodox Christianity and education; and ongoing works of poetry, fiction, and children's literature.

**Archpriest Chad Hatfield** is the President of St Vladimir's Orthodox Theological Seminary, Yonkers, New York. Prior to that he served as Dean of St Herman Orthodox Theological Seminary in Kodiak, Alaska. He holds a D. Min. from Pittsburgh Theological Seminary and a D.D. from Nashotah House Seminary.

**Archpriest Peter Heers, D.Th.,** is the Headmaster of Three Hierarchs Academy in Florence, Arizona and Lecturer of Dogmatic Theology in the Certificate of Theological Studies Program operated by Holy Trinity Seminary in Jordanville, New York, where he previously was the instructor of Old and New Testament. He is the author of *The Missionary Origins of Modern Ecumenism: Milestones Leading up to 1920* (Uncut Mountain Press, 2007), and *The Ecclesiological Renovation of the Second Vatican Council: An Orthodox Examination of Rome's Ecumenical Theology Regarding Baptism and the Church* (Uncut Mountain Press, 2015). Fr Peter has also translated several books into English from Greek. He holds a doctoral degree in Dogmatic Theology from the Theological School of the University of Thessalonika, Greece.

**Dr Edith Mary Humphrey** is the William F. Orr Professor of New Testament at Pittsburgh Theological Seminary. She earned her bachelor's (with honors) from Victoria University (University of Toronto) and received her doctorate from McGill University, Montreal, where she was awarded the Governor General's Gold Medal for her work on the New Testament and Christian Origins. The author of numerous articles on the literary and rhetorical study of the Bible, she has also written seven books: *Further Up and Further In: Orthodox Conversations with C. S. Lewis* on Scripture and Theology (St Vladimir's Press, 2017), *Scripture and Tradition: What the Bible Really Says* (Baker Academic, 2013); *Grand Entrance: Worship on Earth as in Heaven* (Brazos, 2010); *And I Turned to See the Voice: The Rhetoric of Vision in the New Testament* (Baker Academic, 2007); *Ecstasy and Intimacy: When the Holy Spirit Meets the Human Spirit* (Eerdmans, 2005); the *Sheffield Guide to Joseph and Aseneth* (Continuum/Sheffield, 2000); and *The Ladies and the Cities: Transformation and Apocalyptic Identity in Joseph and Aseneth, 4 Ezra, the Apocalypse and The Shepherd of Hermas* (Sheffield, 1995).

**Fr Johannes L. Jacobse** holds a B.A. from the University of Minnesota and an M.Div. from St Vladimir's Orthodox Theological Seminary. He edits the websites Orthodoxy Today and Another City, and is founder and president of the American Orthodox Institute. A former fellow at the Hubert H. Humphrey Institute of Public Affairs at the University of Minnesota, he now serves as rector of St Peter the Apostle Antiochian Orthodox Church in Bonita Springs, Florida.

**Kh. Frederica Mathewes-Green** received her B.A. in English from the University of South Carolina and her M.A. in Theological Studies from Virginia Episcopal Theological Seminary.

She has authored ten books on a variety of subjects including *Facing East: A Pilgrim's Journey into the Mystery of Orthodox* (Harper San Francisco, 1997); *At the Corner of East and Now: A Modern Life in Ancient Christian Orthodoxy* (Conciliar Press, 2009); *The Illumined Heart: The Ancient Christian Path of Transformation* (Paraclete Press, 2001); and *Welcome to the Orthodox Church: An Introduction to Eastern Christianity* (Paraclete Press, 2015) and penned more than 700 essays in such diverse publications as the *Washington Post, Christianity Today, Smithsonian,* and the *Wall Street Journal.* She has been a regular commentator for National Public Radio (NPR), a columnist for the *Religion News Service, Beliefnet.com,* and *Christianity Today,* and a podcaster for Ancient Faith Radio. She has appeared as a speaker over 500 times at colleges and universities, including Yale, Harvard, Princeton, Wellesley, Cornell, Baylor, Calvin College, and Westmont. She has been interviewed over 700 times on venues like Prime Time Live, the 700 Club, NPR, PBS, *Time, Newsweek,* and the *New York Times.*

**Archpriest John E. Parker III** is Dean of St Tikhon Orthodox Theological Seminary. Fr John earned his Bachelor of Arts degree in Spanish at the College of William and Mary, Williamsburg, Virginia, a Master of Divinity degree from Trinity Episcopal School for Ministry, Ambridge, Pennsylvania, and a Master of Theology degree at St Vladimir's Orthodox Theological Seminary, Yonkers, New York. In 2011, Fr John was appointed Chair of the Department of Evangelization of the Orthodox Church in America. More recently he earned his Doctor of Ministry degree at Saint Vladimir's Seminary with a project titled "Radechesis: A Radical Return to the Roots of Christian Catechism."

**Subdeacon Alfred Kentigern Paul Siewers, Ph.D.,** is Associate Professor of English at Bucknell University and 2018–2019 William E. Simon Research Fellow in Religion and Public Life in the James Madison Program at Princeton. He holds a B.A. in History from Brown University, M.A. in Early British Studies from the University of Wales (Aberystwyth), an M.S.J. from the Medill School of Journalism, Chicago, and a Ph.D. in English from the University of Illinois. His publications include Co-Editor, *The Totalitarian Legacy of the Bolshevik Revolution* (Lexington Books, 2019); Co-Editor, *Glory and Honor: Orthodox Christian Resources on Marriage* (St Vladimir's Seminary Press, 2015); Editor and contributor, *Re-Imagining Nature: Environmental Humanities and Ecosemiotics* (Bucknell, 2013); "*The Periphyseon*, the Irish 'Otherworld,' and Early Medieval Nature," in *Eriugena and Creation* (Brepols, 2014); "The Green Otherworlds of Early English Literature" in *The Cambridge Companion to Environment and Literature* (Cambridge, 2013). He codirects the Bucknell Program for American Leadership and Citizenship. A former award-winning journalist for the *Chicago Sun-Times*, his recent public writings have appeared in *The Federalist, The American Conservative,* and *Public Discourse* blogs.

**Archpriest Alexander F. C. Webster, Ph.D.,** is Dean and Professor of Moral Theology *Emeritus* at Holy Trinity Seminary (ROCOR) in Jordanville, New York. He earned an A.B. from the University of Pennsylvania, an M.A. from Columbia University Teachers College, an M.T.S. from Harvard University Divinity School, and a Ph.D. from the University of Pittsburgh. He has authored four books including *The Virtue of War: Reclaiming the Classic Christian Traditions East and West* (coauthored with Dr Darrell Cole of Drew University, Regina Orthodox Press, 2004), The *Pacifist Option: The Moral Argument Against War in Eastern Orthodox Theology* (International Scholars Publications, 1998), and *The Price of Prophecy: Orthodox Churches on Peace, Freedom, and Security* (William Eerdmans 2nd ed., 1995) and published hundreds of scholarly articles and op-ed essays—primarily on topics pertaining to Orthodox moral theology, war and peace, military ethics and U.S. defense policy, civic virtue, and religion in Eastern Europe. He retired from the U.S. Army in June 2010 as a chaplain in the rank of Colonel after more than twenty-four years of service.

Note: Secular institutional affiliations are given for identification purposes only; the authors' views are their own as Orthodox Christian scholars and writers.

# Notes

1. See the work of the Orthodox literary scholar Harold Weatherby, *Mirrors of Celestial Grace: Patristic Theology in Spenser's Allegory* (Toronto: University of Toronto Press, 1994).

2. Faramerz Dabhoiwala, *The Origins of Sex: A History of the First Sexual Revolution* (Oxford: Oxford University Press, 2012), especially 85–7, 100–10, 116–28, 149–52.

3. Percy Bysshe Shelley, *Queen Mab*, note to V.189, quoted in Dabhoiwala, *Origins of Sex*, 126.

4. Kate Julian, "Why Are Young People Having So Little Sex?", https://theatlantic.com/magazine/archive/2018/12/the-sex-recession/573949/ (accessed February 20, 2019).

5. See Dionysius the Areopagite, *Divine Names*, chap. 4 (PG 4 693B).

6. Ibid., 4.7. Dionysius plays here with the similarity between *kallon*, beautiful, and *kaloun*, calling.

7. Akathist Hymn, Troparion. For the Greek text see *The Akathist Hymn*, ed. and trans. Father George Papadeas (Athens, Greece: Patmos Press, 1972). Many translations can be found online. Most of those that follow are taken from Papadeas, but for that of the opening hymn (below, n. 12) I have preferred http://ww1.antiochian.org/sites/default/files/sacred_music/Trop%20-%20Akathist-With%20mystic.pdf (accessed March 5, 2019). That of the Kontakion (below, n. 16) is one commonly used in the Greek Archdiocese, available at, e.g., https://stgeorgelawrence.org/bulletins/Sundbllt-20180311.pdf (accessed September 4, 2019).

8. Num. 6:2, 21, II Chron. 30:19, I Macc. 14:36 (LXX); cf. Gerhard Kittel, ed., *Theological Dictionary of the New Testament* (Grand Rapids: Eerdmans, 1964), vol. 1, 122–4.

9. The pagan use of this term enshrined a considerable double standard, in that *sōphrosunē* for a woman consisted in no sex outside of marriage combined with a modest disposition, whereas that for a man consisted in control over the sexual appetites, although not to the exclusion of occasional indulgence in prostitutes and slave girls. Christian usage erased this distinction, making the former standard applicable to all. See Kyle Harper, *From Shame to Sin: The Christian Transformation of Sexual Morality in Late Antiquity* (Cambridge, MA: Harvard University Press, 2013), 41–2, 52–5; Helen North, *Sophrosyne: Self-Knowledge and Self-Restraint in Greek Literature* (Ithaca, NY: Cornell University Press, 1966), 243–4, 248–9, 312–16.

10. See the entries for the relevant terms in G.W.H. Lampe, ed., *A Patristic Greek Lexicon* (Oxford: Clarendon Press, 1961); also North, *Sophrosyne*, 328–53.

11. John Chrysostom, *Homilies on Ephesians* 20.8 (PG 62 146).

12. Akathist Hymn, Apolytikion.

13. Akathist Hymn, Troparia of the Fourth and Fifth Odes.

14. Akathist Hymn, Eirmos of the Seventh Ode.
15. Akathist Hymn, Troparia of the Eighth Ode.
16. Akathist Hymn, Kontakion.
17. Akathist Hymn, First Prayer to the Theotokos.
18. *Marketed at everybody* Randy Olson, "A Look at Sex, Drugs, Violence, and Cursing in Films Over Time Through MPAA Ratings," *Randal S. Olson* (January 12, 2014), http://www.randalolson.com/2014/01/12/a-look-at-sex-drugs-violence-and-cursing-in-film-over-time-through-mpaa-ratings/ (accessed June 25, 2019).
19. *Porn is addictive* Adi Jaffe, "Internet Porn Addiction: Why Is Free Porn So Irresistible?," *Psychology Today* (November 11, 2011), https://www.psychologytoday.com/us/blog/all-about-addiction/201111/internet-porn-addiction-why-is-free-porn-so-irresistible (accessed June 25, 2019).
20. *"I kept worrying"* Martin Amis, "A Rough Trade," *The Guardian* (March 16, 2001), https://www.theguardian.com/books/2001/mar/17/society.martinamis1 (accessed June 25, 2019).
21. *Two-thirds of men* "New Survey of Porn Use: Men and Women Watching in Startling Numbers," Church Militant (January 18, 2016), https://www.churchmilitant.com/news/article/new-survey-of-porn-use-shows-startling-stats-for-men-and-women (accessed June 25, 2019).
22. *Humans are herd animals* Noam Shpancer, "You Are a Conformist (That Is, You Are Human)," *Psychology Today* (December 5, 2010), https://www.psychologytoday.com/us/blog/insight-therapy/201012/you-are-conformist-is-you-are-human (accessed June 25, 2019).
23. *Extremely hip* Robert Simonson, "Why Can't Hollywood Get Drinking Right," Punch (April 23, 2018), https://punchdrink.com/articles/why-cant-hollywood-movies-get-drinks-drinking-cocktails-right/ (accessed June 25, 2019).
24. *The word is "loneliness"* Neil Howe, "Millennials and the Loneliness Epidemic," *Forbes* (May 3, 2019), https://www.forbes.com/sites/neilhowe/2019/05/03/millennials-and-the-loneliness-epidemic/#390ef0077676 (accessed June 25, 2019).
25. *Deus absconditus* is a hidden God, seemingly indifferent to his creation.
26. The Bogomils were a dualist religious sect originating in tenth-century Bulgaria and flourishing for several hundred years in the Balkans.
27. Pavel Florensky, *At the Crossroads of Science and Mysticism: On the Cultural-Historical Place and Premises of the Christian World-Understanding*, trans. Boris Jakim (Kettering, OH: Semantron Press, 2014), 120–2.
28. Eric Voegelin, *Order and History, Volume Four, The Ecumenic Age* (Baton Rouge: Louisiana State University Press, 1974), 22.
29. Cited in Hans Jonas, *The Gnostic Religion* (Boston: Beacon Press, 2001), 322.
30. Cited in Jonas, ibid., 323.
31. Ibid.
32. Eric Voegelin, *Science, Politics, and Gnosticism* (Wilmington, DE: ISI Books, 2004), 69–72.
33. Jacob Taubes, *Occidental Eschatology*, trans. David Ratmako (Stanford: Stanford Univ. Press, 2009), 34–40.
34. Voegelin, *Science, Politics, and Gnosticism*, 26f.

35. Eric Voegelin, *The New Science of Politics: An Introduction* (Chicago: University of Chicago Press) 1987, 169.

36. Ibid.

37. Florensky, *At the Crossroads of Science and Mysticism*, 82. See also his earlier critique: "Is not Tolstoy's *Kreuzer Sonata*, that typical product of the [Russian] intelligentsia, foul and blasphemous? Does not the look of condescending aversion and foulness at the same time, that people of a 'scientific' worldview cast at the body, deny the body in its mysterious depth, in its mystical roots …" Pavel Florensky, *The Pillar and Ground of the Truth: An Essay in Orthodox Theodicy in Twelve Letters*, trans. Boris Jakim (Princeton: Princeton University Press, 1997), 213.

38. Jonas, *The Gnostic Religion*, 273f.

39. Albert Camus, *The Rebel*, trans. Anthony Bower (New York: Alfred A. Knopf, 1991), 37.

40. Ibid., 44.

41. Citing Descartes, Heidegger maintains that the "fundamental certainty" of modern consciousness is "the *fundamentum absolutum inconcussum* of the *me cogitare = me esse*," Martin Heidegger, "The Age of the World Picture," in Heidegger, *Off the Beaten Track*, ed. and trans. Julian Young and Kenneth Haynes (Cambridge: Cambridge University Press, 2002), 83.

42. This is most thematically discussed in the chapter on "Self-Consciousness" in Hegel's *Phenomenology of Spirit*.

43. Søren Kierkegaard, *The Sickness unto Death: A Christian Psychological Exposition for Upbuilding and Awakening*, trans Howard V. Hong and Edna H. Hong (Princeton: Princeton University Press, 1980), 131.

44. *Geronda* is the Greek word for an Elder or a Staretz.

45. Archimandrite Dionysios, *The Enemy Within*, 1, Sisterhood of St Nina, 2018; italics added.

46. Christos Yannaras, "Comma," trans. Elizabeth Theokritoff, in *Synaxis, Volume 1: Anthropology, Environment, Creation* (Montreal: Alexander Press, 2007), 232.

47. This distinction is also recognized and consistently sustained throughout the important recent book-length study, which is recommended for its comprehensive coverage of the topic of transgenderism as a social phenomenon. See Ryan Anderson, *When Harry Became Sally: Responding to the Transgender Moment* (New York: Encounter Books, 2018).

48. See https://acpeds.org/the-college-speaks/position-statements/gender-ideology-harms-children

49. Irenaeus of Lyons explains the teachings of the Gnostic Basileides (*c*.130) thus: for Basileides, "salvation belongs to the soul alone, for the body is by nature subject to corruption. [. . .] he holds also the practice of other religious rites, and of every kind of lust, a matter of perfect indifference." See Irenaeus, *Ad Haer.* 1.19.3.

50. This is the basis for the Christian allegations of sexual immorality against the Gnostics, who supposedly declared immunity from any sin in that their souls or selves were not tainted by the licentious sexual/bodily activity. Irenaeus, in describing the Valentinian strain of Gnostic teaching, explains that "it also comes to pass, that the 'most perfect' among them addict themselves without fear to all those kinds of forbidden deeds of which the Scriptures assure us that 'they who do such things shall not inherit the kingdom of God.' [. . .] And committing many other abominations and impieties, they run

us down (who from the fear of God guard against sinning even in thought and word) as utterly contemptible and ignorant persons, while they highly exalt themselves, and claim to be perfect, and the elect seed." See Irenaeus *Ad. Haer.* 1.1.11–12.

51. As Peter Brown has noted, for Valentinus, "the very element of otherness condensed in the polarity of male and female, as in that between spirit and its opposites, matter and mere soul, must vanish. The otherness of matter was not an eternal aspect of the universe, as pagan philosophers tended to think. Matter was an ephemeral accident: it had resulted from a tragic dislocation of the spiritual world. The otherness of all that was not pure spirit would be healed: the female would be swallowed up in the male. It would not simply be disciplined by the male; it would become male." See Peter Brown, *The Body and Society: Men, Women, and Sexual Renunciation in Early Christianity* (New York: Columbia University Press, 1988), 113.

52. As Brown notes, Gnostic circles treasured moments such as the following from the apocryphal Gospel of Thomas, which seemed to provide "an image of the sweet and irresistible absorption of the woman, the perpetual inferior other, into her guiding principle, the male: Simon Peter said to them, 'Let Mary [Magdalene] leave us, for women are not worthy of life.' Jesus said, 'I myself shall lead her and make her male.'" See Brown, *The Body and Society,* 113. See the *Gospel of Thomas,* II, 2 114.

53. Worth noting as well is the eschatological rejuvenation of all things described by John of Patmos in *Revelation* in terms of the heavenly Jerusalem *coming down to* the new earth, in what could perhaps be understood as an "apocalyptic incarnation," a way of visualizing *theosis.*

54. This elitism can be discerned in the double standard found in Gnostic teachers like Valentinus had toward non-Gnostic Christians. According to Irenaeus, "they maintain that good works are necessary to us, for that otherwise it is impossible to be saved. But as to themselves, they hold that they shall be entirely and undoubtedly saved, not by means of conduct, but because they are spiritual by nature." See Irenaeus, *Ad. Haer.* 1.1.11.

55. See John Behr, *The Way to Nicaea* (Crestwood, NY: St Vladimir's Seminary Press, 2001); and *The Nicene Faith* (Crestwood, NY: St Vladimir's Seminary Press, 2004).

56. Let me be crystal clear here that I am talking in particular about a discursive or ideational perspective, and *not* about the particular individual persons who may adhere to this perspective, regardless of whether they themselves are suffering from gender dysphoria or are defending the validity of transgender identity from a place of wanting to help garner respect for, and alleviate the pain of, those who are.

57. In his article "The Strange Persistence of Guilt," Wilfred McClay offers a piercing analysis of the contemporary association of victimhood and moral innocence in secular culture, tracing the moral logic at work in a society without traditional means for the absolution of personal guilt and ascetic spirituality, such as the concept of repentance and the sacrament of confession. See Wilfred McClay, "The Strange Persistence of Guilt," *The Hedgehog Review* 19:1 (Spring 2017). Accessible at https://hedgehogreview. com/issues/the-post-modern-self/articles/the-strange-persistence-of-guilt

58. For a recent example, see https://www.cbsnews.com/news/connecticut-transgender-athletes-face-federal-discrimination-complaint-from-females-over-title-ix-violations/.

59. For more on how both liberal and conservative organizations, but in particular the former, tend to discriminate against dissenters, see Jonathan Haidt, *The Righteous Mind: Why Good People Are Divided by Politics and Religion* (New York: Random House, 2012).

60. Lisa Littman's study suggests that the correlation between external social factors such as social media usage and the assumption of a transgender identity by teens is significant and meaningful. See Lisa Littman, "Parent Reports of Adolescents and Young Adults Perceived to Show Signs of a Rapid Onset of Gender Dysphoria," *PLOS ONE* 14:3 (2019). Accessible at: https://journals.plos.org/plosone/article?id=10.1371/journal.pone.0202330

61. On the devastating impact of "new media" on the spiritual life, see Jean-Claude Larchet, *The New Media Epidemic: The Undermining of Society, Family, and Our Own Soul* (Jordanville NY: The Printshop of St Job of Pochaev, 2019). For more on Taylor's notion of the buffered self, see Charles Taylor, *A Secular Age* (Cambridge, MA: Belknap Press of Harvard University, 2007).

62. Jordan Peterson's point here is salient: that while it is within the power of government to *forbid* certain uses of language defined as "hate speech," a government overreaches into totalitarianism when it forces people *to say only certain things rather than others*.

63. See Jacques Ellul, *The Technological Society* (New York: Random House, 1967). Similarly, Martin Heidegger's essay "The Question Concerning Technology" rightly argued that modern man has come to see the entire natural world as "standing-reserve" of energy whose significance, in a disenchanted cosmos, depends solely on their usefulness for human activity. See Martin Heidegger, "The Question Concerning Technology," in *Basic Writings* (London: HarperCollins, 2008), 307–41.

64. Francis Bacon, inventor of the scientific method, famously wrote that Nature will be "bound into service, hounded in her wanderings and put on the rack and tortured for her secrets." See his *Novum Organum*.

65. For example, here are a few recent reports on such "externalities," to use a term from economics, of smartphone production and usage. See https://www.theguardian.com/global-development/2018/oct/12/phone-misery-children-congo-cobalt-mines-drc; https://www.theguardian.com/technology/2018/jul/14/mobile-phones-cancer-inconvenient-truths; and https://www.theguardian.com/technology/2017/jun/18/foxconn-life-death-forbidden-city-longhua-suicide-apple-iphone-brian-merchant-one-device-extract.

66. What this means in terms of scientific advancements is clear enough, if still desperately requiring moral guidance; the development of bioethics to keep pace with various biotechnologies—from gene splicing to womb implantation in men—takes utmost priority. What salvific technology means when it comes to political or economic crises is less obvious, but still imaginable; both of these are realms in which the power of materialist thinking is relatively predominant. But when it comes to psychological and especially spiritual dimensions, a technological worldview assumes subtler forms, through increasingly refined biochemical treatments or techniques of meditation and so-called self-realization, for instance. The growing popularity of yoga is a good example of how, in our modern society, forms of quasi-spiritual practice that fit snugly with a technological/materialist worldview are gaining increasing popularity. Slavoj Zizek also has a fascinating and provocative lecture on Buddhist meditative practices and global capitalism as an unsuspected alliance between forms of spiritualized materialism. See https://www.youtube.com/watch?v=qkTUQYxEUjs

67. See https://greatergood.berkeley.edu/article/item/people_who_trust_technology_are_happier

68. See https://www.thepublicdiscourse.com/2019/02/49686/

69. On the topic of sexual education in schools and its role in the promotion of transgender ideology, California passed legislation in May 2019 supporting a new curriculum for public schools that takes an aggressive stance on this front, starting in Kindergarten. See https://www.washingtonpost.com/education/2019/05/10/california-is-overhauling-sex-education-guidance-schools-religious-conservatives-dont-like-it/?utm_term=.72219c4c8e4b. For the curriculum itself, see https://www.cde.ca.gov/ci/he/cf/index.asp

70. See https://www.docdroid.net/nm1XeFs/bowden-decision-feb-27-2019.pdf

71. See https://www.transgendertrend.com

72. The letter is available to be downloaded here: https://gendercriticalresources.com/Support/showthread.php?tid=1758

73. See Mark Cherry, "Individually Directed Informed Consent and the Decline of the Family in the West," in *Family-Oriented Informed Consent: East Asian & American Perspectives*, ed. Ruiping Fan (Dordrecht: Springer, 2015), 43–62.

74. See Friedrich Nietzsche, *The Will to Power*, trans. Walter Kaufmann and R.J. Hollingdale. (New York: Vintage Books, 1968).

75. David Bentley Hart, "Christ and Nothing (No Other God)," in *In the Aftermath: Provocations and Laments* (Grand Rapids, MI: Eerdmans, 2009).

76. See Christopher Ferrara, *Liberty; or, the God That Failed: Policing the Sacred and Constructing the Myths of the Secular State, from Locke to Obama* (Tacoma, WA: Angelico Press, 2012).

77. Michael Gillespie, David Bradshaw, John Milbank, David Bentley Hart, and other scholars have explored the genealogy of voluntarism, tracing its influence on culture. Significantly, Rene Descartes himself was raised by voluntarist Jesuits, and the terrifying idea of a "deceiver God" that looms so large behind his philosophy of "total doubt" unfortunately goes hand in hand with the elevation of the *human* will in opposition to a skewed vision of the divine will. See Michael Gillespie, *Nihilism before Nietzsche* (Chicago: University of Chicago Press, 1996).

78. Despite it being commonly used as a rationale for the necessity of gender transition, psychological stability does not accompany the embrace of a transgender identity. See https://www.acpeds.org/the-college-speaks/position-statements/gender-ideology-harms-children

79. See here for the document itself: https://www.glsen.org/article/transgender-model-district-policy

80. This model district policy document is a marvel of layered ambiguity. One thing to notice about it is that its definition of "gender identity" is amazingly similar to the clinical definition of gender dysphoria, but the document adds a positive spin on it, as rooted in the voluntarist principle that something chosen is therefore good. Values being subjectively founded, that is, legitimized by the very act of being freely adopted by an individual or group, they can be repurposed in differing and even opposite ideological directions depending on the larger governing assumptions or meta-values at work. Sociologists such as Bruno Latour have shown how this strategic if, when it comes to ideology, potentially unconscious act of rhetorical shuttling between subjective and objective regimes of knowledge or discourse—at one moment appealing to inaccessible subjective identity and at the next moment appealing to science's objective criteria—is a defining characteristic of modern thought. See Bruno Latour, *We*

*Have Never Been Modern* (Cambridge, MA: Harvard University Press, 1993) and also his *Reassembling the Social: An Introduction to Actor-Network Theory* (Oxford: Oxford University Press, 2005).

81. See chapter three, "Detransitioners Tell Their Stories," in Ryan Anderson, *When Harry Became Sally: Responding to the Transgender Moment* (New York: Encounter Books, 2018).

82. Unfortunately, as Littman's study suggests, this climate infects even the approaches of medical and psychiatric clinics. See https://journals.plos.org/plosone/article?id= 10.1371/journal.pone.0202330

83. Jean-Claude Larchet, *The Theology of the Body* (Crestwood, NY: St. Vladimir's Press, 2017).

84. Ibid., 34, 57.

85. Ibid., 35.

86. See https://www.cardplayer.com/poker-news/21342-americans-lost-116-9b-gambling-in- 2016-report and also https://www.economist.com/graphic-detail/2017/02/09/the-worlds- biggest-gamblers.

87. 40 million adults in the U.S. visit internet pornography sites on a regular basis.
    - 1 in 5 internet searches on a mobile device are for pornography.
    - Men who are happily married are 61 percent less likely to look at porn.
    - 20 percent of men admit to viewing pornography at work.
    - 88 percent of porn scenes contain physical aggression. 49 percent contain verbal aggression. (From: https://www.psychguides.com/guides/porn-addiction/)

88. See CBS's *60 Minutes* report on screen time and its effects on the brain development of children here: https://www.cbsnews.com/news/groundbreaking-study-examines- effects-of-screen-time-on-kids-60-minutes/

89. See https://www.nytimes.com/interactive/2017/06/05/upshot/opioid-epidemic-drug- overdose-deaths-are-rising-faster-than-ever.html Chris Hedges has also provided a comprehensive and sobering coverage of the opioid crisis. See Chris Hedges, *America: The Farewell Tour* (New York: Simon & Schuster, 2018), chapter 2, "Heroin."

90. The effect of opioids on the brain provides a helpful lens for how all the technological enhancements of pleasure function: "Opioids target the brain's reward system by flooding the circuit with dopamine. Dopamine is a neurotransmitter present in regions of the brain that regulate movement, emotion, cognition, motivation, and feelings of pleasure. The overstimulation of this system, which rewards our natural behaviors, produces the euphoric effects sought by people who misuse drugs and teaches them to repeat the behavior." https://www.naabt.org/faq_answers.cfm?ID=6

91. See Bruce K. Alexander, *The Globalization of Addiction: A Study in Poverty of the Spirit* (New York: Oxford University Press, 2008).

92. See Christian Smith, *Lost in Transition: The Dark Side of Emerging Adulthood* (New York: Oxford University Press, 2011) and *Souls in Transition: The Religious and Spiritual Sides of Emerging Adults* (New York: Oxford University Press, 2009).

93. Progressive socialism, for example, always includes its false claim to take care of the poor, masking its aggressive atheism and failed economics. As Karl Marx notes: "Nothing is easier than to give Christian asceticism a Socialist tinge. Has not Christianity declaimed against private property, against marriage, against the State? Has it not preached in the place of these, charity and poverty, celibacy and mortification of the

flesh, monastic life and Mother Church? Christian Socialism is but the holy water with which the priest consecrates the heart-burnings of the aristocrat" (1978, 492).

94. Consider Gianni Vattimo on this point: "The truth that, according to Jesus, shall make us free is not the objective truth of science or even that of theology: likewise, the Bible is not a cosmological treatise or a handbook of anthropology or theology. The scriptural revelation was not delivered to give us knowledge of how we are, what God is like, what the 'natures' of things or the laws of geometry are, and so on, as if we could be saved through the 'knowledge' of truth. The only truth revealed to us by Scripture, the one that can never be demythologized in the course of time – since it is not an experimental, logical, or metaphysical statement but a call to practice – is the truth of love, of charity" (2005, 51). For Vattimo, the Bible is no more than a set of moral sentiments to be interpreted in terms of contemporary progressive concerns with egalitarian social justice.

95. God gave seven commandments to Noah and his sons, the Gentles, but 613 to Moses and the Jews. "Seven precepts were the sons of Noah commanded: social laws; to refrain from blasphemy; idolatry; adultery; bloodshed; robbery; and eating flesh cut from a living animal. R. Hanania b. Gamaliel said: Also not to partake of the blood drawn from a living animal. R. Hidka added emasculation. R. Simeon added sorcery. . . . R. Eleazar added the forbidden mixture [in plants and animals]" (Sanhedrin 56a – b) (Epstein, 1994). For an engaging discussion of the ways in which Jewish law does not apply to Gentiles, see Rabbi Steinsaltz (2005).

96. Consider Immanuel Kant (1724–1804), who held that the Bible as a religious text ought to be "forced into a moral dress, in preference to the verbal and literal meaning, whenever this last savours nothing of morality, or perhaps tends even to snap our moral springs" (Kant, 1838, 141). Kant recognized that if the nature and content of the right, the good, and the virtuous were determined by God's willing them to be right, good, and virtuous, then significant tension would exist between ordinary moral philosophy and God's commands. Kant deflated Christianity into a moral perspective, a set of moral sentiments, an account of moral duty. "Every body must at once perceive, that when this lively and singularly popular narrative is divested of its mystic veil, its spirit and meaning are practically valid and obligatory, at all times, and for the whole world, in as much as they lay before every man a vivid outline of his duty. The moral suggested by the narrative is, that there is absolutely no salvation for mankind apart from their adopting into their inmost sentiments genuine moral principles" (Kant, 1838, 102).

97. Joseph Fuchs concluded similarly that there was nothing distinctive about Christian morality:

> Christians and non-Christians face the same moral questions, and both must seek their solution in genuinely human reflection and according to the same norms . . . ; e.g., whether adultery and premarital intercourse are morally right or can be so, whether the wealthy nations of the world must help the poor nations and to what extent, whether birth control is justified and should be provided, and what types of birth control are worthy of the dignity of the human person. Such questions are questions for all of humanity. If, therefore, our church and other human communities do not always reach the same conclusions, this is not due to the fact that there exists a different morality for Christians from that for non-Christians. (Fuchs 1980, 11)

98. Charles Curran, for example, asserted that Christians and non-Christians share the same morality: "Obviously a personal acknowledgment of Jesus as Lord affects at least the consciousness of the individual and his thematic reflections on his consciousness, but the Christian and the explicitly non-Christian can and do arrive at the same ethical conclusions and can and do share the same general ethical attitudes" (Curran, 1976, 20).

99. Euthanasia and autonomous choice have become so normalized that a teenaged girl in the Netherlands, who reportedly suffered from post-traumatic stress disorder, depression, and anorexia, was recently permitted to refuse medical treatment, food, and water, with the understanding that she would be permitted to die. See https// independent.co.uk/news/world/europe/euthanasia-clinic-suicide-depression-rape-anorexia-netherlands-teenager-noa-pothoven-a8944356.html

100. Following such key figures, Christian bioethics gradually lost its public prominence. It faded from importance, H.T. Engelhardt Jr. argues, precisely because it failed to be authentically Christian. As Engelhardt documents: "After them, it appeared that Christian bioethics was marginalized and lost its salience" (Engelhardt, 2014, 146–7).

101. Consider, for example, Gianna Vattimo who argues that Roman Catholicism needs to radically reform its bioethics in line with contemporary secular thought and the actual lives of its members. As Santiago Zabala summarizes Vattimo's position: "The fact that today most practicing Catholics find their own sexual ethics contrary to the ones preached by the Church amounts to an appeal for the privatization of religion. ... Today, there are few Catholics who do not favor freedom of decision regarding birth control, the marriage of priests, the ordination of women, the free election of bishops by priests, the use of condoms as a precaution against AIDS, the admission to communion of divorcees who remarry, the legalization of abortion ..." (2005, 16). For many Christians, they argue, sexual purity, divorce, abortion, and so forth, have ceased to be important moral issues (see also Rorty, Vattimo and Zabala, 2005, 79).

102. Frank Bruni of the *New York Times* concludes more aggressively: "church leaders must be made 'to take homosexuality off the sin list'" (2015, SR3).

103. As of 2012, Iceland was leading Europe with 66.9 percent of children born outside of marriage; Bulgaria was not far behind with 59.1 percent, Estonia 58.4 percent, Norway 55 percent, and Sweden 54 percent. For the twenty-eight member states of the European Union, the total percentage of children born out of wedlock was approximately 40 percent (Eurostat, 2015: https://ec.europa.eu/eurostat/en/web/products-statistical-books/-/KS-05-14-031). In the United States, the statistics were very similar. In 2013, 40.6 percent of all children were born to unmarried mothers (Martin et al., 2015).

104. The Centers for Disease Control estimates the annual direct health costs of treating sexually transmitted disease in the United States at approximately 17 billion dollars (Centers for Disease Control National Prevention Information Network, STDs Today, 2013). Other estimates place the direct health costs for treating just eight of the major sexually transmitted diseases (chlamydia, gonorrhea, hepatitis B, HIV, human papillomavirus, genital herpes simplex virus type 2, trichomoniasis, and syphilis) at as much as 23 billion dollars per year (Chesson et al. computed the range as 13.9–23 billion dollars in 2010 (2011)).

105. As Mary Jo Iozzio notes: "While eugenics may not be institutionalized with anything like an official position, it holds normative ideological power and is practiced widely

in reproductive medicine and the selective abortion of fetuses; it has become commonplace under the cloak of routine prenatal genetic testing – from the 10th to 20th week of pregnancy, chorionic villus sampling, amniocentesis, and/or maternal serum screening to detect chromosomal and/or genetic variance (in the US, pregnancy termination rates following a diagnosis of Down Syndrome range from 67–92 percent)." (2017, 242).

106. Consider, for example, the 2008 California Supreme Court case *North Coast Women's Care Group v. Benitez*, 44 Cal. 4th 1145 (2008) ruling that the refusal to provide assisted reproductive medicine to a lesbian couple based on the physician's religious views violated state law.

107. See www.nwsurrogacycenter.com. Prospective homosexual fathers can even browse through their list of currently available surrogates, download sample expenses, and contractual details.

108. In the UK, the National Health Services has seen a significant increase in referrals to their Gender Identity Development Services, which is their service for transgender children: "84 children aged between 3 and 7 were referred last year, compared to 20 in 2012/13. The number of children referred to the service under the age of ten had also seen a four-fold increase, from 36 in 2012/13 to 165 last year. Last year there were a total of 2016 referrals for youngsters aged between three and 18, more than six times more than the 314 referrals five years previously" (Turner, 2017).

109. It is worth remembering that the first canon of the first council at Niceae (325 AD) forbade castration. "If anyone has been operated upon by surgeons for a disease, or has been excised by barbarians, let him remain in the clergy. But if anyone has excised himself when well, he must be dismissed even if he is examined after being in the clergy. And henceforth no such person must be promoted to holy orders. But as is self-evident, though such is the case as regards those who affect the matter and dare to excise themselves, if any persons have been eunuchized by barbarians or their lords, but are otherwise found to be worthy, the Canon admits such persons to the clergy" (canon I, First Council of Nicaea, Nicodemus and Agapius, 1957, 163). Apostolic canons XXII, XXIII, and XXIV from the first-century AD tied purposeful self-mutilation to moral and spiritual condemnation. "Individuals who castrate themselves are castigated as self-murderers, plotters against their own lives, and enemies of God's creation. Let no one who has mutilated himself become a clergyman; for he is a murderer of himself, and an enemy of God's creation" (Apostolic canon XXII, Nicodemus and Agapius, 1957, 84). "If anyone who is a clergyman should mutilate himself, let him be deposed from office. For he is a self-murderer" (Apolistic canon XXIII, Nicodemus and Agapius, 1957, 85). "Any layman who has mutilated himself shall be excommunicated for three years. For he is a plotter against his own life" (Apostolic canon XXIV, Nicodemus and Agapius, 1957, 85). Castration which results from hatred of one's body or sex, or as a physical means to help one control sinful passions, is mutilation which inappropriately rejects the fundamental sexual and gendered nature of God's creation; it thereby constitutes a grave moral evil.

110. H. Tristram Engelhardt Jr. argued similarly: "[To] enter worthily into the Liturgy, into communion, the soul must first be prepared ascetically. Traditional Christian bioethics is spiritually therapeutic, liturgical, and Eucharistic, because true moral knowledge comes from union with God, which can only be achieved after spiritual therapy, after

freeing the heart from passions . . ., and because the Christian community achieves, celebrates, and ratifies that union in liturgical worship, all of which conveys theological knowledge" (Engelhardt, 2000, 188).

111. "there is no independent scholarly practice either as a moral philosophy or as an academic theology (e.g., moral theology) that can bring into question that which one knows religiously. Although the claims of a religiously informed morality can be at tension with those of a secular morality or with the requirements of moral philosophy and academic theology, the latter are not accepted as having the authority to reshape the former." (Engelhardt, 2007, 110–11).

112. René Girard, *I See Satan Fall Like Lightning*, trans. James G. Williams (Maryknoll, NY: Orbis Books, 2001), 160; my emphasis.

113. Hexameron, Homily 1.6 (NPNF 2, vol. VIII, p. 55; my emphasis). Saint Basil also says, "I want creation to penetrate you with so much admiration that everywhere, wherever you may be, the least plant may bring to you the clear remembrance of the Creator. If you see the grass of the fields, think of human nature and remember the comparison of the wise Isaiah, 'All flesh is grass' [Is. 40:6]" (Hexameron, Homily 5.2; NPNF 2, VIII, p. 76). As St Ephrem the Syrian said, "because that Being is hidden, He has depicted it by means of what is visible" (quoted by myself in *The Soul's Longing: An Orthodox Christian Perspective on Biblical Interpretation* [South Canaan, PA: St. Tikhon's Monastery Press, 2016], 84).

114. Quoted by St Nikolai Velimirovich in *The Universe As Symbols and Signs: An Essay on Mysticism in the Eastern Church* (Libertyville, IL: Serbian St. Sava Monastery, 1950), 2–3.

115. Ibid.

116. Quaestiones ad Thalassium 51; quoted by Paul M. Blowers, *Exegesis and Spiritual Pedagogy in Maximus the Confessor: An Investigation of the Quaestiones ad Thalassium* (Notre Dame, IN: University of Notre Dame Press, 1991), 110. This language is meant to indicate that real knowledge of God is possible in this way.

117. Mary Sanford, "'How Do You Read?': Theology and Hermeneutics in the Interpretation of New Testament Parables," unpublished doctoral dissertation, University of Kent, Canterbury, UK, 1984.

118. See *The Soul's Longing* for a description.

119. An idea which perhaps came from Aristotle, and/or from just looking at things in a superficial way.

120. See Hans Boersma, *Heavenly Participation: The Weaving of a Sacramental Tapestry* (Grand Rapids, MI: Eerdmans Publishing, 2011), especially ch. 3, pp. 57ff.

121. https://www.realclearscience.com/blog/2013/11/male_and_female_cells_are_not_the_same.html (accessed September 6, 2018).

122. Ibid.

123. Richard M. Weaver, *Ideas Have Consequences* (Chicago: University of Chicago Press, 1948; 2013 edition), 18; my emphasis.

124. For a more in-depth discussion of this, see "By Whose Authority?" by Drs. David and Mary Ford, forthcoming in the online journal *Christian Bioethics*.

125. Gabriele Kuby, *The Global Sexual Revolution: The Destruction of Freedom in the Name of Freedom*, trans. James P. Kirchner (Lifesite/Angelico Press, 2015), 47.

126. Only in order to impose itself as the ultimate meta-narrative.

127. Weaver, *Ideas Have Consequences*, 37.

128. And for such ideas she has received Guggenheim and Rockefeller fellowships, and a $1.5 million Andrew Mellon award. She received a special prize at Yale for her achievements in "lesbian and gay studies," the 50,000 Euro Theodor Adorno prize, and an honorary doctorate in Switzerland. So we see that these ideas are no longer extremely fringe ideas, but they are being mainstreamed very deliberately and aggressively.

129. This was a very popular way of looking at reality in the nineteenth century; Fichte, Darwin, and many others all assumed this basic framework.

130. St Nikolai of Zicha, *Homilies*, trans. Mother Maria (Birmingham, UK: Lazarica Press, 1998), vol. 2, 169.

131. This has been true of secularists from the "Enlightenment" onward; see Mary Ford, *The Soul's Longing*, especially chapters 3 and 6.

132. (Bishop) Alexander Golitzin, *Mystagogy: A Monastic Reading of Dionysius Areopagita* (Collegeville, MN: Liturgical Press, 2013), xix–xxi.

133. Ibid., 163; quoting St Dionysius's Celestial Hierarchy III.1.

134. Ibid., 161. Furthermore, each "reason-endowed being, whether human or angel, discovers within its respective hierarchy its own true place or meaning, i.e., its reality," and rises to the "active apprehension of that same reality and . . . its source in God," enabling it to become "godlike" in union with God (ibid.).

135. St Nikolai of Zicha, *Homilies*, 170; my emphasis.

136. This observation appears to have been introduced in his second chapter of his 1920 *Puto russkogo bogosloviya*, translated as *Ways of Russian Theology*, in *Collected Works of Georges Florovsky, Vol. 5* (Belmont, Mass: Nordland, 1979).

137. Lewis's conceit of the "Amphibious Human Being" is found in *The Screwtape Letters* (1942; New York: HarperCollins, 1996), 37. The description by Screwtape is intended to be disgusting, and diminishes human persons by calling them "half spirit and half animal," but it surely is a distortion of the helpful insight that we make our life both among the animals and in God's presence.

138. *For the Life of the World* (Yonkers, NY: St. Vladimir's Seminary Press, 2018), 21–2. It is helpful to remember the etymological connection between the Latin word *pons* (meaning "bridge") and the priestly connotation of "pontiff."

139. See Moses Gaster's entry "Androgynous," in the 1906 *Jewish Encyclopedia*, available online at http://www.jewishencyclopedia.com/articles/1508-androgynos-hermaphrodite (accessed June 2019). Paul Evdokimov, in *Woman and the Salvation of the World: A Christian Anthropology on the Charisms of Women* (1983; New York: St. Vladimir's Press, ET 1994), seemingly follows the lead of the rabbis, when he asserts on pages 138–39 that male and female are two halves that must find completion in each other, and that a single man or woman is not a complete human being.

140. We must admit that there is a tension in Orthodoxy regarding the permanence of the marriage bond. There is a stream, arguably seen in St Maximus the Confessor (*Ambiguum* 41), that considers the distinction between male and female to be merely God's prevenient concession to the fall. As such, it will disappear at the resurrection, when our glorified bodies will be genderless in every respect; further, there will be no special relationships in the Kingdom, because everything will be centered on Christ. Then there is another tradition, seen in St John Chrysostom's consolation of the young widow (*Ad viduam juniorem*), that recognizes a deep continuity between relationships here and now, and that emphasizes marriage (though not carnal relations) as

continuing beyond death. Saint John promised that young woman that she would see her husband face to face, receiving him back with a beauty even more glorious than the rays of the sun, and even that he might visit her in visions while she awaited her own death. My plea here is that we recognize this tension, as we grapple with the mystery of the resurrection and marriage, and not overuse Jesus's exchange with the Sadducees so as to resolve this problem prematurely.

141. Alexander Schmemann, *The Virgin Mary* (Celebration of the Faith, vol. III; Yonkers, NY: St. Vladimir's Press, 2001), 65.

142. Schmemann, *The Virgin Mary,* 91.

143. Ibid.

144. Homily 26, *Homilies on the Epistle of Paul to the Corinthians* in ed. P. Schaff, *A Select Library of Nicene and Post-Nicene Fathers of the Christian Church, Vol. XII* (New York: Christian Literature Company, 1989), 150. Later in the homily, he points out that radical submission was accentuated because of the woman's disobedience, and was not foundational. Moreover, toward the end of the homily, he rails against male domination expressed in terms of violence or physical discipline of wives.

145. For differences among the fathers regarding the retention of personal characteristics in the eschaton, including the elements of gender and sexual organs, see Elizabeth Clark, *The Origenist Controversy: The Cultural Construction of an Early Christian Debate* (Princeton: Princeton University Press, 1992) and Carolyn Walker Bynum, *The Resurrection of the Body in Western Christianity 200–1336* (New York: Columbia University Press, 1995).

146. It is odd that Evdokimov, in *Woman and the Salvation of the World,* in speculating about the resurrected state, finds help in Emmanuel Swedenborg rather than the fathers, when he declares that the male person and the female person are two halves that must find completion in each other: "Swedenborg gives a luminous explanation of [Jesus's words in Mark 12:25]: the masculine and the feminine (in their totality) find one another again in the form of one single angel" (184). I would counter that to see the human mystery this way would be like saying that the Father *contains* the Son, and so there would be an emanation, rather than a true eternal begetting. It seems to be a modalist form of anthropology, rather than acknowledgment of God's original purpose in creating male and female, as one-yet-two.

147. Surely the dynamic of the story in Genesis suggests both a unity and a distinction, not a half-and-half situation, or else a celibate person is not complete. Jungian archetypes in Evdokimov's work, *Woman and the Salvation of the World,* seem more dominant than the fathers: Evdokimov was a daring theologian and is certainly worth reading. However, much of his work is located, it would seem, in the area of pious opinion, and not established doctrine. Moreover, as Fr Maxym Lysack (Protopresbyter, Christ the Saviour Orthodox Church in Ottawa, and PhD specialist in Maximus, Palamas, and spiritual theology) has suggested to me in private conversation about Evdokimov's work, it seems that Evdokimov, in describing the resurrected state, follows fathers like St Gregory of Nyssa, who owe a debt to Origen, who himself was not condemned until the Fifth Ecumenical Council. Indeed, of real concern to Origen, as he dealt with Genesis and the creation stories, was the connection of anthropology to cosmology (as also we see in Evagrius). Not surprisingly, an extra-biblical cosmology, based on polarities, also shapes Origen's anthropology: namely, the polarity of male–female, to

be resolved at the consummation of all things. We might ask, is Origen, and are those who follow him, imposing an extra layer on the Genesis text, and thus making it carry an unnecessary burden, a burden foreign to the writer? Is it necessary to understand reality in terms of polarities that need to be resolved?

148. Eight of these boundaries were formulated in my monograph *Further Up and Further In: Orthodox Conversations with C. S. Lewis on Scripture and Theology* (Yonkers, NY: St. Vladimir's Press, 2017), 271–2. A ninth (the fifth in the list) has been added for the purpose of this chapter.

149. I first became aware of the incipient debate between evangelical "egalitarians" and "complementarians" when preparing for a 2008 conference at Wheaton College, which issued in a paper entitled "The Gift of the Father—Looking at Salvation History Upside Down," in *Trinitarian Theology for the Church: Scripture, Community, Worship*, ed. D. T. Treier and David E. Lauber (Downer's Grove, IL: InterVarsity Press, 2009), 79–201. A perusal of that paper will help readers to understand how evangelical "egalitarians" initially formulated their critique of evangelical "complementarians" by means of Trinitarian theology. Kevin Giles (*The Trinity & Subordinationism: The Doctrine of God & the Contemporary Gender Debate* [IVP, 2002] and *Jesus and the Father*) seems catalyzed by concerns of social egalitarianism, and reads Gregory according to this focus. Robert Letham (*The Holy Trinity: In Scripture, History, Theology and Worship* [Phillipsburg: P&R Publishing, 2004]) is more measured, and accepts the term *taxis*, but not hierarchy. T.F. Torrance's work (*The Trinitarian Faith: The Evangelical Theology of the Ancient Catholic Church* [Edinburgh: T&T Clark, 1995] and "The Doctrine of the Holy Trinity—Gregory Nazianzen and John Calvin," *Calvin Studies 5* [eds. John H. Leith and W. Stacy Johnson; Richmond, VA: Union Theological Seminary, 1995], 7–19) is, in my view, mostly sane, and wonderfully vigorous. However, Torrance champions St Gregory of Nazianzus over against the other Cappadocians in the matter of *taxis*, but neglects where the saint speaks of the *monarchia* of the Father and of the sense in which He is described as "greater" than the Son. Nor has the skirmish subsided. Most recently, Peter J. Leithart, in "No Son, No Father," pages 119–21 in eds. M.F. Bird and S. Harrower, *Trinity without Hierarchy* (Grand Rapids: Kregel Academic, 2019), has argued that *taxis* and hierarchy should be differentiated, pleading that *taxis* does not imply authority, whereas hierarchy does. Appealing to Athanasius (who obviously was countering the Arian controversy) Leithart problematically imports necessity into the Holy Trinity, confusing logical and necessary causes (i.e., the Father *needs* the Son to be Father!). The entire collection of essays is prefaced by a short piece in which evangelical complementarians such as Wayne Grudem and Bruce Ware are accused of being semi-Arians, but without careful evidence of this charge, and against their own explicit confessions. It is helpful to remember that the concept of Father as both *aitia* (cause) and *archē* (font; beginning) is common to both the Roman Catholic and the Orthodox communions. The burden of proof, therefore, lies with those Protestants who urge a radical qualification or even denial of *taxis* in the Godhead, such as the title *Trinity without Hierarchy* implies. For a more detailed account of the nine boundaries, and of this particular controversy, see the published version of my paper given in the 2019 Pro-Ecclesia conference (Baltimore) entitled "Male and Female, the Image of God, and the Significance of Children," where I develop some of the ideas first presented here.

150. On the importance of normative masculine language for God, see Edith M. Humphrey, "Why We Worship God as Father, Son, and Holy Spirit," *Crux* 32:2 (1996), 2–12, and section IIC of Edith M. Humphrey, *Ecstasy and Intimacy: When the Holy Spirit Meets the Human Spirit* (Grand Rapids: Eerdmans, 2005).

151. In the children's novel entitled *The Voyage of the Dawn Treader,* Lucy Pevensie comes upon a magic book that contains "a spell for the refreshment of the spirit." It is actually a compelling story, full of images that remain in her imagination far after she has forgotten all the details of the narrative. Lewis knew well the power of images: we, too, as Orthodox, use them and are refreshed by them, throughout our liturgies.

152. C.S. Lewis, *Perelandra,* in *The Cosmic Trilogy* (1943; London: Pan/Macmillan, 1990), 331.

153. Fr. John Romanides: https://thoughtsintrusive.wordpress.com/2013/01/20/definition-of-dogma/

154. Portions of this essay draw on sections of a substantially different article, "Totalitarian Transhumanism vs. Christian *Theosis*: From Russian Orthodoxy with Love," appearing in an upcoming special issue of the *Journal of Christian Bioethics* (2020) on sexual ethics.

155. St Ignatius (Brianchaninov), *The Field: Cultivating Salvation,* trans. Nicholas Kotar (Jordanville, NY: Holy Trinity Publications, 2016), Chapter 17, location 2005–2015 (Kindle edition).

156. For a summary scholarly case for foundational Christian aspects of America's founding, see Mark David Hall, *Did America Have a Christian Founding?* (Nashville, TN: Nelson Books, 2019).

157. This at a time of increasing questioning of political assumptions about the science of sexuality, including the genetic determinism of same sex identities, as in a recent study on the complex factors involved with same-sex attraction. See Paul Sullins, "'Born That Way' No More: The New Science of Sexual Orientation," *Public Discourse* (September 30, 2019), https://www.thepublicdiscourse.com/2019/09/57342/ (accessed October 12, 2019).

158. Project Veritas, "Insider Blows Whistle & Exec Reveals Google Plan to Prevent Trump Situation in 2020 on Hidden Cam," *Project Veritas* (June 24, 2019), https://www.projectveritas.com/2019/06/24/insider-blows-whistle-exec-reveals-google-plan-to-prevent-trump-situation-in-2020-on-hidden-cam/ (accessed September 1, 2019). On the developing consensus of cyber "hive minds" see also Shoshana Zuboff, *The Age of Surveillance Capitalism: The Fight for a Human Future at the New Frontier of Power* (New York: Public Affairs, 2019).

159. Shoshana Zuboff, *The Age of Surveillance Capitalism: The Fight for a Human Future at the New Frontier of Power*; James Adams, "Sexbot Apocalypse," *Spectator* (June 17, 2019), https://spectator.us/sexbot-apocalypse/

160. Hannah Arendt, *The Origins of Totalitarianism* (New York: Harcourt, Brace, Jovanivich, 1973).

161. Stéphane Courtois, "Lenin and the Bolshevik Revolution," in *The Totalitarian Legacy of the Bolshevik Revolution,* ed. Alexander Riley and Alfred Kentigern Siewers (Latham, MD: Rowman and Littlefield, 2019), 1–29, at 8.

162. Claude Lefort, "The Image of the Body and Totalitarianism," in *The Great Lie: Classic and Recent Appraisals of Ideology and Totalitarianism,* ed. Flagg Taylor IV (Wilmington, DE: ISI Books, 2011), 177–91, at 182.

163. Eric Voegelin, *New Science of Politics* (Chicago: University of Chicago Press, 1952), and *Science, Politics, and Gnosticism: Two Essays*, ed. Ellis Sandoz (Washington, DC: Regnery Publishing, 1997).

164. Statistics and trends cited in "America's Millennial Baby Bust," editorial, *Wall Street Journal* (May 29, 2019), A14; Justin Dyer, "John Quincy Adams contra Patrick Deneen: Marriage, Family, and the Story of the American Founding," in *Public Discourse* (February. 20, 2019), https://thepublicdiscourse.com/2019/02/48330/, and in James Adams, "Sexbot Apocalypse," *Spectator* (June 17, 2019), https://spectator.us/sexbot-apocalypse/.

165. Jack Jenkins, "'Nones' Now as Big as Evangelicals, Catholics in the United States," *Religion News Service* (March 21, 2019), https://religionnews.com/2019/03/21/nones-now-as-big-as-evangelicals-catholics-in-the-us/

166. In *Planned Parenthood* v. *Casey*, 1992, Justice Anthony Kennedy wrote that liberty is "the right to define one's own concept of existence, of meaning, of the universe, and of the mystery of human life," a point that he upheld again in *Lawrence v. Texas* defending public homosexual rights. See William J. Haun, "'The Mystery of Life' Makes Law a Mystery," *Public Discourse* (July 26, 2013), https://thepublicdiscourse.com/2013/07/10091/. Kennedy did ambiguously later seek to qualify the coercive nature of the approach in the 2018 Supreme Court ruling *Masterpiece Cakeshop, Ltd. v. Colorado Civil Rights Commission,* although weakly.

167. See, for example, the ongoing Masterpiece Cakeshop saga, which has been in court from 2012 to the present: Nico Lang, "Masterpiece Cakeshop Owner in Court Again for Denying LGBTQ Customer," *NBC News* (April 11, 2020), https://nbcnews.com/feature/nbc-out/masterpiece-cakeshop-owner-court-again-denying-lgbtq-customer-n1184656

168. Jess Bravin, "Supreme Court Strikes Down Ban on Immoral or Scandalous Trademarks," *The Wall Street Journal* (June 24, 2019), https://wsj.com/articles/supreme-court-strikes-down-ban-on-immoral-or-scandalous-trademarks-11561387715

169. Scott Alexander, "Gay Rites are Civil Rights," *Slate Star Codex* (July 8, 2019), https://slatestarcodex.com/2019/07/08/gay-rites-are-civil-rites/; James A. Lindsay and Mike Nayna, "Postmodern Religion and the Faith of Social Justice," *Aero Magazine* (December 18, 2018), https://areomagazine.com/2018/12/18/postmodern-religion-and-the-faith-of-social-justice/

170. English transcript of *Financial Times* interview with Putin from Russian government website (June 27, 2019), http://en.kremlin.ru/events/president/news/60836

171. Slavoj Žižek, "Transgender Ideology is Naïve and Incompatible with Freud," *Spectator* (May 31, 2019), https://spectator.us/transgender-dogma-naive-freud/

172. Cited in Lefort, "The Image of the Body and Totalitarianism," 184.

173. Harry Farley, "Astonishing Church Growth in Russia Sees Record Number Training for Priesthood," *Russian Faith* (June 23, 2019) https://russian-faith.com/astonishing-church-growth-russia-sees-record-number-training-priesthood-n2265

174. Bill Muehlenberg, "Faith, Family, and Freedom in Today's Russia," *Russian Faith* (June 20, 2019), https://russian-faith.com/trends/faith-family-and-freedom-todays-russia-n2249

175. On Locke and these issues, see D.C. Schindler, *Freedom from Reality: The Diabolical Quality of Modern Liberalism* (Notre Dame, IN: University of Notre Dame Press, 2017).

176. Lionel Barber, Henry Foy, and Alex Barker, "Vladimir Putin says Liberalism has 'become obsolete,'" *Financial Times* (June 27, 2019), https://ft.com/content/670039ec-98f3-11e9-9573-ee5cbb98ed36

177. See, for example, "His Holiness Patriarch Kirill Meets with President of Billy Graham Evangelistic Association, Mr. Franklin Graham," Russian Orthodox Church Department for External Relations (March 5, 2019), https://mospat.ru/en/2019/03/05/news171189/

178. "Russia Passes Anti-Gay Law," The Associated Press in *The Guardian*, https://theguardian.com/world/2013/jun/30/russia-passes-anti-gay-law

179. C.S. Lewis, *The Abolition of Man* (New York: HarperOne, 2015), appendix.

180. Hélène Barthélemy, "How the World Congress of Families Serves Russian Orthodox Political Interests" (May 16, 2018), https://splcenter.org/hatewatch/2018/05/16/how-world-congress-families-serves-russian-orthodox-political-interests. Jeremy Tedesco, "How Long Will Amazon Follow Southern Poverty Law Center 'Hate Group' Slander," *The Daily Signal* (June 5, 2019), https://dailysignal.com/2019/06/05/how-long-will-amazon-follow-southern-poverty-law-centers-hate-group-slander/

181. Nun Cornelia Rees, "A Provocation by a Provocateur," *Orthodox Christianity* (October 12, 2019), OrthodoxChristian.com/124602.html (accessed October 12, 2019).

182. S. L. Frank, *The Unknowable: An Ontological Introduction to the Philosophy of Religion*, trans. Boris Jakim (Akron, OH: Ohio University Press, 1983), 47.

183. Ibid., 116–17.

184. S. L. Frank, *The Spiritual Foundations of Society: An Introduction to Social Philosophy*, trans. Boris Jakim (Athens, OH: Ohio University Press, 1987), 148.

185. On the administrative technocratic state, see (among others) Eric Voegelin, *The New Science of Politics, Order and History* (Chicago: University of Chicago Press, 1987).

186. The psychoanalytic theorist Julia Kristeva, herself of Bulgarian Orthodox background, has written of that in part. Kristeva (drawing on Lacan) describes the Imaginary in a triad with elements of the Real and the Symbolic, a secular model for the cultural formation of the self, which she paralleled with the Christian Trinity (the Real related to the Father, the Imaginary related to the Son as the Image of God, and the Symbolic to the Holy Spirit). Kristeva argued in 1989 that in Orthodox Christian cultures, following Trinitarian theology without the Latin addition of the *filioque* to the Nicene Creed, the Imaginary was balanced more equally by the Real and the Symbolic, in the process of how culture shaped the self. See Julia Kristeva, chapter on "Dostoevsky, the Writing of Suffering, and Forgiveness," in *Black Sun: Depression and Melancholia*, trans. Leon S. Roudiez (New York: Columbia University Press, 1989), 173–218. For more on this, see my "Introduction: Song, Tree, and Spring: Environmental Meaning and Environmental Humanities," in Alfred Kentigern Siewers, *Re-Imagining Nature: Environmental Humanities and Ecosemiotics* (Lewisburg, PA: Bucknell University Press, 2015), 1–44. Kristeva later would argue that the relational identity fostered by the prototype Trinity, continued in the Orthodox East, was responsible for dictatorial regimes there. But the inconsistency of that political argument (made in support of her own transition from Bulgarian to French culture as an emigrant) is evident in her appreciation of French colonial operations, the totalitarian regime of Mao, and the Soviet crushing of the Prague Spring, as well as the atheism, in historically Orthodox

lands, of the Communist regimes in power there, which she reportedly served as a Bulgarian spy in France.

187. Peter Brown, *The Body and Society: Men, Women, and Sexual Renunciation in Early Christianity* (New York: Columbia University Press, 2008), xlv–slvi.

188. Fr. Andrew Louth, "The Body in Western Catholic Christianity," in *Religion and the Body*, ed. Sarah Coakley (Cambridge: Cambridge University Press, 1997), 113–30, at 129.

189. Nicolas Zernov, *Moscow the Third Room* (London: Society for Promoting Christian Knowledge, 1937), 21.

190. Richard Pevear, citing Frank, in Dostoevsky, *The Adolescent*, trans. Richard Pevear and Larissa Volokhonsky (New York: Vintage, 2003), vii, f.n.

191. On which, see Stéphane Courtois, "Lenin and the Bolshevik Revolution.".

192. Lefort, "The Image of the Body and Totalitarianism," 184.

193. Anthony N. Kaldellis, *The Byzantine Republic: People and Power in New Rome* (Cambridge, MA: Harvard University Press, 2015), ix.

194. This is the major thesis in Frank, *The Spiritual Foundations of Society: An Introduction to Social Philosophy*, throughout. See also S. L. Frank, *The Light Shineth in Darkness: An Essay in Christian Ethics and Social Philosophy*, trans. Boris Jakim (Athens, OH: Ohio University Press, 1989), 136–40.

195. H. Tristram Engelhardt, Jr., *The Foundations of Christian Bioethics* (Lisse, The Netherlands: Swets & Zeitlinger, 2000), 246–7.

196. St Basil, *Ascetical Works*, The Fathers of the Church, vol. 9, trans. Sr. M. Monica Wagner (Washington, DC: Catholic Univ. of America Press, 1962), 233 (response to Question 2 in The Long Rules).

197. Vladimir Lossky, *The Mystical Theology of the Eastern Church* (Crestwood, NY: St Vladimir's Seminary Press, 1997), 101, 126.

198. St Maximus the Confessor, "Two Hundred Texts on Theology: First Century," in *The Philokalia*, vol. 2, ed. and trans. G.E.H. Palmer, Philip Sherrard, Kallistos Ware (London: Faber and Faber, 1981), 127.

199. St John of Damascus, "The Philosophical Chapters," in *Writings*, trans. Frederic H. Chase, Jr. (Middleton, DE: Ex Fontibus, 2015), 8.

200. St Maximus the Confessor, *Ambigua ad Iohannem* 7 and 22. See, for example, Fr. Nicholas Constans, ed. and trans., *On Difficulties in the Church Fathers*, vol. 1 (Cambridge, MA: Harvard University Press, 2014), 75–141, and 448–51. The philosopher and patristic scholar David Bradshaw concludes that the association of divine energies with *logoi* in the *Ambigua* involves a distinction in which the energies are known effectively through the *logoi* (personal communication).

201. Alexander Dugin, *The Fourth Political Theory*, trans. Mark Sleboda and Michael Millerman (London: Arktos, 2012), 189.

202. Ibid., 190.

203. Alexander Dugin, *Martin Heidegger: The Philosophy of a New Beginning*, trans. Nina Kouprionova (Augusta, GA: Washington Summit, 2014).

204. Dugin, *The Fourth Political Theory*, 192.

205. Biblical quotations here follow the King James (or Authorized) Version in the *New Cambridge Paragraph Bible with Apocrypha* (Cambridge: Cambridge University Press, 2011), in consultation with the *Orthodox Study Bible*, ed. St Athanasius Academy (Nashville, TN: Thomas Nelson, 2008).

206. On marital asceticism in Orthodox Christianity, see as a summary Fr. Josian Trenham, *Marriage and Virginity According to St. John Chrysostom* (Platina, CA: St Herman of Alaska Monastery, 2013).

207. Hieromonk Luke (Murianka), "New Age Philosophy, Orthodox Thought, and Marriage," https://jordanville.org/files/Articles/New_Age_Philosophy.pdf. This originally appeared in *Orthodox Life*, no. 3, 1997.

208. St Maximus the Confessor, *On Difficulties in the Church Fathers: The Ambigua*, vol. 2, Nicholas Constas, ed. and trans., Dumbarton Oaks Medieval Library 29 (Cambridge, MA: Harvard Univ. Press, 2014), *Ambigua* 67:10, pp. 296–9. See also Doru Costache, "Living above Gender: Insights from Saint Maximus the Confessor," *Journal of Early Christian Studies* 21 (2013), 261–90.

209. Hieromonk Damascene Christiansen in a note to Fr Seraphim Rose, *Genesis, Creation, and Early Man: The Orthodox Christian Vision*, 2nd ed. (Platina, CA: St Herman of Alaska BrotherhoBood, 2011), 203.

210. Lefort, "The Image of the Body and Totalitarianism," 177–91 (originally published in 1955); Igor R. Shafarevich, *The Socialist Phenomenon*, trans. William Tjalsma (Harper & Row, 1980).

211. Ibid., 281.

212. Oscar Lopex, "LGBT Suicide Risk at Crisis Proportions among LGBT+ Youth—U.S. Research," *Reuters* (June 27, 2019), https://reuters.com/article/usa-lgbt-suicide/suicide-risk-at-crisis-proportions-among-lgbt-youth-us-research-idUSL2N23YoIo; [no space here, since the citation of Stanton is also in n50]; Glenn T. Stanton, "CA Legislators Blame Religious People for High LGBT Suicide Rates," https://thefederalist.com/2019/06/27/ca-legislators-blame-religious-people-high-lgbt-suicide-rates/

213. Julie Bindel, "The Truth behind America's Most Famous Gay Hate Murder," *The Guardian* (October 26, 2014), https://theguardian.com/world/2014/oct/26/the-truth-behind-americas-most-famous-gay-hate-murder-matthew-shepard

214. Ryan Anderson, "Sex Reassignment Doesn't Work: Here Is the Evidence," *Heritage Foundation* (March 9, 2018), https://heritage.org/gender/commentary/sex-reassignment-doesnt-work-here-the-evidence

215. Lisa Littman, "Rapid-Onset Gender Dysphoria in Adolescents and Young Adults: Parent Reports," *PLOS* 1:14 (2018), https://journals.plos.org/plosone/article?id=10.1371/journal.pone.0202330. Note that the study reported on in the article predictably was controversial, which was revised in response to criticisms to highlight its basis in "parent perspectives."

216. Slavoj Žižek, "Transgender Ideology Is Naïve and Incompatible with Freud," *Spectator* (May 31, 2019), https://spectator.us/transgender-dogma-naive-freud/

217. Rod Dreher, "Some Woman's Husband, Some Kids' Father," *American Conservative* (June 27, 2019), https://theamericanconservative.com/dreher/transgender-christine-benvenuto-joy-ladin/?fbclid=IwAR3V9oymoql-jNXXG1gXz8peQX41h5IlSPTD-N9UDXZsahpoOkM8534UDadM

218. George Yancey, *Dehumanizing Christians: Cultural Competition in a Multicultural World* (New York: Routledge, 2017).

219. See Justin Dyer, "John Quincy Adams contra Patrick Deneen: Marriage, Family, and the Story of the American Founding," *Public Discourse* (February. 19, 2019), https://thepublicdiscourse.com/2019/02/48330/

220. "John Adams to Massachusetts Militia," *Founders Online, National Archives* (October. 11, 1798), https://founders.archives.gov/documents/Adams/99-02-02-3102

221. Holy Synod of the Russian Orthodox Church (Department for External Church Relations, 2006), https://mospat.ru/en/documents/dignity-freedom-rights/ii/, which cites the passage from St Gregory of Nyssa's *Sermon on the Dead*.

222. Patriarch Kirill, "Address by His Holiness Patriarch Kirill of Moscow and All Russia at the Solemn Act Marking the 10th Anniversary of the 2009 Local Council and Patriarchal Enthronement," The Russian Orthodox Church Department for External Church Relations (January 31, 2019), https://mospat.ru/en/2019/01/31/news169822/. The translation is slightly edited in my own translation.

223. David Gelernter, "Giving Up Darwin," *The Claremont Review of Books* (Spring 2019), 104–9. For an Orthodox Christian perspective, see Fr. Seraphim Rose, *Genesis, Creation, and Early Man: The Orthodox Christian Vision*, ed. Fr. Damascene Christiansen, 2nd ed. (Platina, CA: St Herman of Alaska Press, 2010).

224. St. Theophan the Recluse, *Raising Them Right: A Saint's Advice on Raising Children* (Mount Herman, CA: Conciliar Press, 1989), 66–7.

225. Bp. Irenaios of Ekaterinburg, *On the Upbringing of Children* (Wildwood, CA: St. Xenia Skete, 1991), 24–5.

226. St. John Chrysostom, *An Address on Vainglory and the Right Way for Parents to Bring Up Their Children*, in M. L. W. Laistner, *Christianity and Pagan Culture* (Ithaca: Cornell University Press, 1951), 96; translation and emphasis mine.

227. For example, see Robbie Low's article, "The Truth about Men and Church," in *Touchstone Magazine* (June, 2003), http://www.touchstonemag.com/archives/article.php?id=16-05-024-v (accessed July 12, 2019).

228. This talk is available online at http://orthodoxinfo.com/praxis/marriage.aspx (accessed July 12, 2019).

229. David and Mary Ford, and Alf Kentigern Siewers, eds., *Glory and Honor: Orthodox Christian Resources for Marriage* (Yonkers, NY: St. Vladimir's Seminary Press, 2016).

230. See my talk, "The Home as a Little Church: The Wisdom of St. John Chrysostom" at https://orthodox-stl.org/little_church.html (accessed July 12, 2019).

231. Dr. Jean-Claude Larchet, *The New Media Epidemic: The Undermining of Society, Family, and Our Own Soul* (Jordanville, NY: Holy Trinity Publications, 2019).

232. See https://www.projectmexico.org (accessed September 3, 2019).

233. For a magnificent refutation of these errors, see Benjamin Wiker and Jonathan Witt, *A Meaningful World: How the Arts and Sciences Reveal the Genius of Nature* (Downers Grove, IL: IVP Academic, 2006).

234. See http://www.crownthem.org/sage/ (accessed July 12, 2019).

235. Dr. Philip Mamalakis, *Parenting Toward the Kingdom: Orthodox Christian Principles of Child-Rearing* (Chesterton, IN: Ancient Faith Publishing, 2016).

236. "On Vainglory and the Proper Upbringing of Children," in Laistner, 119–20.

237. Homily III on Philemon; *Nicene and Post-Nicene Fathers*, first series, vol. XIII, 557; emphasis mine.

238. Homily II on Titus; NPNF 1, XIII, 524–25; translation and emphasis mine.

239. Pornography, a particularly toxic affliction for young men, is becoming normalized. See my article in the *Minneapolis Star and Tribune*: "Pornography Is an Affliction for Young Men. And It's Been Mainstreamed. It Comes from the Depths of Hell to Destroy

Their Characters before They Can Grow into a Healthy Sense of Who They Are", http://www.startribune.com/pornography-is-an-affliction-for-young-men-and-it-s-been-mainstreamed/413461753/ (accessed January 27, 2019).

240. I use the term "sexual self-abuse" ("self-abuse," in short) as formerly used in "polite company" instead of the crude or the ostensibly clinical terms preferred in American society today. The latter implies a behaviorist understanding that mutes the relational dimension necessary for healing.

241. "An Appeal for Theological Affirmation," https://worldview.carnegiecouncil.org/archive/worldview/1975/04/2511.html (accessed October 23, 2019). Seven additional religious leaders signed the final document, including Fr. Thomas Hopko, at that time a professor of theology at St. Vladimir's Orthodox Theological Seminary.

242. Alexander Schmemann, *For the Life of the World: Sacraments and Orthodoxy* (Yonkers: St. Vladimir's Seminary Press, 2018 [original edition, 1973]), 139.

243. Ibid.; italics in the original.

244. Ibid., 139–40; italics in the original.

245. Ibid., 140; italics in the original.

246. Ibid.; italics added.

247. Ibid.

248. See the latest Pew Research Center Religion & Public Life report released on October 17, 2019: *In U.S., Decline of Christianity Continues at Rapid Pace: An update on America's changing religious landscape*, https://pewforum.org/2019/10/17/in-u-s-decline-of-christianity-continues-at-rapid-pace/ (accessed October 23, 2019).

249. Alexander Schmemann, *The Eucharist* (Crestwood: St. Vladimir's Seminary Press, 1998), 10.

250. *In U.S., Decline of Christianity Continues at Rapid Pace: An update on America's changing religious landscape* (accessed October 23, 2019).

251. See *Homily of St. John Chrysostom:* "Against Those Who Have Abandoned the Church and Deserted it for Hippodromes and Theatres," http://tertullian.org/fathers/chrysostom_against_theatres_and_circuses.htm (accessed January 28, 2019).

252. Robert P. George, *Conscience and Its Enemies: Confronting the Dogmas of Liberal Secularism* (Wilmington, DE: ISI Books, 2013), 9.

253. Rodney Stark, *The Triumph of Faith: Why the World Is More Religious Than Ever* (Wilmington: ISI Books, 2015), 193.

254. Ibid., 196.

255. Supreme Court of the United States, *Obergefell v. Hodges*, Justice Alito, with whom Justice Scalia and Justice Thomas join, dissenting (June 26, 2015), https://law.cornell.edu/supremecourt/text/14-556#writing-14-556_DISSENT_7 (accessed October 23, 2019).

256. H. Richard Niebuhr, *Christ and Culture* (New York: Harper and Row, 1951).

257. St. Benedict of Nursia, *St. Benedict's Rule for Monasteries*, trans. Leonard J. Doyle (Collegeville, MN: The Liturgical Press, 1948), Chap. 1, p. 6.

258. Alisdair MacIntyre, *After Virtue*, 2nd ed. (Notre Dame, IN: University of Notre Dame Press,1984), 263.

259. The term was introduced in a book coauthored by Christian Smith and Melinda Lundquist Denton, *Soul Searching: The Religious and Spiritual Lives of American Teenagers* (New York: Oxford University Press, 2005).

260. Rod Dreher, *The Benedict Option: A Strategy for Christians in a Post-Christian Nation* (New York: Sentinel, 2017), 11.

261. Paul Connerton, *How Societies Remember* (Cambridge: Cambridge University Press, 1989).

262. Mary Douglas, *Natural Symbols: Explorations in Cosmology* (London and New York: Routledge, 1996).

263. Connerton, *How Societies Remember*; see Chapter 1, 6–40.

264. Connerton, *How Societies Remember*, 23.

265. Douglas, *Natural Symbols*, 41.

266. Philip Rieff, *The Triumph of the Therapeutic: Uses of Faith after Freud* (Chicago: University of Chicago Press, 1966).

267. Ibid., 17.

268. Peter Brown, *The Body and Society: Men, Women, and Sexual Renunciation in Early Christianity* (New York: Columbia University Press, 2008), xlv–xlvi.

269. Douglas, *Natural Symbols*, 44.

270. Alasdair MacIntyre, *After Virtue: A Study in Moral Theory* (2nd ed.; Notre Dame, IN: University of Notre Dame Press, 1984), 263.

271. Rod Dreher, *The Benedict Option: A Strategy for Christians in a Post-Christian Nation* (New York: Sentinel, 2017), 2, 18.

272. "(JP 1–02)—A line which indicates the most forward positions of friendly forces in any kind of military operation at a specific time. The FLOT normally identifies the forward location of covering and screening forces. (Army)—The FLOT may be at, beyond, or short of the FEBA [i.e., Forward Edge of the Battle Area]. An enemy FLOT indicates the forwardmost position of hostile forces. . . .": https://www.globalsecurity.org/military/library/policy/army/fm/101-5-1/f545-f.htm (accessed May 17, 2019).

273. Ibid., 82, 184.

274. "Benedict Option or Constantine Project: Part 2," Circe Institute (March 15, 2017), https://www.circeinstitute.org/blog/benedict-or-constantine-part-2 (accessed May 17, 2019). Orthodox Jewish political commentator Ben Shapiro echoed that concern when he spoke to a gathering of Roman Catholic business leaders at a Legatus conference in California in January 2019. LifeSiteNews reported: "Shapiro predicted that state governments in the U.S. will assail religious schools on the basis of LGBTQ laws, revoke their accreditation and ultimately eliminate the non-profit status of religious institutions. 'It will come into the home, too,' said Shapiro, 'and kids will be removed from homes because if it is repressive to teach kids about traditional values in schools, certainly it is more repressive to teach traditional values at home.'" That scenario hits close to home: the hard-won accreditation and reaccreditations of Holy Trinity Seminary by the New York State Board of Regents may be an early target of the radical left in higher education. See https://www.lifesitenews.com/news/ben-shapiro-this-time-leftist-radicals-are-coming-for-catholics-first (accessed May 17, 2019).

275. "Benedict Option or Constantine Project: Part 2," Circe Institute, March 15, 2017.

276. Ibid.

277. "Benedict Option or Constantine Project: Part 1," Circe Institute (March 15, 2017), https://www.circeinstitute.org/blog/benedict-option-or-constantine-project (accessed May 17, 2019).

278. https://www.poynter.org/reporting-editing/2014/today-in-media-history-mr-dooley-the-job-of-the-newspaper-is-to-comfort-the-afflicted-and-afflict-the-comfortable/(accessed May 17, 2019).

279. Joshua Steely, "Must Say No," *Touchstone Magazine* 32:5 (September/October 2019), 23.

280. Frederick B. Chary, *The Bulgarian Jews and the Final Solution 1940–1944* (Pittsburgh: University of Pittsburgh Press, 1972), 149, quoted in Alexander F. C. Webster, *The Romanian Legionary Movement An Orthodox Christian Assessment of Anti-Semitism* (Carl Beck Papers, no. 502; Pittsburgh: University of Pittsburgh Center for Russian and East European Studies, 1986), 5.

281. Irene Archos, "Mother Maria of Paris Says 'OXI!' to the Nazi Mass Murder Machine" (November 2, 2015), https://greekamericangirl.com/mother-maria-of-paris-says-oxi-to-the-nazi-mass-murder-machine/ (accessed May 17, 2019).

282. Alexander F.C. Webster, "Death of a Patriarch," *The Wall Street Journal* (April 15, 2005), W13.

283. If I may be permitted a personal note, I was blessed to witness that seminal Commencement Address in person as a graduating M.T.S. student from Harvard Divinity School, with then Bishop-Elect Maximus Aghiourgoussis as the special guest of my wife and myself. It was one of the most significant public events in my entire life.

284. "Metropolitan Onuphry Calls on Poroshenko to Change Ukraine's Course to One of Peace, Unity" (March 22, 2019), http://orthochristian.com/120097.html (accessed May 17, 2019).

# Bibliography

Alexander, Bruce K. 2008. *The Globalization of Addiction: A Study in Poverty of the Spirit.* New York: Oxford University Press.

Anderson, Ryan. 2018. *When Harry Became Sally: Responding to the Transgender Moment.* New York: Encounter Books.

Arendt, Hannah. 1973. *The Origins of Totalitarianism.* New York: Harcourt, Brace, Jovanivich.

Basil, St. 1962. Ascetical Works: The Long Rules. In *The Fathers of the Church*, vol. 9, ed. R.J. Deferrari et al., trans. M.M. Sister and C.S.C Wagner. Washington, DC: The Catholic University of America Press.

Basil, St. 1962. *Ascetical Works, The Fathers of the Church*, vol. 9, trans. Sr. M. Monica Wagner. Washington, DC: Catholic Univ. of America Press, 233.

Behr, John. 2001. *The Way to Nicaea.* Crestwood, NY: St Vladmir's Seminary Press.

Behr, John. 2004. *The Nicene Faith.* Crestwood, NY: St Vladimir's Seminary Press.

Benedict of Nurisa, St. 1948. *St. Benedict's Rule for Monasteries*, trans. Leonard J. Doyle. Collegeville, MN: The Liturgical Press.

Boersma, Hans. 2011. *Heavenly Participation: The Weaving of a Sacramental Tapestry.* Grand Rapids, MI: Eerdmans Publishing.

Brown, Peter. 1988. *The Body and Society: Men, Women, and Sexual Renunciation in Early Christianity.* New York: Columbia University Press, 113.

Brown, Peter. 2008. *The Body and Society: Men, Women, and Sexual Renunciation in Early Christianity.* New York: Columbia University Press, xlv–xlvi.

Bruni, Frank. Same Sex Sinners. *New York Times*, April 5, 2015, p. SR3.

Bynum, Carolyn Walker. 1995. *The Resurrection of the Body in Western Christianity 200–1336.* New York: Columbia University Press.

Camus, Albert. 1991. *The Rebel*, trans. Anthony Bower. New York: Alfred A. Knopf, 37.

Centers for Disease Control and Prevention. 2013. CDC Fact Sheet, STD trends in the United States, 2011 National Data for Chlamydia, Gonorrhea, and Syphilis. www.cdc.gov/std/stats11/trends-2011.pdf (accessed July 28, 2015).

Chary, Frederick B. 1972. *The Bulgarian Jews and the Final Solution 1940–1944.* Pittsburgh: University of Pittsburgh Press, 149.

Cherry, M.J. 2010a. Human Rights, Social Justice, and Other Secular Evils: Why Christian Ethics and Christian Bioethics must be Traditionally Christian. *St. Vladimir's Theological Quarterly* 54: 133–63.

Cherry, Mark. 2015. Individually Directed Informed Consent and the Decline of the Family in the West. In *Family-Oriented Informed Consent: East Asian & American Perspectives*, ed. Ruiping Fan, 43–62. Dordrecht: Springer.

Cherry, N.J. 2010b. Parental Authority and Pediatric Bioethical Decision Making. *The Journal of Medicine and Philosophy* 35: 553–72.

Chesson, Harrell W., Thomas L. Gift, Kwame Owusu-Edusei Jr., Guoyu Tao, Ana P. Johnson, and Charlotte K. Kent. 2011. A Brief Review of the Estimated Economic Burden of Sexually Transmitted Diseases in the United States: Inflation-adjusted updates of Previously Published Cost Studies. *Sexually Transmitted Disease* 38 (10): 889–91.

Chrysostom, J. St. 2004. Homily III on Colossians. In *Nicene and Post-Nicene Fathers*, vol. 13, ed. P. Schaff, 270–5. Peabody, MA: Hendrickson Publishers.

Chrysostom, St. John. 1951. *An Address on Vainglory and the Right Way for Parents to Bring Up Their Children*, in M. L. W. Laistner, *Christianity and Pagan Culture*. Ithaca: Cornell University Press, 96.

Clark, Elizabeth. 1992. *The Origenist Controversy: The Cultural Construction of an Early Christian Debate*. Princeton: Princeton University Press.

Clark, P.A. 2008. Richard McCormick, SJ and Dual Epistemology. *Christian Bioethics* 14: 236–71.

Connerton, Paul. 1989. *How Societies Remember*. Cambridge: Cambridge University Press.

Constans, Fr. Nicholas, ed. and trans. 2014. *On Difficulties in the Church Fathers*, vol. 1. Cambridge, MA: Harvard University Press, 75–141, and 448–51.

Courtois, Stéphane. 2019. Lenin and the Bolshevik Revolution. In *The Totalitarian Legacy of the Bolshevik Revolution*, ed. Alexander Riley and Alfred Kentigern Siewers, 1–29. Latham, MD: Rowman and Littlefield.

Cox, J. 2013. "The Only Safe Guide Is Love": Models of Engaging Luther's Ethical Hermeneutic for Theological Responses to the Affirmation of Same-sex Sexuality. *A Journal of Theology* 52 (4): 365–72.

Curran, C. 1976. *Catholic Moral Theology in Dialogue*. Notre Dame, IN: University of Notre Dame Press.

Dabhoiwala, Faramerz. 2012. *The Origins of Sex: A History of the First Sexual Revolution*. Oxford: Oxford University Press.

Douglas, Mary. 1996. *Natural Symbols: Explorations in Cosmology*. London and New York: Routledge.

Dreher, Rod. 2017. *The Benedict Option: A Strategy for Christians in a Post-Christian Nation*. New York: Sentinel, 2, 11, 18.

Dugin, Alexander. 2012. *The Fourth Political Theory*, trans. Mark Sleboda and Michael Millerman. London: Arktos, 189.

Dugin, Alexander. 2014. *Martin Heidegger: The Philosophy of a New Beginning*, trans. Nina Kouprionova. Augusta, GA: Washington Summit.

Engelhardt, H.T., Jr. 1996. *The Foundations of Bioethics*, second edition. New York: Oxford University Press.

Engelhardt, H.T., Jr. 2000. *The Foundations of Christian Bioethics*. Lisse: Swetz & Zeitlinger.

Engelhardt, H.T., Jr. 2007. The Euthyphro's Dilemma Reconsidered: A Variation on a Theme from Brody on Halakhic Method. In *Pluralistic Casuistry: Moral Arguments, Economic Realities, and Political Theory*, ed. M.J. Cherry and A. Iltis, 109–30. Dordrecht: Springer.

Engelhardt, H.T., Jr. 2014. The Recent History of Christian Bioethics Critically Reassessed. *Christian Bioethics* 20 (2): 146–67.

Engelhardt, H.T., Jr. 2017. *After God: Morality & Bioethics in a Secular Age*. Yonkers: St. Vladimir's Seminary Press.

Epstein, I., ed. 1994. Sanhedrin. Babylonian Talmud, trans. Jacob Shachter. London: Soncino Press.

Evagrios the Solitary. 1988. On Prayer. In *The Philokalia*, 3 vols., ed. Sts. Nikodimos and Markarios, trans. G.E.H. Palmer, Philip Sherrard and Kallistos Ware, vol. 1, 55–71. Boston: Faber and Faber.

Ferrara, Christopher. 2012. *Liberty; or, the God That Failed: Policing the Sacred and Constructing the Myths of the Secular State, from Locke to Obama*. Tacoma, WA: Angelico Press.

Florensky, Pavel. 1997. *The Pillar and Ground of the Truth: An Essay in Orthodox Theodicy in Twelve Letters*, trans. Boris Jakim. Princeton: Princeton University Press, 213.

Florensky, Pavel. 2014. *At the Crossroads of Science and Mysticism: On the Cultural-Historical Place and Premises of the Christian World-Understanding*, trans. Boris Jakim. Kettering, OH: Semantron Press, 120–2.

Ford, David and Mary and Alf Kentigern Siewers, eds. 2016. *Glory and Honor: Orthodox Christian Resources for Marriage*. Yonkers, NY: St. Vladimir's Seminary Press.

Francis, Pope. 2013. *Apostolic Exhortation Evangelii Gaudium of the Holy Father Francis to the Bishops, Clergy, Consecrated Persons and the Lay Faithful on the Proclamation of the Gospel in Today's World*. Vatican City: Vatican Press.

Frank, S.L. 1983. *The Unknowable: An Ontological Introduction to the Philosophy of Religion*, trans. Boris Jakim. Akron, OH: Ohio University Press, 47.

Frank, S.L. 1987. *The Spiritual Foundations of Society: An Introduction to Social Philosophy*, trans. Boris Jakim. Athens, OH: Ohio University Press, 148.

Frank, S.L. 1989. *The Light Shineth in Darkness: An Essay in Christian Ethics and Social Philosophy*, trans. Boris Jakim. Athens, OH: Ohio University Press, 136–40.

Freedman, L. 2014. Forgiveness in the Abortion Clinic. *Atrium: The Report of the Northwestern Medical Humanities and Bioethics Program* 12 (Winter): 6–8.

Fuchs, J. 1980. Is There a Specifically Christian Morality? In *Readings in Moral Theology No. 2: The Distinctiveness of Christian Ethics*, ed. C. Curran and R. McCormick, 3–20. New York: Paulist Press.

Gelernter, David. 2019. Giving Up Darwin. *The Claremont Review of Books* (Spring): 104–9.

George, Robert P. 2013. *Conscience and Its Enemies: Confronting the Dogmas of Liberal Secularism*. Wilmington, DE: ISI Books, 9.

Gillespie, Michael. 1996. *Nihilism before Nietzsche*. Chicago: University of Chicago Press.

Girard, René. 2001. *I See Satan Fall Like Lightning*, trans. James G. Williams, 160. Maryknoll, NY: Orbis Books.

Golitzin, Alexander. 2013. *Mystagogy: A Monastic Reading of Dionysius Areopagita*. Collegeville, MN: Liturgical Press, xix–xxi.

Haidt, Jonathan. 2012. *The Righteous Mind: Why Good People Are Divided by Politics and Religion*. New York: Random House.

Hall, Mark David. 2019. *Did America Have a Christian Founding?* Nashville, TN: Nelson Books.

Harper, Kyle. 2013. *From Shame to Sin: The Christian Transformation of Sexual Morality in Late Antiquity*. Cambridge, MA: Harvard University Press, 41–2, 52–5.

Hart, David Bentley. 2009. Christ and Nothing (No Other God). In *In the Aftermath: Provocations and Laments*. Grand Rapids, MI: Eerdmans, 1–19.

Heidegger, Martin. 2002. The Age of the World Picture. In Heidegger, *Off the Beaten Track*, ed. and trans. Julian Young and Kenneth Haynes, 83. Cambridge: Cambridge University Press.

Heidegger, Martin, 2008. The Question Concerning Technology. In Basic Writings, London: HarperCollins. 307–41.

Holland, S., K. Labacqz, and L. Zoloth. 2001. *The Human Embryonic Stem Cell Debate*. Cambridge: MIT Press.

Humphrey, Edith M. 1996. Why We Worship God as Father, Son, and Holy Spirit. *Crux* 32 (2): 2–12.

Humphrey, Edith M. 2005. *Ecstasy and Intimacy: When the Holy Spirit Meets the Human Spirit*. Grand Rapids: Eerdmans.

Ignatius (Brianchaninov), St. 2016. *The Field: Cultivating Salvation*, trans. Nicholas Kotar. Jordanville, NY: Holy Trinity Publications.

Irenaios of Ekaterinburg. 1991. *On the Upbringing of Children*. Wildwood, CA: St. Xenia Skete, 24–5.

Iozzio, M. J. 2017. Radical Dependence and the Imago Dei: Bioethical Implications of Access to Healthcare for People with Disabilities. *Christian Bioethics* 23: 234–60.

Jacques Ellul. 1967. *The Technological Society*. New York: Random House.

James, King. 2011. *New Cambridge Paragraph Bible with Apocrypha*. Cambridge: Cambridge University Press.

Jaggar, A. 2009. Abortion Rights and Gender Justice Worldwide: An Essay in Political Philosophy. In *Abortion: Three Perspectives*, ed. M. Tooley, C. Wolf-Devine, P. E. Devine, and A. Jaggar, 120–82. New York: Oxford University Press.

Joffe, C. 2011. Working with Dr. Tiller: Staff Recollections of Women's Health Care Services of Wichita. *Sexual & Reproductive Health* 43: 199–204.

John of Damascus, St. 2015. The Philosophical Chapters. In *Writings*, trans. Frederic H. Chase, Jr., 8. Middleton, DE: Ex Fontibus.

Jonas, Hans. 2001. *The Gnostic Religion*. Boston: Beacon Press, 322.

Kaldellis, Anthony N. 2015. *The Byzantine Republic: People and Power in New Rome*. Cambridge, MA: Harvard University Press, ix.

Kant, I. 1838. *Religion within the Boundary of Pure Reason*, trans. J.W. Semple. Edinburgh: Thomas Clark.

Kierkegaard, Søren. 1980. *The Sickness unto Death: A Christian Psychological Exposition for Upbuilding and Awakening*, trans. Howard V. Hong and Edna H. Hong. Princeton: Princeton University Press, 131.

Kittel, Gerhard, ed. 1964. *Theological Dictionary of the New Testament*. Grand Rapids: Eerdmans, vol. 1, 122–4.

Kuby, Gabriele. 2015. *The Global Sexual Revolution: The Destruction of Freedom in the Name of Freedom*, trans. James P. Kirchner. Lifesite/Angelico Press, 47.

Lachs, J. 2014. Physician Assisted Suicide Is Ethical. In *Contemporary Debates in Bioethics*, ed. A. Caplan and R. Arp, 203–12. Chichester, UK: Wiley Blackwell.

Lampe, G.W.H., ed. 1961. *A Patristic Greek Lexicon*. Oxford: Clarendon Press.

Larchet, Jean-Claude. 2017. *The Theology of the Body*. Crestwood, NY: St. Vladimir's Press.

Larchet, Jean-Claude. 2019. *The New Media Epidemic: The Undermining of Society, Family, and Our Own Soul*. Jordanville NY: The Printshop of St Job of Pochaev.

Larchet, Dr. Jean-Claude. 2019. *The New Media Epidemic: The Undermining of Society, Family, and Our Own Soul*. Jordanville, NY: Holy Trinity Publications.

Latour, Bruno. 1993. *We Have Never Been Modern*. Cambridge, MA: Harvard University Press.

Latour, Bruno. 2005. *Reassembling the Social: An Introduction to Actor-Network Theory*. Oxford: Oxford University Press.

Lefort, Claude. 2011. The Image of the Body and Totalitarianism. In *The Great Lie: Classic and Recent Appraisals of Ideology and Totalitarianism*, ed. Flagg Taylor IV, 177–91. Wilmington, DE: ISI Books.

Lewis, C.S. 1990. *Perelandra*. In *The Cosmic Trilogy*. 1943; London: Pan/Macmillan, 331.

Lewis, C.S. 2015. *The Abolition of Man*. New York: HarperOne.

Lindeman, R. 2015. Down Syndrome Screening Isn't about Public Health. It's about Eliminating a Group of People. *The Washington Post*, June 16. [Online] Available: www.washingtonpost.com/posteverything/wp/2015/06/16/down-syndrome-screening-isnt-aboutpublic-health-its-about-eliminating-a-group-of-people/

Lossky, V. 1957. *The Mystical Theology of the Eastern Church*. Cambridge, United Kingdom: James Clarke & Co Ltd.

Lossky, Vladimir. 1997. *The Mystical Theology of the Eastern Church*. Crestwood, NY: St. Vladimir's Seminary Press, 101, 126.

Louth, Fr. Andrew. 1997. The Body in Western Catholic Christianity. In *Religion and the Body*, ed. Sarah Coakley, 113–30. Cambridge: Cambridge University Press.

MacIntyre, Alasdair. 1984. *After Virtue: A Study in Moral Theory*, 2nd ed. Notre Dame, IN: University of Notre Dame Press, 263.

Maguire, D. C. 2001. *Sacred Choices: The Right to Contraception and Abortion in Ten World Religions*. Minneapolis, MN: Fortress Press.

Mamalakis, Dr. Philip. 2016. *Parenting toward the Kingdom: Orthodox Christian Principles of Child-Rearing*. Chesterton, IN: Ancient Faith Publishing.

Mansfield, C., S. Hopfer, and T.M. Marteau. 1999. Termination Rates after Prenatal Diagnosis of Down Syndrome, Spina bifida, Anencephaly, and Turner and Klinefelter Syndromes: A Systematic Literature Review. European Concerted Action: DADA (Decision-making after diagnosis of a fetal abnormality). *Prenatal Diagnosis* 19: 808–12.

Martin, Joyce, A., Brady E. Hamilton, Michelle J. K. Osterman, Sally Curtin, and T.K. Matthews. 2015. Births: Final Data for 2013. *National Vital Statistics Reports* 64 (1): 1–65.

Marx, K. 1978. Manifesto of the Communist Party. In *The Marx-Engels Reader*. 2nd ed., ed. R. C. Tucker, 469–500. New York: W. W. Norton.

Maximus the Confessor, St. 1981. Four Hundred Texts on Love. In *The Philokalia*, 4 vols., ed. Sts. Nikodimos and Markarios, trans. G.E.H. Palmer, Philip Sherrard and Kallistos Ware, vol. 2, 52–113. London: Faber and Faber Limited.

Maximus the Confessor, St. 1981. Two Hundred Texts on Theology: First Century. In *The Philokalia*, vol. 2, ed. and trans. G.E.H. Palmer, Philip Sherrard, Kallistos Ware, 127. London: Faber and Faber.

Maximus the Confessor, St. 2014. *On Difficulties in the Church Fathers: The Ambigua*, vol. 2, Nicholas Constas, ed. and trans., Dumbarton Oaks Medieval Library 29. Cambridge, MA: Harvard University Press.

McCormick, R. 1989. *The Critical Calling: Moral Dilemmas Since Vatican II.* Washington, DC: Georgetown University Press.

Nagel, T. 2009. *Secular Philosophy and the Religious Temperament: Essays 2002–2008.* New York: Oxford University Press.

Natoli, J.L., D.L. Ackerman, S. McDermott, and J.G. Edwards. 2012. Prenatal Diagnosis of Down Syndrome: A Systematic Review of Termination Rates (1995–2011). *Prenatal Diagnosis* 32: 142–53.

Nicodemus and Agapius, Sts. 1957. *The Rudder.* Chicago: The Orthodox Christian Educational Society.

Nietzsche, Friedrich. 1968. *The Will to Power*, trans. Walter Kaufmann and R.J. Hollingdale. New York: Vintage Books.

North, Helen. 1966. *Sophrosyne: Self-Knowledge and Self-Restraint in Greek Literature.* Ithaca, NY: Cornell University Press, 243–4, 248–9, 312–16.

Reinhard, Kathryn L. 2012. Conscience, Interdependence, and Embodied Difference: What Paul's Ecclesial Principles can Offer the Contemporary Church. *Anglican Theological Review* 94 (3): 403–28.

Richard Niebuhr, H. 1951. *Christ and Culture.* New York: Harper and Row.

Rieff, Philip. 1966. *The Triumph of the Therapeutic: Uses of Faith After Freud.* Chicago: University of Chicago Press.

Rorty, R. 2004. Foreword. In *Nihilism and Emancipation: Ethics, Politics, and Law*, ed. S. Zabala, ix–xx. New York: Columbia University Press.

Rorty, R., G. Vattimo and S. Zabala. 2005. What Is Religion's Future after Metaphysics? In Rorty, R. and Vattimo G. *The Future of Religion*, ed. S. Zabala, 55–84. New York: Columbia University Press.

Rose, Fr. Seraphim. 2010. *Genesis, Creation, and Early Man: The Orthodox Christian Vision*, ed. Fr. Damascene Christiansen, 2nd ed. Platina, CA: St. Herman of Alaska Press.

Rose, Fr. Seraphim. 2011. *Genesis, Creation, and Early Man: The Orthodox Christian Vision*, 2nd ed. Platina, CA: St. Herman of Alaska BrotherhoBood, 203.

Sanford, Mary. 1984. "How Do You Read?": Theology and Hermeneutics in the Interpretation of New Testament Parables. unpublished doctoral dissertation, University of Kent, Canterbury, UK.

Schindler, D.C. 2017. *Freedom from Reality: The Diabolical Quality of Modern Liberalism.* Notre Dame, IN: University of Notre Dame Press.

Schmemann, Alexander. 1998. *The Eucharist.* Crestwood: St. Vladimir's Seminary Press, 10.

Schmemann, Alexander. 2001. *The Virgin Mary* (Celebration of the Faith, vol. III). Yonkers, NY: St. Vladimir's Press, 65.

Schmemann, Alexander. 2018. *For the Life of the World: Sacraments and Orthodoxy* [original edition, 1973]. Yonkers: St. Vladimir's Seminary Press, 139.

Shafarevich, Igor R. 1980. *The Socialist Phenomenon*, trans. William Tjalsma. Harper & Row.

Smith, Christian. 2009. *Souls in Transition: The Religious and Spiritual Sides of Emerging Adults.* New York: Oxford University Press.

Smith, Christian. 2011. *Lost in Transition: The Dark Side of Emerging Adulthood.* New York: Oxford University Press.

Smith, Christian and Melinda Lundquist Denton. 2005. *Soul Searching: The Religious and Spiritual Lives of American Teenagers.* New York: Oxford University Press.

Stark, Rodney. 2015. *The Triumph of Faith: Why the World Is More Religious than Ever*. Wilmington: ISI Books, 193.

Steely, Joshua. 2019. Must Say No. *Touchstone Magazine* 32 (5) (September/October): 23.

Steinsaltz, A. 2005. Peace without Conciliation: The Irrelevance of "Toleration" in Judaism, *Common Knowledge* 11 (1): 41–7.

Tachibana, M., P. Amato, M. Sparman, J. Woodward, D.M. Sanchis, H. Ma, N.M. Gutierrez et al. 2013. Towards Germline Gene Therapy of Inherited Mitochondrial Diseases. *Nature* 493: 627–31.

Taubes, Jacob. 2009. *Occidental Eschatology*, trans. David Ratmako. Stanford: Stanford University Press, 34–40.

Tavare, A. 2012. Scientists are to Investigate "three parent IVF" for Preventing Mitochondrial Diseases. *British Medical Journal* 344: e540.

Taylor, Charles. 2007. *A Secular Age*. Cambridge, MA: Belknap Press of Harvard University.

Theophan the Recluse, St. 1989. *Raising Them Right: A Saint's Advice on Raising Children*. Mount Herman, CA: Conciliar Press, 66–7.

Trenham, Fr. Josian. 2013. *Marriage and Virginity According to St. John Chrysostom*. Platina, CA: St. Herman of Alaska Monastery.

Turner, C. 2017. Number of Children Being Referred to Gender Identity Clinics Has Quadrupled in Five Years. Telegraph, July 8, 2017. https://www.telegraph.co.uk/news/2017/07/08/number-children-referred-gender-identity-clinics-has-quadrupled/

Vattimo, G. 2005. The Age of Interpretation. In Rorty, R. and Vattimo G., *The Future of Religion*, ed. S. Zabala, 43–54. New York: Columbia University Press.

Velimirovich, Nikolai. 1950. *The Universe as Symbols and Signs: An Essay on Mysticism in the Eastern Church*. Libertyville, IL: Serbian St. Sava Monastery, 2–3.

Voegelin, Eric. 1952. *New Science of Politics*. Chicago: University of Chicago Press.

Voegelin, Eric. 1974. *Order and History, Volume Four, The Ecumenic Age*. Baton Rouge: Louisiana State University Press, 22.

Voegelin, Eric. 1987. *The New Science of Politics: An Introduction*. Chicago: Univ. of Chicago Press, 169.

Voegelin, Eric. 1997. *Science, Politics, and Gnosticism: Two Essays*, ed. Ellis Sandoz. Washington, DC: Regnery Publishing.

Voegelin, Eric. 2004. *Science, Politics, and Gnosticism*. Wilmington, DE: ISI Books, 69–72.

Walter, J. 1980. Christian Ethics: Distinctive and Specific? In *Readings in Moral Theology No. 2: The Distinctiveness of Christian Ethics*, ed. C. Curran and R. McCormick, 90–110. New York: Paulist Press.

Waters, B. and R. Cole-Turner. 2003. *God and the Embryo: Religious Voices on Stem Cells and Cloning*. Washington, DC: Georgetown University Press.

Weatherby, Harold. 1994. *Mirrors of Celestial Grace: Patristic Theology in Spenser's Allegory*. Toronto: University of Toronto Press.

Weaver, Richard M. 1948. *Ideas Have Consequences*. 2013 edition. Chicago: University of Chicago Press.

Webster, F. C. 1986. *The Romanian Legionary Movement an Orthodox Christian Assessment of Anti-Semitism* (Carl Beck Papers, no. 502). Pittsburgh: University of Pittsburgh Center for·Russian and East European Studies, 5.

Wiker, Benjamin and Jonathan Witt. 2006. *A Meaningful World: How the Arts and Sciences Reveal the Genius of Nature*. Downers Grove, IL: IVP Academic.

Yancey, George. 2017. *Dehumanizing Christians: Cultural Competition in a Multicultural World*. New York: Routledge.

Yannaras, Christos. 2007. Comma, trans. Elizabeth Theokritoff, in *Synaxis, Volume 1: Anthropology, Environment, Creation*. Montreal: Alexander Press, 232.

Zabala, S. 2005. A Religion without Theists or Atheists. In Rorty, R. and Vattimo G., *The Future of Religion*, ed. S. Zabala, 1–28. New York: Columbia University Press.

Zernov, Nicolas. 1937. *Moscow the Third Room*. London: Society for Promoting Christian Knowledge, 21.

## HOLY TRINITY
## PUBLICATIONS
### JORDANVILLE, NEW YORK

 PRINTSHOP OF
SAINT JOB OF POCHAEV

 HOLY TRINITY
SEMINARY PRESS

Selected recent titles from Holy Trinity Publications:

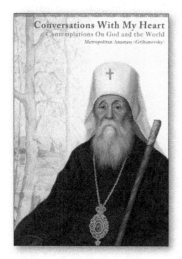

ISBN: 9780884654728

# Conversations with My Heart
## Contemplations on God and the World

*By Metropolitan Anastasy (Gribanovsky)*

Metropolitan Anastasy was the second primate of the Russian Orthodox Church Abroad (1936–1964). These reflections from his diary, which he writes "are part of my very essence," offer the groanings of his heart and musings on the eternal mercy of God. They draw upon wisdom from sources as diverse as writers of classical antiquity, authors, composers and inventors of the age of enlightenment, offering unique perspectives on these. This volume also contains a short life of the author written by Archbishop Averky (Taushev).

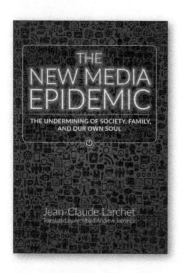

ISBN: 9780884654711

# The New Media Epidemic
## The Undermining of Society, Family, and Our Own Soul

*By Jean-Claude Larchet*

If we realize how gravely sick is our civilization, we may gain strength to resist. Philosopher and patrologist Dr Jean-Claude Larchet, renowned for his examinations of patristic writings on the causes and consequences of spiritual and physical illness, here tackles the pressing question of the societal and personal effects of our use of new media. His meticulous diagnosis concludes with a discussion of the ways individuals might limit and counteract the deleterious consequences of this new epidemic.